GOLF SCHOOLS

The complete guide to
hundreds of instruction programs
for adults and juniors

Barbara Wolf *with* Zelda Kaplan

First Person Press
25 Allen Road, Swampscott, Massachusetts 01907

Cover design — Leslie Haimes
Book design — Leslie Haimes with First Person Press

Library of Congress Cataloging-in-Publication-Data
Wolf, Barbara
Golf Schools — The Complete Guide to Hundreds of Instruction Programs for Adults and Juniors
Barbara Wolf with Zelda Kaplan Includes index.
1. Golf - study and teaching - U.S. - Directories 2. Sports camps - U.S. - Directories
II Title
GV 981.K37 1994 796.352'3 - dc20   93-5184
                                    CIP
ISBN 0-9635307-1-2

Printed in the United States of America

We are grateful to all those
who willingly and in a timely
fashion provided information
for this book, especially the
numerous golf professionals
and their staffs.

We dedicate this effort to:
*— Our long-suffering golf
instructors who have provided us
with sufficient skill to chew up some
of our nation's finest courses*
and to
*— Our husbands, Bert and Harold,
who have told us at least a thousand
times to keep our heads down.*
The authors,

Barbara Wolf
Zelda Kaplan

First Person Press
25 Allen Road
Swampscott, Massachusetts 01907

Ken Venturi

Foreword

At every level of play and across a lifetime, the game of golf delivers enormous thrills and rewards. Ask any golfer: Few things provide greater elation than making a really fine shot. That feeling stays with you and inspires you to want to play better and better golf. I know few greater passions than wanting to elevate your game and there is no better place to do it than at a golf school.

Golf is a game of habits – good habits and bad ones. Over a full and rewarding career of playing and teaching, I have concluded that complete immersion in the game, over a weekend or for three or five days, is the route to conditioning a player to unlearn bad habits and make the necessary changes which lead to playing better. And for beginners, whether young people or adults, a concentrated, well-rounded few days of instruction is an invaluable start.

With some authority, I can tell you there are no short cuts to learning and progressing. There are no gimmicks to developing a sound, consistent, well managed, intelligent game. It takes hard work, commitment and expert schooling in fundamentals: the address, the grip and the shape of the swing. It takes sustained teaching and practice and fine-tuning of your short game. It takes experience where it counts, on the course, with qualified instructors, to grasp the concepts of what is needed to score well. All of these are the mainstays of a good golf school.

An extended period of nurturing and strengthening your game at a golf school is a sound and lasting investment. But be cautious. Golf information comes in lots of packages with lots of fancy trimmings. Pick carefully and thoughtfully. Enroll in the very best school you can manage, with the very best reputation and system behind it. Take a long hard look at the program and at the people who teach. Ask a lot of questions. Satisfy yourself that you have made an educated choice – not an impetuous one based on location or price alone.

This book deals with just about every aspect of golf schools to help you make a smart selection. It explains in detail the who, what, where, when and how-much of hundreds of programs for adults and juniors. The book leaves it to me, however, to tell you *why* a golf school should figure in your plan to improve your game.

To be a fine golfer means being a perpetual student – and golf school weighs heavily in a total instruction plan. I'm enthusiastic about such schools because they pull together all the elements of learning and allow you to surround yourself with like-minded people who are serious about their game. They place you in a congenial and relaxed setting and allow you to concentrate. Golf schools give you access to the very latest systems and technology and expose you to the finest talents the industry has to offer. So put a golf school on your schedule. You'll count it among the best investments you could possibly make in your game.

1964 U.S. Open Champion and one of television's most qualified golf commentators, Ken Venturi has been named by the PGA of America among its ten "Living Legends in Golf Instruction." He plays a central role in Ken Venturi Golf Training Centers.

Table of Contents

How To Use This Book

Golf Schools abound. To the best of our knowledge, in 1975 thirteen "live-in" golf schools were operating in this country. This year we were able to document more than a hundred such schools conducting instruction for adults at more than 200 different vacation spots. Plus we've discovered an equal number of specialized programs for junior golfers. How do you find the information in these pages that you need in order to decide on the right school for you? Read on.

Methods and Programs

Schools are arranged according to states and alphabetically. The headquarters for each school is clearly identified with the symbol of a visor. Such master listings contain the school's philosophy and method of instruction, the various programs and sites where sessions are conducted. Here you will find the hours of instruction, class size, student/teacher ratio and specifics such as how many nights and meals are included in every program. A pricing symbol ($) gives you an idea of what the school will cost. (More about that below) In the Index at the back of the book, you will find the page for each Headquarters in bold print.

Listings for Resorts

A school may operate only one or many teaching sites. Each teaching location for adults is listed separately and contains a description of where you will stay and the golf courses on which you will play. The "Info," notation in the resort listing refers you back to the school's headquarters for a review of programs and methods.

Commuter Programs

Many schools offer appealing packages composed of instruction, lodging and meals. However, nearly all schools reserve a number of "commuter" spots, permitting students to make their own accommodations. And in fact, a growing number of schools operate commuter programs exclusively. These schools will recommend discounted area lodging and will even make the arrangements for you. Commuter tuition entitles students to instruction, use of practice facilities and, in most cases, green and cart fees.

How Much Will It Cost?

There is a golf school for every inclination and every pocketbook. Recognizing that golf school is an investment in a sport you will play for a lifetime, golf educators urge students to shop reputation and excellence, not merely economy.

Relative Pricing Scale

Schools range from under $1,000 for a 5-day program with lodging and all meals to $10,000 for three days of private instruction with a famous teaching pro at a topnotch resort. For the purpose of providing an idea of what golf schools cost, *we have compared prices based on an all-inclusive 5-day program.* For schools with shorter or less complete or commuter-only programs, we have extrapolated prices. Fees are indicated by $ symbols as follows:

$ – Less than $999 for 5 days instruction, 5 nights lodging, all meals and unlimited golf.

$$ – $1,000 to $1,499 for the same 5-day package; this is in the low-average range.

$$-$$$ – $1,500-$2,999. Costs creep up to high-average due to seasonal variations, fewer nights or meals, or add-ons (green fees, amenities, tips).

$$$-$$$$ – $3,000-$4,999 range for 5-day programs situated at luxurious resorts or headed by a well-known pro. Or perhaps with smaller classes or sophisticated technology. Many special programs such as Low Handicap, VIP, or Playing Schools are in this category.

$$$$$ – $5,000 to $10,000/week–usually those with world-class teachers, private or semi-private instruction, located at the finest resorts.

Hidden Charges

It is prudent to find out exactly what you are paying for when you opt for a golf school package. Ask about taxes, gratuitites, charges for bag storage, club and shoe cleaning, green and cart fees. If you are staying in a condo or villa, inquire whether there is an extra charge for maid service. You will certainly want to know the costs for a non-student guest in your room, for children and for supplements for single occupancy.

Tipping Your Pro

Should you offer a parting gratuity to your teaching pro? It is entirely up to you. However, it is never wrong, especially if you have had significant contact with that person and you sensed his or her concern for your well-being. Consider $10 or $12 per full day of instruction at an average priced school.

ADULT SCHOOLS

ALABAMA

GULF SHORES

Arnold Palmer Golf Academy

Craft Farms Cotton Creek Club
Gulf Shores, AL 36547; 205 968-7766

2-day; spring

Rates: $$$, tuition only*

Info: Arnold Palmer Golf Academy, 800 523-5999. See page 49 for programs and methods.

*School arranges accommodations at the nearby Perdido Beach Resort (27200 Perdido Beach Blvd., Orange Beach, AL 36561, 800 634-8001), a luxurious AAA Four-Diamond, 345-room, Mediterranean-style vacation destination. Situated directly on the white sandy beach fronting the Gulf, Perdido Beach offers tennis, pool, state-of-the-art health and fitness club, children's program. Renown for Creole cuisine. Area is rich in outdoor recreation and history. Located between Mobile and Pensacola, FL.

■ Instruction at Cotton Creek Club/Craft Farms, a private, 18-hole, Arnold Palmer course with practice facility; additional nine holes under construction. Total of four courses available to guests of Perdido Beach Resort.

POINT CLEAR

John Jacobs Practical Golf Schools

Marriott's Grand Hotel at Lakewood Golf Club
Scenic Hwy 98, Point Clear, AL 36564; 800 228-9290   205 928-9201

5-day (M-F), Feb-May, Sept-Oct; 4-day (M-Thu), June-July; 4-day midweek (Thu-Sun), Aug; 2-day weekend, Mar-July, Sept-Oct; Women's Golf Conference, Aug*

Rates: $$

Info: John Jacobs Practical Golf Schools, 800 472-5007. See page 6 for programs and methods.

* Women's Golf Conference: 4 days instruction, 3 nights, 2 rounds, breakfasts, dinners, networking, career seminars, speakers.

A rambling cypress structure dating from 1847, The Marriott Grand Hotel is called "The Queen of Southern Resorts." Sixteen cottages accommodate 308 guests. Offers assorted dining, equestrian sports, bowling, croquet, tennis, swimming, fishing, biking, water sports; 40-slip marina, and cruises on the resort's 53-foot yacht, the Hatteras. Located 50 minutes from Mobile Airport; 49 miles west of Pensacola, FL.

■ Dogwood and Azalea courses total 36 holes at Marriott's Lakewood Golf Club. The pair has earned Silver Medals among GOLF Magazine's "Top 50 Resort Courses in the U.S."

TUSCALOOSA

Golf Digest Instruction Schools

NorthRiver
P.O. Box 48999, Tuscaloosa, AL 35404
800 622-2029   205 345-0202

5-day VIP; March-May

Rates: $$$$

Info: Golf Digest Instruction Schools, 800 243-6121. See page 29 for programs and methods.

A luxurious private resort situated on Lake Tuscaloosa, NorthRiver offers indoor/outdoor Golf Club pool, marina and lake sports, spa, fitness instruction and refined dining. Accommodations in 58 deluxe rooms and 25 two- and three-bedroom villas.

⚑ An 18-hole, 6,700-yard, par 71, Gary Player and Ron Kirby course.

ARIZONA

LITCHFIELD PARK

John Jacobs Practical Golf Schools

The Wigwam
451 N. Litchfield Rd., Litchfield, AZ 85340
800 327-0396   602 935-3811

5-day, Jan-May; 4-day mid-week, Oct-Dec; 2-day weekend, Jan-May
Short Game School, Low Handicap School, Playing School*

Rates: $$-$$$ (Special schools $$$); weekend commuter rates, inquire about lodging

Info: John Jacobs Practical Golf Schools, 800 472-5007. See page 6 for programs and methods.

*Four-day Short Game School (Nov and Dec): chipping, pitching and sand shots; includes John Jacobs Precision Putting Program. Four-day Low Handicap (Dec): 0-10 handicaps, emphasis on the short game, course management and mental aspects. Four-day Playing School (Nov and Dec): 3:1 student/teacher ratio, 18-holes on-course training daily.

The luxurious, 75-year-old Wigwam, newly renovated to the tune of $45 million, continues to offer the charm and ambiance of authentic old Arizona. Provides tennis, equestrian sports, health clubs, a trap and skeet club, pools, volleyball and croquet court, numerous dining and lounge options. Accommodations in 331 guest casitas. Located 30 minutes from Phoenix Sky Harbor International Airport.

⚑ Three celebrated championship courses, 54 holes, all awarded Silver Medals by GOLF Magazine. Laid out in 1964, the original Robert Trent Jones Gold Course measures 7,074 yards. With 96 threatening bunkers and plentiful water, it demands skill and intelligence. The shorter and wider Blue Course, also a Jones design, stretches 5,960 yards. The West Course, created in the early 70s by Robert "Red" Lawrence, lulls players into complacency until the last four holes, perhaps the toughest combination in the state.

MESA

Professional Golf Schools of America

Arizona Golf Resort
425 S. Power Rd., Mesa, AZ 85206; 800 528-8282   602 832-3202

5-day; 3-day, M-W or F-Sun; Nov-June

Rates: $$

Info: Professional Golf Schools of America, 800 447-2744. See page 36 for programs and methods.

Arizona Golf Resort, 30 minutes from Phoenix Airport, offers 162 rooms with kitchenettes or fully appointed lakeside or fairway casitas and suites. Hotel features spas, tennis, cycling, swimming and a refined restaurant on its lushly planted, 150-acre Spanish-style campus.

■ 18-hole, 6,574-yard, par-71, resort course with fearsome, extra-large greens inviting three putts, and par three holes measuring 200 yards and then some.

PHOENIX

Bill Skelley School of Golf

Gold Canyon Ranch
6100 S. Kings Ranch Rd., Gold Canyon, AZ 85219; 800 624-6445   602 982-9090

5-day, 3-day; Jan-May

Rates: $$-$$$

Info: Bill Skelley School of Golf, 800 541-7707. See page 40 for programs and methods.

Located on the site of the Lost Dutchman Mine, the resort offers tennis, cycling, trail rides, varied dining, against a spectacular mountain backdrop. Accommodations in private, mountain-side casitas with wet bars, fireplaces, many with spas.

■ An 18-hole, 6,400-yard, Hardin and Nash/Cavanaugh-design with a variety of challenges.

PHOENIX

Exceller Programs Golf Schools

Pointe Hilton Resort at Tapatio Cliffs - The Pointe Golf Club on Lookout Mountain
11111 N. 7th St., Phoenix, AZ 85020; 602 866-7500

5-day, 4-day, 2-day; Sept-May

Rates: $$-$$$

Info: Exceller Programs Golf Schools, 800 424-7438. See page 4 for programs and methods.

High above the Valley of the Sun, the resort village offers unmatched vistas in an atmosphere reminiscent of the old Southwest. Guests are housed in 584 two-room suites with balconies, stocked refrigerators, honor bars, two TVs and computerized safes. Three dining rooms, six pools, spa and fitness center, 15 tennis courts, full equestrian program.

■ Bill Johnston-designed, 18-hole, par 72 course, loops about the slopes and arroyos of the Phoenix Mountain Preserve. Pointe Lookout Mountain Golf Club, site of the Arizona Classic, teams up with its 18-hole sister course to the south, The Pointe Golf Club on South Mountain.

PHOENIX

Mazda Golf Clinics for Executive Women
Moon Valley Country Club, February
Info: 800 262-7888. See page 73 for programs and methods.

PHOENIX

Paradise Golf Schools
Gold Canyon Ranch
6100 S. Kings Ranch Rd., Gold Canyon, AZ 85219; 800 624-6445   602 982-9090
5-day; 3-day, F-Sun; Masters program*; Sept-June
Rates: $$$
Info: Paradise Golf Schools, 800 624-3543. See page 41 for programs and methods.

*Masters Program: $$$$; same format as 3-day or 5-day programs plus 6-8 hours instruction, 1:1, with sought-after, Class-A, PGA Pro Jim Wright.

On the outskirts of Phoenix, at the base of the fabled Superstition Mountain, the resort is known for spectacular scenery, dining, tennis, swimming, congenial cookouts. Extensive equestrian program features hay rides, old Western trail rides and lessons.

⬛ A challenging 18-hole, 6,400-yard, Hardin and Nash/Cavanaugh creation.

PHOENIX

Swing Masters
1018 East Indian School Rd, Phoenix, AZ 85014; 800 752-9162
Director: Dana Hickman
2-day; Nov-May
Rates $$, tuition only*

Program is based on the strengths and abilities of golfers at all levels. Instructors work within students' skills and proficiency, refining and reinforcing instead of instituting radical change. Six hours daily instruction provided by attentive PGA and LPGA professionals, 5:1 student/teacher ratio. Includes green fees, video analysis, instruction booklet, daily lunch. Two-day programs begin Tues, Thu or Sat.

*Discounted lodging at the 160-suite Orange Tree Golf and Conference Resort (10601 N. 56th St, Scottsdale, AZ 85254; 602-948-6100); inquire about school-hotel specials.

⬛ USGA-rated championship course at Orange Tree Resort, 6,837 yards, designed by Johnny Bulla. Complete practice facilities.

SCOTTSDALE

Exceller Programs Golf Schools
7500 E. Butherus, Scottsdale, AZ 85260
800 424-7438   602 998-1038
Director: Dave Bisbee

5-day, 4-day, 2-day programs; 3-day holiday weekends; Women's Only programs, Business Women's Conference; Junior programs (see page 126)

Rates: $$-$$$

Locations: Phoenix, AZ; Rancho Mirage, CA; Howey-in-the-Hills, FL; Amherst, NH; Roscoe, NY; Park City, UT. Women's Only programs: Amherst, NH, July; Roscoe, NY, Sept

Exceller's "Links of Learning" comprises three vital steps to improvement: mechanical, physical and mental. PGA and LPGA instructors are certified in Exceller's own five-step instructional process. The school makes use of video technology, monitors each student's progress, and reinforces learning with physical and mental exercises, demonstrations and personalized practice. Exceller incorporates course management and shot-visualization techniques with daily on-course instruction to make the transition from the practice tee to the 1st tee.

Five hours daily instruction; maximum 5:1 student/teacher ratio, entire class limited to 25. Video analysis, daily on-course instruction, closing tournament. Includes green fees and carts, instruction manual and maintenance program. Five-day program provides 6 nights, 5 breakfasts and lunches, 2 dinner parties; four-day program: 5 nights, 4 breakfasts and lunches, 2 dinner parties; two-day program: 2 nights, 2 breakfasts and lunches.

SCOTTSDALE

Golf Digest Instruction Schools

Troon North Golf Club
10320 East Dynamite Blvd., Scottsdale, AZ 85255
602 585-5300

3-day, 2-day weekend, 3-day Low Handicap, Mini-schools; Oct-May

Rates: $$$$, tuition only*

Info: Golf Digest Instruction Schools, 800 243-6121. See page 29 for programs and methods.

* School suggests accommodations at The Scottsdale Princess, 7575 East Princess Dr., Scottsdale, 800 344-4758 or 602 585-4848; discounted rate includes 4 nights, breakfasts, transportation to Troon North. See page 8 for details.

■ At the base of Pinnacle Peak, Troon North Golf Club, part of an 1,800-acre resort, provides outstanding learning facilities and 18 championship holes designed by Weiskopf and Morrish. Like numerous southwestern courses, this one is in the "desert links" style, the result of a scarcity of water. Outcroppings of rock loom over greens; arroyos, canyons and desert washes comprise hazards; fairways are de-emphasized. Course plays 7,008 yards from championship tees.

> *According to golf writer Pat Seeleg in Golfweek magazine, the higher your handicap, the more progress you can expect to make at golf school. Students with realistic expectations are the ones who profit the most. So don't hope for miracles.*

Golf Schools of Scottsdale

La Posada Resort
4949 E. Lincoln Dr. Suite 102, Scottsdale, AZ 85253
800 356-6678   602 998-4800
Director: Ray R. Almada
3-day, 4-day and 5-day; Mini-Schools; VIP, Short Game and Low Handicap Schools, 1-day Quick Fix School; year round
Rates: $$-$$$$*

Thirty years of teaching golf has taught Ray Almada to custom design programs to students' needs and desires. Attention is paid to fundamentals. Skills are put to the test in afternoon play. Classes limited to 30; 5:1 student/teacher ratio (2:1 or 1:1 in VIP programs); includes complimentary green fees and carts following class, Sony "Caddy Cam" video analysis, club storage, playing lessons in selected programs. Deluxe accommodations according to duration of program, breakfasts and lunches, refreshments during class, welcome reception.

*Accommodations and year-round programs at Red Lion's La Posada Resort (address above). Summer sites only: Denver and Colorado Springs, CO and Lake Havasu, AZ. Rates vary according to site and season.

◼ Golf at neighboring Tatum Ranch Golf Club and Rancho Manana, among 113 Scottsdale area courses to play.

> *Wear two gloves. Hands take serious abuse when you are hitting hundreds of balls. But don't invest in a right and a left. If you're a righty, buy two lefts. Turn one inside out for the short time you'll need a right glove.*

John Jacobs Practical Golf Schools

7825 E. Redfield Rd, Scottsdale, AZ 85260-6977
800 472-5007
Director: John Jacobs
4-day, 4-day mid-week, 5-day, 2-day weekend, special programs
Rates: $$-$$$

Other locations: More than 600 separate sessions at 16 resorts in AL, AZ, CA, CO, FL, HI, MI, MO, NJ, NY, TX, UT, WI, WY, plus Europe, China

Since 1971, John Jacobs instruction has been providing students with an understanding of the principles of practical golf and the theory of ball flight, thus making each student his or her own best teacher. The approach leads to consistency, confidence in one's golfing skills and ultimately to lower scores. Programs are coed, for Ladies Only, Juniors, Seniors or families and tailored for golfers of every ability. Special programs include VIP (low student/teacher ratio, Lake Geneva, WI and Orlando, FL), Short Game, Low Handicap, and seminars for Professional Women (Atlantic City, NJ, June; Scottsdale, AZ, July; Point Clear, AL, Aug; Marco Island, FL, Sept)

Five hours daily classes, 5:1 student/teacher ratio; students grouped according to ability. Includes video analysis, instruction manual, unlimited use of practice facilities, bag storage. Complimentary green fees and cart after class.

Five-day program (M-F) includes six nights (Sun-F), 6 breakfasts, 5 lunches, 2 banquets, 4 cocktail parties. Four-day program (M-Thu): 5 nights (Sun-Thu), 5 breakfasts, 4 lunches, 2 banquets, 3 cocktail parties. Four-day midweek program (Thu-Sun): 4 nights, 4 breakfasts, 4 lunches, 1 dinner, 2 cocktail parties. Two-day weekend program (Sat and Sun): 2 nights, 2 breakfasts, 2 lunches, 2 dinners, 1 wine and cheese party. Commuter rate (no lodging, includes lunches) applies to weekend programs at many sites; school helps students make lodging arrangements.

S C O T T S D A L E

John Jacobs Practical Golf Schools

Marriott's Camelback Inn and Golf Club
7847 North Mockingbird Lane, Scottsdale, AZ 85253; 800 24-CAMEL   602 948-6770

5-day, 4-day, 2-day weekend; year round

Rates: $$$$, John Jacobs Golf School is conducted on the premises; hotel guests enroll at commuter rate.

Info: John Jacobs Practical Schools, 800 472-5007. See page 6 for programs and methods.

A Mobil Five Star, AAA Five Diamond resort offering the luxurious Camelback Spa, a complete fitness facility for beauty and health treatments to nourish and revitalize body and mind. Jogging, cycling and walking trails; tennis, volleyball, three outdoor pools with whirlpools. Lodging in casita-style villas for more than 400 guests. Located 15 minutes from Phoenix Airport.

■ At Camelback Golf Club, two championship USGA courses – the long, 18-hole, Jack Snyder Indian Bend Course and the earlier, more compact, 18-hole, 6,559-yard Padre Course designed by Red Lawrence. Award-winning pro shop.

S C O T T S D A L E

John Jacobs Practical Golf Schools

Marriott's Fairfield Inn
13440 N. Scottsdale Rd., Scottsdale, AZ 85254; 602 483-0042

5-day; year round

Rates: $

Info: John Jacobs Practical Golf Schools, 800 472-5007. See page 6 for programs and methods.

Marriott's Fairfield Inn offers economical lodging reflecting thoughtful hospitality. Pool and sun deck. Located 20 minutes from Phoenix Airport. Call Inn directly for accommodations.

■ Instruction at Camelback Golf Club, Scottsdale; guests provide own transportation.

8   ARIZONA

S C O T T S D A L E

John Jacobs Practical Golf Schools

Marriott's Mountain Shadows Resort and Golf Club
5641 E. Lincoln Dr., Scottsdale, AZ 85253
800 228-9290   602-948-7111

5-day, Sept-May; 4-day, June-Aug; 2-day weekends*; Women's Conference**

Rates: $$-$$$

Info: John Jacobs Practical Golf Schools, 800 472-5007. See page 6 for programs and methods.

*Weekend programs: resort guests, June-Aug; commuter rates, Oct-May.
**Women's Golf Conference, July: 4 days instruction, 3 nights, 2 rounds, break-fasts, dinners, networking, seminars, women speakers

The resort is a 70-acre oasis boasting prize-winning dining, fitness center, three pools and varied recreation; more than 300 guests are lodged in private villas. Located 15 minutes from Phoenix Airport.

▣ Mountain Shadows Resort Course is a 9-hole, par 3, executive. Instruction and play at Camelback Golf Club, Scottsdale; guests provide own transportation. See previous page for details.

S C O T T S D A L E

Nicklaus Flick Golf School

Scottsdale Princess
7575 East Princess Dr., Scottsdale, AZ 85255; 800 344-4758   602 585-4848

Desert Mountain Golf Club, 10333 Rockaway Hills, Scottsdale, AZ 85262,
602 252-4244

Master Golf I (3-day); Feb-May, Oct-Nov

Rates: $$$$-$$$$$

Info: Nicklaus Flick Golf School, 800 642-5528. See page 44 for programs and methods.

Resembling a great and luxurious estate, the Mexican Colonial-style resort presents a blending of high style comfort and southwestern charm. Six-hundred guest rooms, suites, and casitas are grouped near pools and tennis courts (including a 10,000-seat stadium court); offers Spa and Fitness Center, and a host of recreational and dining opportunities.

▣ Three Jack Nicklaus-designed championship courses and practice facilities; site of the Senior Tour's "Tradition" event. Renegade Course (designed with multiple tees and different pin placements so players of varying skills can enjoy the same course simultaneously) was recently voted by Golf Digest as one of America's greatest golf courses.

S C O T T S D A L E

Stratton-Scottsdale Golf School

Regal McCormick Ranch
7401 N. Scottsdale Rd., Scottsdale AZ 85253; 800 222-8888
Director: Keith Lyford

5-day, 3-day; 2-day, Thu-F or Sat-Sun; Nov-May*

Rates: $$

Info: Stratton-Scottsdale Golf Schools, P.O. Box 6349, Scottsdale, AZ 85258; 800 238-2424, winter; 800 843-6867, summer. See page 116 for programs and methods.

AAA Four Diamond, 125-room, lakeside resort surrounded by the austere beauty of the Sonoran Desert. Offers entertainment, dining, swimming, canoeing, tennis, in beautifully landscaped surroundings.

◧ A comprehensive training facility with simulated course conditions and target green. Two 18-hole courses, Pine and Palm, amidst stunning desert scenery.

*Arizona programs differ from school's summer sessions at Stratton Mountain, VT. Provides 5 hours daily instruction, 5:1 student/teacher ratio, video and photo analysis, complimentary play after instruction, unlimited use of practice facilities, instruction booklet; 3 and 5-day programs include on-course instruction and welcome reception. Accommodations: 5 nights, 3 nights or 2 nights; lunches.

SCOTTSDALE

Swing's The Thing Golf Schools

Tournament Players Club of Scottsdale TPC Stadium Course
17020 N. Hayden Rd., Scottsdale, AZ 85255
602 585-3600

Thunderbird Inn
7515 East Butherus, Scottsdale, AZ 85260
800 334-1977   602 951-4000

3-day VIP program (2 or 3 nights); Feb-Mar

Rates: $$$, VIP program limited to 12 participants.

Info: Swing's The Thing Golf School, 800 221-6661. See page 98 for programs and methods.

Lodging in 2-room suites, all with wet bars, refrigerators, two TVs; pool, dining, conveniently located to recreation, minutes from Phoenix Sky Harbor Airport.

◧ The Tom Weiskopf-Jay Morrish TPC Stadium Course with its huge grass stadium mounds is among the finest of all the stadium courses commissioned by Deane Beman and the PGA Tour. Home to the Phoenix Open, the course plays 6,992 from tournament tees.

Please mention "Golf Schools: The Complete Guide" when contacting schools. The pros at the various schools have been extremely helpful to First Person Press. Let us know which schools you have chosen using the form at the back of the book.

▰▪▰▪▰▪▰▪▰▪▰▪▰▪▰▪▰▪▰▪▰▪▰▪▰▪▰▪▰▪▰▪▰▪▰▪

SEDONA

S.E.A. (Sports Enhancement Associates, Inc.)
Nice Shot! Golf Schools

7256 Highway 179, P.O. Box 2788, Sedona, AZ 86336
800 345-4245   602 284-9000

Sedona Golf Resort, 7260 Highway 179, Sedona, AZ 86336; 602 284-9355

President: Chuck Hogan; Director: Mike Altman

5-day Sedona Experience; 3½-day Golfers School; 3½-day Experts Only School (for low handicap and collegiate players); Alumni Conference

Rates: $$-$$$, tuition only; school arranges discounted lodging at area resorts and hotels.

Other locations: Tempe, AZ; Tampa, FL; Brewster, MA; Portland, OR; Dallas, TX

S.E.A. is dedicated to increasing the level of human performance. Ten thousand amateurs and 60 PGA touring professionals have availed themselves of S.E.A.'s innovative methods for accelerated learning, "no pain" practice and preparation, and advanced concentration and relaxation techniques to transport one into the "effortless zone." Players are taught to end their mechanical dependency and replace it with trust in their golf swings and in themselves. Mental and physical aspects of the game are integrated, enabling players to learn more effectively, prepare for tournament play, control pressure and, therefore, score better.

Experts Only Schools (Tampa, FL, Tempe, AZ, Dallas, TX; inquire about dates) for competitive, 0-10 handicap amateurs or pros: 3½ days (25+ hours, Thu-Sun) individual and group instruction from Chuck Hogan, celebrated Tour coach. Teaches techniques for tournament preparation and play, managing pressure, advanced concentration and relaxation. Take-home custom strategy for continued improvement. Open to S.E.A. repeating students regardless of handicap.

The Golfer's School (Brewster MA, July; Portland, OR, Sept): 3½ days (25+ hours, Fri-Mon) instruction for golfers of all abilities. Program divided between classroom, driving range and short game environment. Attention to pre-swing and in-swing fundamentals, practice techniques, confidence building and relaxation.

Sedona Experience, April-June & Oct: 4½ days (32 hours+, M-F) instruction on fundamentals for all levels; includes 27 holes on-course training. Teaches management of inconsistencies, practice routines, accelerated skill learning, relaxation and confidence-building skills. Includes two dinners at area restaurants, all lunches (no lodging).

■ Instruction at the award-winning Sedona Golf Resort, a master-planned community (only course is completed) in the high desert, 90 miles north of Phoenix. Course is an 18-hole, Gary Panks design, in one of the most spectacular settings in the Southwest. Complete practice facility.

TEMPE

S.E.A. Experts Only Golf School

Fiesta Inn
2100 S. Priest Ave., Tempe, AZ 85282; 800 528-6481

3½ day Experts Only School (0-10 handicap and collegiate players), Thu-Sun; Feb, March, Oct, Nov

Rates: $$-$$$, tuition only*

Info: Sports Enhancement Associates, 800 345-4245   602 284-9000. See Sedona, previous page, for program and method.

*Discounted accommodations at The Fiesta Inn, a 270-room southwestern-style hotel with 110 mini-suites, on 33 landscaped acres; exercise room and sauna, concierge service, pool, tennis, jogging trails, dining.

■ Practice facility on the premises with lighted driving range, short game instruction area.

T U C S O N

Arnold Palmer Golf Academy

Star Pass Golf Club, 3645 W 22nd St., Tucson, AZ 85745
602 622-4300

3-day; April & May

Rates: $$$, tuition only; school will suggest nearby accommodations.

Info: Arnold Palmer Golf Academy, 800 523-5999. See page 44 for programs and methods.

■ Starr Pass, an Arnold Palmer, 18-hole course, is a new addition to the Arnold Palmer Management Company. Cut from the foothills of the Tucson Mountains, Starr Pass is one of the sites for the PGA Northern Telecom Tucson Open. Rated by Golf Digest among the top 10 courses in Arizona.

T U C S O N

Craft-Zavichas Golf School

Tucson National Golf and Conference Resort
2727 West Club Drive, Tucson, AZ 85741
800 528-4856   602 297-2271

3-day, W-Sun or Sun-Th, Feb and April; 5-day and 5-day Women Only, M-F, Feb-April*

Rates: $$-$$$

Info: Craft-Zavichas Golf School, 800 858-9633. See page 26 for programs and methods.

Tucson National Golf and Conference Resort is a sprawling, 650-acre vacation spot in Arizona's high desert. Renown spa offers every known recipe to pamper and induce well-being. Accommodations in 167 villa suites; two restaurants, pool, tennis; grounds crisscrossed with southwestern-style covered colonnades and punctuated with fountains.

■ Three gently rolling nines are the site of NBC's annual Tucson Open.

* Programs and accommodations differ from school's Colorado site. Five-day program provides 25+ hours instruction, on-course lessons, 5 days unlimited play; provides 7 days, 6 nights, 2 banquets, 5 lunches. Five-day Women Only program provides 30+ hours LPGA instruction, on-course strategy session, scramble Pro-Am tournament, 5 days unlimited play; provides 7 days, 6 nights, 3 banquets, 5 lunches. Three-day program includes 15+ hours instruction, 3 days unlimited play; provides 5 days, 4 nights, one banquet, 2 receptions, 3 lunches. See page 26 for details of instruction.

ARKANSAS

Jack Fleck College of Golf Knowledge

Lil' Bit A Heaven Golf Club
Rt. 1, Box 140, Magazine, AR 72943
501 969-2203

Director: Jack Fleck

3-day and 5-day; late spring to fall

Rates: $, tuition only; inquire about nearby motel lodging; peace and quiet guaranteed in the Ozarks countryside.

At the base of Magazine Mountain near Booneville, 110 miles west of Little Rock, legendary, 1955 U.S. Open winner, Jack Fleck (he defeated Ben Hogan), personally trains golfers of all levels, from amateurs to top pros. Jack, for 53 years a professional golfer, and his son Craig, maximize students' natural abilities and stress the mental game to instill confidence, composure and consistency. Nutrition and fitness training is available under the direction of Dr. Mariann (Jack's wife), a Ph.D. in health sciences. Full day instruction and play, 1:1 student/teacher ratio, classes limited to 3-5 students. Class tournament.

■ The Flecks' 18-hole Lil' Bit A Heaven Golf Club, "never before designed or built in the history of golf," is billed as a thinking man's, shot maker's course. Full practice facility.

Many schools encourage consultation with instructors after you return home. Some even promise lifetime contact. Don't be shy.
Ask your teacher if he or she will critique a videotape of your swing in the future. Send it with a stamped, self-addressed, return mailer.

CALIFORNIA

The Golf Academy at Aviara

7447 Batiquitos Dr., Carlsbad, CA 92009
800 433-7468, 619 438-4539

Co-directors: Kip Puterbaugh, Dr. Jim Suttie

4-day and 3-day; Jan-May

Rates: $$$, tuition only. The Academy will help students find accommodations at nearby resorts. Inquire about lodging package with neighboring La Costa Resort (see following listing).

Kip Puterbaugh, named by GOLF Magazine one of the 50 best instructors in America, is teamed with Dr. Jim Suttie, 1991 finalist for PGA Teacher of the Year. Students learn swing fundamentals and gain an understanding of an effective swing through studying video footage of golf greats. Through daily state-of-the-art videotaping and analysis, students and instructor pinpoint aspects for personalized correction. A customized beginner's curriculum is offered and all programs are tailored to the needs of individuals.

Full day instruction, 8:30 am to 5 pm, on all aspects, includes videotaped on-course training; 5:1 student/teacher ratio, with Puterbaugh and/or Suttie in attendance. Complimentary green fees and carts; take-home videotape with instructional voice-over for continued learning. Includes lunch. Located 30 minutes from San Diego's Lindberg Field, five minutes from Palomar Airport.

◖ School is based in the luxurious California-style clubhouse overlooking the 18th hole of the Arnold Palmer-designed Aviara Resort course, ranked one of the country's 10 best new resort courses in 1991. Students practice on fairway quality grass tees and on slopes designed to simulate difficult lies. Full use of clubhouse facilities, private lockers, showers, sauna.

C A R L S B A D
La Costa School of Golf

La Costa Resort and Spa
Costa Del Mar Rd., Carlsbad, CA 92009
800 653-7888   619 438-9111 ex. 4258

Director: Carl Welty

Hourly, half-day and full-day, for guests of the resort; year round

Rates: $$, tuition only; rate varies according to number in your party; La Costa "Stay and Learn" packages ($$$$$) include tuition and lodging.

Work on your game where Couples, Love, Norman, Kite, Strange and a host of others have improved their's. Pro Carl Welty has assembled an unsurpassed array of technical and video aids to analyze students' games, to help them visualize an optimum swing and to make effective corrections. Welty, founder of the school in 1984 and a pioneer in the use of video technology in teaching golf, has been rated by Golf Illustrated among its Top Teaching Pros. Program provides entirely individualized instruction; 1:1 or 2:1 with your golfing partner(s). Majority of teaching takes place on the course and in the indoor, hi-tech, video studio/ driving station.

La Costa ranks among the leading resorts of the world, with 1,000 acres of manicured grounds, championship sporting facilities and haute cuisine. Offers 23 tennis courts under the supervision of Pancho Segura, a total spa and fitness program including spa menu; lodging in deluxe rooms or 1-, 2- or 3-bedroom suites in 30 chateaus, 24 villas, plus private residences.

◖ Boasts two 18-hole courses designed by Joe Lee and Dick Wilson, among the most challenging anywhere. La Costa is home to the annual MONY and Infiniti tournaments.

CARMEL
Golf Digest Instruction Schools
Quail Lodge Resort and Golf Club
8205 Valley Greens Dr., Carmel, CA 93923; 408 624-1581

3-day; June and Sept.

Rates: $$$$

Info: Golf Digest Instruction Schools, 800 243-6121. See page 29 for programs and methods.

Located minutes from Big Sur, Quail Lodge is among Mobil's elite Five Star resorts. Rustic in decor and luxurious in character, the lakeside layout is set on 850 acres. Accommodations in deluxe rooms, suites and executive villas. Offers tennis, jogging trails, refined dining.

■ 18-hole, 6141 yard, par 71, Robert Muir Graves design, home to the annual Women's California Amateur Division and Men's California State Handicap Division; 17 acre practice range.

CARMEL
Paradise Golf Schools
Carmel Valley Ranch
One Old Ranch Rd., Carmel, CA 93923;   800 422-7635

5-day; 3-day, F-Sun; Masters program*; July-Sept

Rates: $$$-$$$$

Info: Paradise Golf Schools, 800 624-3543. See page 41 for programs and methods.

*Masters: $$$$, same format as 3 or 5 day programs plus 6-8 hours instruction, 1:1, with sought after, Class-A, PGA Pro, Jim Wright.

Amidst the rugged hills of the Monterey Peninsula, behind the guarded gates of the 100-suite Carmel Valley Ranch, lies a world of luxury and natural beauty. A gracious staff caters to guests' every need. The ranch-style lodge is characterized by a blend of antiques and early California furnishings with floor to ceiling windows disclosing dramatic views. This is a full amenity resort with five spas dotting the grounds.

■ Pete Dye's 18-hole course incorporates railroad ties, Moorish mounds, deep pot bunkers and three man-made lakes. Elevation changes as much as 400 feet. Four holes border the Carmel River, five more climb the hillside.

LA JOLLA
THE School of Golf Exclusively for Women

Whispering Palms Resort
2252 Caminito Preciosa Sur
La Jolla, CA 92037; 619 270-6230

President: Gilbert Mombach; Director: Shirley Spork

5-day, Sun-F, one week per month; March-June, Sept-Nov

Rates: $$$

Since 1978, women have been instructing women here with the goal of helping each student achieve a sound, confident, consistent swing for a lifetime of enjoyable golf. Director Shirley Spork, twice voted LPGA Teacher of the Year and named one of America's outstanding teachers by Golf Digest, believes there is nothing like watching yourself in action to learn what you're doing wrong and to chart improvement. Therefore, video analysis and step-by-step photography play an important role here – as does watchful, customized teaching by a staff of women, all Master or Class A pros expert in the art of communication and attuned to the finesse women need to lower their handicaps.

Curriculum designed for women who have had at least six private lessons. Provides seven hours daily instruction, including on-course teaching; 6:1 student/teacher ratio on the range; 5:1 on course; class limited to 36. Video analysis and personalized tape for at-home learning, instruction notebook, unlimited use of practice facilities; Pro-am scramble tournament. Includes 5 nights, all meals (commuter includes lunches, two dinners, no lodging). Provides San Diego Airport transfers, 30 minutes away.

Set in the rolling hills of Rancho Santa Fe, Whispering Palms Resort is entirely dedicated to golf. Lodging in four spacious buildings; pool.

◼ 27-hole, David Rainville course; school has nine holes for its exclusive use.

LOS ANGELES

Mazda Golf Clinics for Executive Women

Los Coyotes Country Club, March
Info: 800 262-7888. See page **73** for programs and methods.

NAPA

Heritage Golf Schools

Silverado Country Club and Resort
1600 Atlas Peak Rd., Napa, CA 94558
800 532-0500   707 257-0200

3-day, F-Sun or M-W; Aug

Rates: $$$$

Info: Heritage Golf Schools, 800 362-1469. See page 60 for programs and methods.

An Italianate-French mansion set on 1,200 acres in the heart of California's famous wine district has been transformed into an unparalleled resort. Guests accommodated in 280 private and personalized studios and suites clustered around pools and gardens. Outstanding dining at the resort and in the immediate area dotted with 20 wineries. Silverado enjoys the largest tennis complex in Northern California, a magnificent view of the Mayacamas Mountains, and a year round mean temperature of 72° F.

◼ Two celebrated courses designed by Robert Trent Jones Jr. Count on a dozen water crossings on the newest, the South Course, a par 72. The North course has been recognized by the National Groundskeepers Association for excellence. The pair are home to the Transamerica Championship, a senior PGA event.

NAPA

John Jacobs Practical Golf Schools

The Inn at Napa Valley
1075 California Blvd., Napa, CA 94559
707 253-9540

The Chardonnay Club, 2555 Jameson Canyon Rd., Napa
800 788-0136

4-day and 2-day weekend; June-Sept.

Rates: $$

Info: John Jacobs Practical Golf Schools, 800 472-5007. See page 6 for programs and methods.

Located in the heart of California's vineyard country, just north of San Francisco, the Inn combines first class amenities with the charm of a French country hotel. Outstanding dining in "Caffe 1991" situated in a landscaped atrium. Guest rooms are spacious, 2-room suites; includes breakfast and afternoon wine tastings. Five minutes from Napa Valley Airport.

■ The Chardonnay Club, 10 miles from the Inn (guests provide own transportation), offers two of California's most scenic courses: the tricky, links-style Vineyards Course and the private Shakespeare Course. Both designed by Algie Pulley, Jr., they grace 325 acres of hillside vineyards, small lakes and canyons.

PALM DESERT

Riley School of Golf

P.O. Box 3695
Palm Desert, CA 92261
 800 847-4539   619 341-1009

Director: Mike Schroder

3-day, 4-day, 5-day; 2-day weekend commuter program

Rates: $$-$$$

Locations: Warner Springs, CA; Myrtle Beach, SC

Director of instruction, Mike Schroder, is a former PGA Tour professional with 20 years teaching experience. He perfected his "Simplify Your Circle" technique in 12 years at his own popular Strand Academy in Myrtle Beach. Emphasis is on fundamentals and building good mechanics to achieve a consistent, confident swing. Classes are kept small to insure individualized attention and to impart an full understanding of the game and all its aspects.

Provides 5 hours daily instruction, 3:1 student/teacher ratio; stop-action video analysis with take-home instructional tape. On-course playing lessons; includes green fees and cart. Optional evening sessions on fitness, course management, rules, and topics of interest. Lifetime follow-up consultation via video or phone. Remembrance gift.

Programs include daily breakfasts and lunches. Five day program provides 5 nights, 2 dinners, cocktail parties; four-day: 4 nights, 1 dinner, cocktail party; three-day: 3 nights, 1 dinner, cocktail party. Commuter programs include lunch. Weekend commuter: 4½ hours instruction, Sat afternoon, Sun morning, 5:1 student/teacher ratio.

PALM SPRINGS AREA
Exceller Programs Golf Schools

Westin Mission Hills Resort Hotel
Dinah Shore and Bob Hope Dr., Rancho Mirage, CA 92270
800 999-8284   619 328-5955

5-day, 4-day, 2 day; Sept-May

Rates: $$-$$$

Info: Exceller Programs Golf Schools, 800 424-7438. See page 4 for programs and methods.

The 512-room, low slung, tile-roofed, luxury hotel features villa accommodations on 360 landscaped acres; spectacular pools, health club, acclaimed dining. Offers every comfort and service in a setting of rare elegance.

◼ Adjacent to the hotel, specially constructed practice facility at the acclaimed 18-hole, Gary Player-designed North Course, voted best new resort course in 1992. Pete Dye-designed second course offers 18-holes and a large private practice facility.

PALM SPRINGS AREA
Golf Digest Instruction Schools

Mission Hills Golf Course
34-600 Mission Hills Dr., Rancho Mirage, CA 92270; 619 321-8484

3-day, 2-day weekend, Mini-schools; Nov-March

Rates: $$$$, tuition only*

Info: Golf Digest Instruction Schools, 800 243-6121. See page 29 for programs and methods.

*Suggested accommodations: Westin Mission Hills Resort Hotel, 800 999-8284, see previous listing; ask school about alternative discounted lodging.

◼ The Resort Course, a Pete Dye design, offers 18-holes and a large private practice facility. Site of the LPGA Dinah Shore event.

PALM SPRINGS AREA
Heritage Golf Schools

La Quinta
49-499 Eisenhower Dr., La Quinta, CA 92253; 800 854-1271   619 564-4111

3-day, F-Sun or M-W; May

Rates: $$$$

Info: Heritage Golf Schools, 800 362-1469. See page 60 for programs and methods.

GOLF Magazine calls La Quinta "one of the finest golf resorts in America." This distinctive early California jewel provides every luxury. Charming casitas, a renown tennis center with stadium facility, shops, health club, refined dining – all in an incomparably landscaped setting.

◼ Instruction at La Quinta's Citrus course, created on the site of a citrus orchard by architect Pete Dye in 1987. Extend your vacation and play unforgettable golf at Pete Dye's Dunes Course, containing one of the toughest holes in America, or PGA West, host of "The Skins Game," both nearby.

PALM SPRINGS AREA

John Jacobs Practical Golf Schools

Marriott's Desert Springs Resort and Spa
74855 Country Club Dr., Palm Desert, CA 92260
619 341-2211

5-day and weekend; Oct- May

Rates: $$$, commuter rate applies on weekends; inquire about accommodations.

Info: John Jacobs Practical Golf Schools, 800 472-5007 See page 6 for programs and methods.

Marriott's Desert Springs presents an unparalleled setting and limitless recreation. Provides a serious tennis facility and instruction, a 27,000 square foot Health and Fitness Spa with every beauty and therapeutic means of achieving well-being, three pools. Offers bocci, basketball, croquet, sand court volleyball; 895 luxurious guest rooms, numerous specialty restaurants. Fully equipped rental villas on site (apply golf school commuter rates to school programs). Located eleven miles from Palm Springs Airport, two-hour drive from Los Angeles.

▶ Two rolling, challenging, championship courses crisscrossing the resort campus and an 18-hole putting course, all designed by Ted Robinson.

PALM SPRINGS AREA

John Jacobs Practical Golf Schools

Marriott's Rancho Los Palmas Resort & Country Club
41000 Bob Hope Dr., Rancho Mirage, CA 92270
800 ILUV-SUN   619 568-2727

5-day and 2-day weekend; Jan-April

Rates: $$$, commuter rate applies on weekends; inquire about accommodations.

Info: John Jacobs Practical Golf Schools, 800 472-5007. See page 6 for programs and methods.

Rancho Los Palmas Resort boasts secluded luxury on 240 lush acres. Accommodations in tile-roofed haciendas or hotel; pools, whirlpools, a complete exercise facility, 25-court tennis center, dining.

▶ Ted Robinson-designed, 27-hole course blends six lakes, 80 bunkers and over 1,500 palm trees with gently rolling terrain at the foot of Mt. San Jacinto. Each of the three nines – North, South and West – displays its own character.

PALM SPRINGS AREA

Swing's The Thing Golf Schools

PGA West Stadium Course, 56-150 PGA Blvd., La Quinta, CA 92253
619 564-PGAW

La Quinta Hotel* or Travelodge**

3-day VIP; Jan-April

Rates $$$*, $$**; VIP instruction limited to 12; provides two or three nights

Info: Swing's The Thing Golf School, 800 221-6661. See page 98 for programs and methods.

*The Spanish-style La Quinta (49-499 Eisenhower Dr., La Quinta, CA 92253, 800

854-1271) is legendary for refinement and luxury; boasts a stadium tennis facility with 40 courts; five pools, varied dining, shops; 640 rooms and suites in adobe haciendas spread among 45 flowering acres.

**The 54-room, centrally located Travelodge (80-651 Hwy. 111, Indio, CA 92201, 800 255-3050), serving the Coachella Valley, offers pool, tennis court, nearby restaurant and lounge.

🏳 As much a sculpture as a course, Pete Dye's PGA West is one of the most difficult – and rewarding – experiences in golf. Some holes have seven or eight different tees to make them playable for golfers of all abilities. Course is located 20 miles east of Palm Springs and minutes from the hotels.

PALO ALTO
Stanford Golf School for Adults

Stanford University
Palo Alto, CA
800 433-6060

Directors: Tim Baldwin and Wally Goodwin

3-day, W-F; Sept

Rates: $$, includes tuition, golf fees and meals; school will help students find accommodations.

Info and registration: Stanford Athletics/Golf Camp, 919 Sir Francis Drake Blvd., Kentfield, CA 94904; 800 433-6060. See page 127 for further details.

Stanford's top-rated varsity coaches, Tim Baldwin and Wally Goodwin, and a staff of PGA professionals, provide 4½ hours of well-rounded instruction daily followed by 18-holes of on-course training with an instructor. Includes personalized videotaped analysis, final day tournament and awards ceremony, golf fees and gift. Daily lunch and two dinners.

🏳 Stanford University Golf Course, 18 holes, with complete practice facility.

Tipping your pro is never wrong. See "How To Use This Book," page vi.

PEBBLE BEACH
Nicklaus Flick Golf School

The Inn at Spanish Bay
2700 17-Mile Dr., Pebble Beach, CA 92953; 800 654-9300

3-day Master Golf I; 3 half-day, Master Golf III; May-Sept

Rates: $$$$$

Info: Nicklaus Flick Golf School, 800 642-5528. See page 44 for programs and methods.

Cradled by the beautiful Del Monte Forest and barely 300 yards from the Pacific, the AAA Four Diamond-rated Inn occupies a 236-acre enclave entirely surrounded by golf. Boasts 254 elegant and luxurious rooms, four outstanding restaurants, tennis, a European spa, pool, miles of neighboring beachfront and hiking trails, an equestrian center, and a handsome club house with every amenity. Located seven miles from Monterey Airport, minutes from the quaint avenues of Carmel-by-the-Sea.

▣ The Links at Spanish Bay, 6,820 from the championship tees, are newly redesigned by the team of Tom Watson, Robert Trent Jones, Jr. and Frank "Sandy Tatum; World class golf is at hand at the quintet of spectacular courses at Pebble Beach: Spanish Bay, Pebble Beach, Spyglass Hill, Del Monte and Poppy Hills.

PEBBLE BEACH

The Golf Clinic, Pebble Beach California

P.O. Box 1129, Pebble Beach, CA 93953
800 321-9401   408 624-5421

Lodge at Pebble Beach and Inn at Spanish Bay*

Co-directors: John Geertsen, Jr. and Ben Alexander

5-day and 3-day programs; 3½-day, 2½-day, and 2-day; year round; Junior program (see page 128)

Rates: $$$$, luxury accommodations included in 5 and 3-day programs; inquire about numerous other lodging opportunities.

Other locations: Waikoloa, HI

Director of instruction, John Geertsen, Jr. uses his own book, "Your Turn for Success!" as the basis for golf teaching. Programs, now in their seventh year, are geared for students at all levels. The school emphasizes easy to understand fundamentals and basic mechanics. Mental aspects of the game are taught individually. Swing concepts are reinforced with discussion, exercises, practice and videotaping. Students receive complete written material and a supporting instructional video to augment continued learning.

Maximum 4:1 student/teacher ratio, class averages 8-12 students, personalized daily instruction. Program includes green fees and carts; optional free golf and cart following supervised play daily; videotaped swing analysis and instructional video, copy of "Your Turn for Success!" Lunches included. Five-day and 3-day programs provide a round at Pebble Beach, Spyglass and Poppy Hills; 5 nights (4 nights in 3-day program), breakfasts, 2 dinners. Shorter programs provide two 9-hole and one 18-hole round at Poppy Hills, daily lunch, no lodging.

*School refers students to a wide range of area lodging. See Inn at Spanish Bay, previous listing. The Lodge at Pebble Beach (17 Mile Dr., Pebble Beach, CA 93953, 800 654-9300) is a landmark along the legendary cypress-lined Monterey Peninsula. Comprised of an 11-room early-California style lodge and 150 rooms in 12 separate buildings, with spectacular views and every comfort. Fine dining, tennis, pools, massage, spa, equestrian program, nature trails and stunning vistas.

▣ Instruction is centered at a private driving range and short game facility at Poppy Hills Course (transportation provided). Students play Poppy Hills, Spyglass Hill (the super-challenging Robert Trent Jones coast and forest course) and the legendary Jack Neville-designed Pebble Beach Golf Links.

SAN DIEGO

The Golf University at San Diego

17550 Bernardo Oaks Dr., San Diego, CA 92128
800 426-0966   619 485-8880
Director: Scott Blanchard
4-day Golf University Program, M-Thu; 3-day weekend, F-Sun; Nov-June
Rates: $$$$, tuition only*

Learning is based on Dr. Ken Blanchard's innovative management concepts in his book "Playing the Greatest Game of Golf." His approach gradually transfers the role of teacher to the student, as golfers learn what they are doing well and where they must improve. Instructors deliver personalized training to players of every level, adapting the curriculum to each. Working together, pairs set goals and work toward reaching them, using a unique personal achievement scorecard.

All programs provide 6+ hours instruction daily, on-course playing lesson(s), videotaped swing evaluation with voice-over analysis, club fitting, instruction manual, free half-day follow-up to continue progress. Lunch daily. Four-day program also includes physical evaluation and exercise program, personal practice program, opening night dinner and cocktail party.

*Accommodations at Rancho Bernardo Inn (800 542-6096 or 619 487-1611) are additional and provide 5-day/4-nights deluxe hacienda room, breakfasts and dinners, green fees at West, Oaks North, and Temecula Creek Inn courses. Commuter rate available. Rancho Bernardo Inn is a celebrated 287-room, early California-style resort with pools, hydrospas, fitness facility, 12 tennis courts, acclaimed dining. Located 30 minutes from San Diego.

▉ 45 holes on site (access to a total of 108). The celebrated West course is a William Francis Bell, 18-hole, 6,388-yard, par 72; plus three executive nines designed by Ted Robinson.

SAN FRANCISCO

Mazda Golf Clinics for Executive Women

Stanford Golf Course, September
Info: 800 262-7888. See page 73 for programs and methods.

SANTA ROSA AREA

America's Favorite Golf Schools

Adobe Creek Golf Club, 1901 Frates, Petaluma, CA 94954; 707 765-3000
Quality Inn, Petaluma
5100 Montero Way, Petaluma, CA 94954; 800 221-2222   707 664-1155
5-day; 3-day, M-W or F-Sun; year round
Rates: $$

Info: America's Favorite Golf Schools, 800 365-6640. See page 36 for programs and methods.

Deluxe 110-room Inn situated at the gateway to wine and redwood country. Boasts in-room private spas and refrigerators; pool, whirlpool, free continental breakfast, dining. Located 40 minutes north of San Francisco.

■ Three miles from the Inn, Adobe Creek Golf Course is the area's newest 18-hole course, a Robert Trent Jones, Jr. challenger with a practice area designed by Jones, himself. Site of Nike Tour qualifier rounds.

WARNER SPRINGS RANCH

Riley School of Golf

Warner Springs Ranch
31652 Highway 79, Warner Springs, CA 92086; 619 782-3555

5-day, 4-day, 3-day; weekend commuter; year round

Rates: $$$

Info: Riley School of Golf, 800 847-4539. See page 16 for programs and methods.

Situated at 3,000 feet in the foothills of Palomar Mountain, the secluded Warner Springs Ranch (in the town of the same name, pop. 200) covers 2,552 rolling acres, one and a half hours northeast of San Diego. Lodging in spacious cottages, many with fireplaces. Spa, health and beauty facilities, high and low ropes courses, fresh water pools and naturally revitalizing hot springs; 15 tennis courts, equestrian center with lessons and guided rides. Dine formally in the Lodge or in two casual restaurants (includes all meals). Private airport.

■ 18-hole course is known for its manicured bent grass greens, treacherous bunkers and challenging landing areas. Tree-lined fairways give way to breathtaking scenic outlooks uncluttered by the advances of civilization.

COLORADO

COLORADO SPRINGS

The Academy of Golf at The Broadmoor

1 Lake Ave.; Colorado Springs, CO 80906; 800 634-7711   719 577-5790

3-day, Fri-Sun or Tu-Thu; June-Sept

Rates: $$$

Info: The Academy of Golf at PGA National, 800 832-6235. See page 52 for programs and methods.

A Colorado landmark, this 550-room, Five Star-Gold Medal oldie offers up-to-the-minute comforts and activities galore: tennis, shooting (trap and skeet), swimming, paddle boating, fishing, hiking, mountain biking, croquet, squash, shuffleboard, acclaimed and varied dining, plus nearly limitless area festivals and events ranging from the Rodeo Hall of Fame to July's annual Pike's Peak Auto Climb. Located 60 miles south of Denver. Includes three nights, breakfasts and lunches.

■ Provides state-of-the-art analyzation equipment, the ultimate practice facility and three pedigreed courses. The East Course, designed in 1918 by Donald Ross, remains challenging and beautifully integrated with nature; plays 7,218 from championship tees, par 72. The West Course, with nine holes constructed in 1950 and a second nine in 1965, is a Robert Trent Jones, Sr. design in the traditional style. Toughest, shortest, newest, and boasting the greatest elevation changes is the Arnold Palmer-Ed Seay South Course.

Programs, prices, locations and personnel change from time to time. Be certain to contact the schools directly to clarify the information contained in these pages.

COLORADO SPRINGS

Academy of Golf Dynamics

Garden of the Gods Resort - Kissing Camels Golf Club
P.O. Box 1677, Colorado Springs, CO 80901;   719 632-5541
3-day midweek, 3-day weekend; spring/summer

Rates: $$$

Info: Academy of Golf Dynamics, 800-879-2008. See page 108 for programs and methods.

A spectacular natural formation of sheer cliffs, towers, and balancing rocks gives this private resort its name. The peerless Garden of the Gods Resort offers gourmet dining, indoor and outdoor tennis, pools, and renown service. The Academy of Golf Dynamics brings its Class A PGA professional staff from Texas to this mountain resort course. Class size limited to 15; 3-day program includes lodging, breakfast and lunch and one round of golf.

■ At the private Kissing Camels Golf Club, the championship 18-hole course designed by Jay Press Maxwell, fair and generous with large greens. It is a mountain-side course located at the base of Pike's Peak at an elevation of 6,400 feet; plays 7,106 yards from the back tees.

COPPER MOUNTAIN

Bill Skelley School of Golf

Copper Mountain Resort - Copper Creek Golf Club
P.O. Box 3415, Copper Mountain, CO 80443
800 458-8386   303 968-2882

5-day, 3-day; June-Sept

Rates: $$

Info: Bill Skelley School of Golf, 800 541-7707 or 305 828-9740. See page 40 for programs and methods.

The jagged Ten Mile Mountain Range and wide open expanses of the Gore Wilderness Area provide a gorgeous backdrop for the AAA Four Diamond-ranked Copper Mountain Resort. Offers a wide variety of activities: rafting, jeep and canoe tours, tennis, hiking, swimming, cycling, horseback riding, and much more. Highlight of the resort is the showcase, $3 million Racquet and Athletic Club with every service and amenity. Located 70 miles west of Denver. Programs provide four or two nights.

■ Challenging, 6,094-yard, par 70, Pete and Perry Dye-designed course, at the highest altitude of any course in America: 9,650 feet. Setting is incomparable for its beauty.

CRESTED BUTTE

John Jacobs Practical Golf Schools

The Lodge at Skyland - Skyland Country Club
385 Country Club Dr., Crested Butte, CO 81225; 800 433-5684   303 349-6131
4-day and 2-day weekend; June-Sept

Rates: $$

Info: John Jacobs Practical Golf Schools, 800 472-5007. See page 6 for programs and methods.

Nestled against the southern slope of towering Mt. Crested Butte in the heart of the majestic Colorado Rockies, Crested Butte is an old mining town, 29 miles from Gunnison Airport and 230 miles southwest of Denver. Skyland's 31,000 square foot clubhouse is home to a restaurant, lounge, indoor swimming pool, racquetball courts and adjoining tennis courts. Lodge offers 49 rooms and condos in a woodland setting. Abundant, stimulating outdoor recreation.

■ Skyland's 7,200 yard, 18-hole, Robert Trent Jones, Jr. course is rated in the top 1% of courses in the U.S. The front nine is wide open American design with four trout streams running through pine and aspen. The back nine features the best of the Scottish links with narrow twisting fairways, elevated tees and two-tiered greens. Number thirteen's 9,000-foot elevation commands magnificent vistas.

> *We'd like to know how you fared. Please comment on your golf school experience, using the form at the back of the book.*
>
>

DURANGO

Innisbrook Golf Institute

Tamarron Resort at Durango
40292 U.S. Hwy. 550 N., Durango, CO 81301
800 678-1000   303 259-2000

5-day program; June-early Sept

Rates: $$$; provides 12 hours instruction, six hours on-course training.

Info: Innisbrook Golf Institute, 800 456-2000. See page 59 for programs and methods.

A world class resort with all the charm of the Old West, situated 18 miles north of Durango, in the towering San Juan mountains. Deluxe accommodations in the rustic main lodge. Breathtaking views from the resort's three restaurants. Horseback riding, hiking, private fishing pond, tennis, full Health Club, indoor/outdoor pool, cookouts, hay rides. Equally distant from Denver and Phoenix; includes round trip airport transfers to Durango Airport.

■ Unparalleled vistas on this thinking man's, 18-hole, Arthur Hills-designed mountain course, 6,885 yards, par 72, challenging for even the best. The fairways abut canyons and sheer rock cliffs and open onto flower-strewn meadows. Rated by Golf Digest among the top 75 resort courses in the country.

GUNNISON

Rocky Mountain Family Golf School

40 W. Littleton Blvd. 201-270
Littleton, CO 80120; 303 932-2664
Director: Ollie Woods
5-day, 4-day, 3-day; June-Aug

Rates: $, tuition only; the school supplies information on motels, many of which offer a discount to golf students; a host of campgrounds dot the area.

Rocky Mountain Golf School makes the golf swing simple and natural. Class A, PGA instructors, with more than 100 years experience among them, employ video and graph checks to monitor progress. They stress the mental aspects of the game, using a method devised by Dr. Fred Barnabei. More than 50% of students at this enjoyable, 17-year-old school are back to sharpen their game. Families and golfers at all levels are welcome.

Furnishes four hours daily staff instruction, 8:1 student teacher ratio, class limited to 32. Full use of facilities, sequence photographs, video replay, electronic swing analyzer, Dave Pelz putting methods, complimentary round of golf, evening session on mental skills in 4- and 5-day sessions.

Rocky Mountain Golf School urges participants to take advantage of the fabulous countryside in the Gunnison area. Enjoy river rafting, backpacking, fishing, sightseeing, mountaineering – and, of course, golf. Direct flights to Gunnison Airport from major U.S. cities.

■ Non-regulation, par 3 course at school's Woods Golf Practice Area. Free 18-hole round at Dos Rios Country Club; additional discounted golf at Dos Rios and Skyland Country Club, a Robert Trent Jones, Jr. course in Crested Butte, rated among top 1% of courses in nation.

> *Pay attention. Golf schools are promoted as fun but, whenever possible, withstand the urge to socialize until lunch or cocktails. And listen to your instructor, not to your spouse or the duffer beside you on the range.*

LITTLETON

America's Favorite Golf School

Lone Tree Resort
9808 Sunningdale Blvd., Littleton, CO 80124; 303 790-0202
5-day; 3-day, M-W or F-Sun; May-Oct
Rates: $$

Info: America's Favorite Golf Schools, 800 365-6640. See page **36** for programs and methods.

Located 20 minutes south of Denver, Lone Tree is a "public country club," offering 15 luxurious suites, swimming, tennis, spa with massage therapy, complimentary continental breakfast.

 An Arnold Palmer, 18-hole, 7,012-yard, scenic course with multiple tees, well bunkered and featuring spectacular views of downtown Denver. Practice is centered on a dedicated range and area simulating on-course play.

M O S C A

Bobby Eldridge Golf School

Great Sand Dunes Country Club and Inn
5303 Hwy. 150, Mosca, CO 81146; 719 378-2356
Director: Bobby Eldridge
3-day, Sun-W; July-Sept
Rates: $$
Info: Bobby Eldridge Golf School, 800 284-9213

The Eldridge philosophy is geared toward helping each student reach his or her own potential. A flexible and attentive staff of PGA pros concentrates on swing fundamentals and creative practice, teaching students how to prevent (and solve) trouble. In classes not exceeding 6:1 student/teacher ratio, students learn how to read greens for improved putting and how to differentiate the techniques needed to improve their short game. Emphasis is placed on choosing the correct club, mastering uneven lies and overcoming bunkers – all the essentials to reduce strokes. Provides 18-20 hours instruction, on-course training, green fees and cart, four nights, all meals, welcoming cocktail party.

One of a kind resort offers authentic Old Western ambience. Total of 15 rooms in the Inn (a former stage coach stop) and in the bunk house and ranch house. Handmade quilts, old cloth tubs, and rustic decor contrast with up-to-the-minute health club with sauna and jacuzzi, pool and acclaimed cuisine by the resort's Danish-born chef. Located five miles from entrance to Great Sand Dunes National Monument, 200 miles south of Denver.

 Located at the base of the Sangre de Cristo Mountain Range in southern Colorado, golfers tee off beneath Great Sand Dunes National Monument, seven magnificent towering peaks, 14,000 feet high. The course is cut from among cottonwoods, cedars and golden aspens and within hailing distance of the third-largest herd of buffalo in the nation. In the Scottish-links style, Great Sand Dunes presents elevated greens and plays 6,816 yards.

P U E B L O

Craft-Zavichas Golf School

600 Dittmer, Pueblo, Colorado 81005
800 858-9633 719 564-4449
Director: Penny Zavichas
3-day, 4-day and 5-day; coed and Women's Only
Rates: $$
Other locations: Tucson, AZ; Klamath Falls, OR
Since 1968, founders Penny Zavichas and Linda Craft, both pioneering LPGA

professionals, have been offering instruction to golfers of all levels. Teaching at Craft-Zavichas is made compatible with natural body balance and flow of motion. According to Penny Zavichas – teaching pro for 33 years, 1973 LPGA Teacher of the Year and niece of legendary Babe Didrickson Zaharias – "The natural golf motion includes an underhand swing and follow-through by the dominant side of your body. Without this, the golfer is inevitably lacking in distance and direction" Students are taught personally and simply to use the dominant sides of their bodies as the source of energy and consistency in the golf swing.

Hours of instruction vary at each of the school's three sites. All sessions insure separate men's and women's classes, maximum 5:1 student/teacher ratio, split video analysis with take-home tape, on-course instruction and strategy sessions, instructional manual, complimentary green fees, cart and unlimited play after class, club storage.

P U E B L O

Craft-Zavichas Golf School

Inn at Pueblo West - Pueblo West Golf Club
251 South McCulloch Blvd, Pueblo West, CO 81007
719 547-2111

4-day, May; 4-day Women Only; June

Rates: $$

Info: Craft-Zavichas Golf School, 800 858-9633. Consult previous listing for programs and methods.

Four day sessions provide 20+ hours instruction, M-Th; 6 days, 5 nights accommodations (Sun-F), 2 banquet receptions, 4 lunches, green fees and cart on school days. Women's Only program: women to women instruction, scramble Pro-Am tournament, evening seminars.

Situated in the high desert at an altitude of 5,000 ft., the 80-room Inn at Pueblo West offers pleasant southwestern-style lodging, personalized atmosphere, pool and tennis facilities, varied dining and abundant sunshine.

◼ Pueblo West Golf Club, 18 holes with ideal practice facility.

S T E A M B O A T   S P R I N G S

Sheraton Steamboat Resort and Conference Center

2200 Village Inn Ct., Steamboat Springs, CO 80477
800 848-8878   303 879-2220

One day program, Fri; private instruction, playing lessons, daily clinics; May-Oct

Rates: $$, tuition only

One-day school is comprised of eight hours personalized instruction and play with full swing and short game review, practice drills, video analysis; 4:1 student/teacher ratio. Includes lunch and all golf fees (no lodging). Culminates in a 9-hole Pro-Am event concentrating on course strategy. Program stresses all aspects of the game with emphasis on individual needs.

Sheraton Steamboat is a full destination, multi-story, 300-room resort with tennis, pools, restaurants, spa; adjacent to shopping. Area offers numerous outdoor activities.

■ Sheraton Steamboat Golf Club boasts a Robert Trent Jones, Jr. 18-hole course at 6,900 foot elevation with spectacular views of the lush Yampa Valley, Flat Top Mountains, Fish Creek Canyon and Mt. Werner. A beautiful, wide river accents seven holes of the back nine.

VAIL

Golf Digest Instruction Schools

Sonnenalp Hotel and Country Club
20 Vail Rd., Vail, CO 81657
800 654-8312   303 476-5656

3-day; June - Aug

Rates: $$$$

Info: Golf Digest Instruction Schools, 800 243-6121. See page 29 for programs and methods.

Located in the center of Vail Village, three separate houses comprise the 165-room, Bavarian family-owned Sonnenalp, known for luxury, friendliness, renowned cuisine, charming and elegant decor. The Sonnenalp's attentive service and attention to detail is legendary. Located 125 miles west of Denver.

■ At Sonnenalp Country Club (1265 Berry Creek Rd., Edwards, CO 81632, 303 926-3533), a short distance from the village, Singletree is rated by Golf Digest as one of America's "Top 50 Resort Courses." In upland rocky terrain in the Scottish style, the Jay Morrish and Bob Cupp course plays 6,423 yards from the middle tees. Generous practice facilities in excellent condition.

VAIL

Vail Golf Club Schools

Vail Golf Club, 1778 Vail Valley Dr., Vail, CO 81657
303 479-2260

Director: Steve Satterstrom

3-day; May-Aug

Rates: $, tuition only*

Golfers of all levels come to groove their swings and gain an understanding of their game in a relaxed atmosphere, 8,000 feet above par. PGA pros treat each student individually, exploring their goals and expectations and utilizing the latest video technology in enhancing their learning experience. School begins where it's at: on the course where instructors videotape students' swings and observe their golfing skills. Twenty hours instruction in classes not exceeding a 4:1 student/teacher ratio; two playing lessons plus on-course short game instruction.

*School suggests lodging at a celebrated, 12-room, bed and breakfast, occupying a handcrafted log structure: the Black Bear Inn. Offers hearty breakfasts and uncommon amenities (303 476-1304).

■ Nestled beneath the towering peaks of the Gore Range, 18-hole Vail Golf Course was laid out by local architects who understood how to route a golf course through the majestic Rocky Mountains. Forested and hilly, with Gore Creek running throughout, the course opens out to reveal fabulous vistas. Plays 7,064 from the champ tees; par 71.

A fabric softener strip tucked into the laces of your golf shoe will likely deter bugs. As will Avon Skin So Soft – more pleasant than conventional insect repellents.

CONNECTICUT

MYSTIC

America's Favorite Golf Schools

Mystic Ramada Inn
Interstate 95 & Route 27, Mystic, CT 06355
800-2-RAMADA   203 536-4281

Stonington Country Club, Taugwonk Rd., Stonington, CT 06378
203 535-4035

5-day; 3-day, M-W or F-Sun; May-Oct

Rates: $$

Info: America's Favorite Golf Schools, 800 365-6640. See page 36 for programs and methods.

The world famous Mystic Seaport offers scenic beauty, seafaring lore, festivals, quaint shops, resort casinos, a Seaquarium, ocean sports without parallel and some of the finest seafood restaurants in New England. The 150-room Ramada Inn is located in the heart of area attractions. Provides indoor pool, game room, sauna, restaurant.

◼ Scenic 3,352-yard, 9-hole layout at Stonington Country Club, all that's necessary to learn and practice. Additional nine holes on the drawing board, plus extensive clubhouse and sports facilities. Area 18-hole courses welcome golfers.

TRUMBULL

Golf Digest Instruction Schools

5520 Park Ave., Box 395, Trumbull, CT 06611-0395
203 373-7130

Director: John D. Hobbins

5-day, 3-day, 2-day; half-day Mini Schools, 2-day weekend schools; special programs for parent/child (ages 12-18), Ladies Only, VIP

Rates: $$$$; unless otherwise noted, programs do not include lodging; school will suggest accommodations.

Locations: Over 250 sessions annually at Tuscaloosa, AL; North Scottsdale, AZ; Carmel and Rancho Mirage, CA; Vail, CO; Tampa, FL; Atlanta and St. Sea Island, GA; Sun Valley, ID; Chicago, IL area; Brewster, MA; Uwharrie Point, NC

The key to Golf Digest's instruction is the talented, handpicked instructors, themselves. The Golf Digest method, instituted in 1971 by Golf Digest magazine, relies primarily on inspired, attentive teaching emphasizing fundamentals, the mental game, course strategy and fitness. Students range from Tour players to rank beginners. Sessions are limited to a maximum of 21 students, with senior staff at every session along with support instructors. Utilizes videotaped analysis and sends students home with his or her own instructional tape and practice program. Teaching sites are designed for learning and are separate from the facilities at each host resort.

Three and five-day regular schools include all-day instruction; five-day program provides two 9-hole playing lessons, complimentary golf after-school, 6 nights lodging (4 nights in 3-day program), all meals. Two-day weekend school, limited to six students, includes lunches, no lodging. Mini-school consists of three half-day sessions, consecutive mornings or afternoons, limited to 6 or 12; includes lunches, no lodging.

Special programs: VIP school at Tuscaloosa, AL provides five days intensive instruction, limited to 16 students with five instructors and 3+ support staff; emphasizes mental aspects with sports psychologist, Dr. Bob Rotella; no meals or lodging. Also 3-day Low Handicap school (handicaps 0-10) and 3-day Short Game schools. Five-day Parent/Child School, Sea Island, GA, see page 139. Golf Digest will base instructional programs at students' home courses across the country.

D E L A W A R E

W I L M I N G T O N

Great Golf Learning Centers

1800 Naamans Rd., Wilmington, DE 19810

800 TEE-OFF-9   302 475-3430

Half-hour individual sessions or prepaid subscription plan

Rate: $-$$, tuition only

Info: Great Golf Learning Centers, 1001 Lower Landing Rd., Suite 303, Blackwood, N.J. 08012; 800 TEE-OFF-9. See page 83 for programs and methods. Call for learning center nearest you.

■ One of 18 franchised learning centers teaching a unique full swing method. Provides 11 hitting stations, 1:1 instruction, Pathfinder® club, videography, PGA teaching pros trained in Great Golf system.

Channel your energies wisely throughout your program. Pace yourself. Conserve your energy during on-range instruction. You'll likely be having afternoon playing lessons or playing golf later in the day. And be sure to stretch well before class.

FLORIDA

AMELIA ISLAND

Ron Philo's Golf School

Amelia Island Plantation
P.O. Box 3000, Amelia Island, FL 32035
800 874-6878

Director: Ron Philo

3-day (Tu-Thu or F-Sun), April-Nov; 3-day Ladies Only, May; 5-day regular program, Oct; 5-day Junior schools (see page 131); lessons and clinics by appointment

Rates: $$-$$$, tuition only; various rates for guests of the resort, club members and commuter students; does not include lodging, meals or golf fees.

Father and son professionals, Ron Philo Sr. and Jr., emphasize that enjoyable golf begins with competence. In a simplified, personalized program, students are made aware of the correct mechanics involved in an efficient and effective golf swing. In small classes, they are taught elements of position and the shape of the golf swing. Instructors stress the importance of the short game as a means of reducing score and help students define realistic short-term and long-term golfing goals.

Provides 4½ hours daily instruction, limited to 15 students, 5:1 student/teacher ratio; individual video analysis with take-home tape, personal notebook and learning guide. Course-ready students receive on-course training in shot-making and management; beginners play learning center, par 3 hole.

Located on the southern end of Amelia Island, the Plantation is a 1,250-acre sanctuary between the Intracoastal Waterway and the Atlantic, 29 miles from Jacksonville Airport (reserve van service 24 hours in advance). Amelia's sugar-white beach is acclaimed as one of the 10 most beautiful in the world. Offers 21 tennis courts, pools, state-of-the art health and fitness center, miles of nature trails, fishing, sailing, water sports. Inn or hotel rooms or lodging in 1-, 2- or 3-bedroom villas equipped with every convenience.

■ World renown, 18-hole, Tom Fazio-designed Long Point Course, plus Amelia Links, 27 holes composed of Oceanside, Oysterbay and Oakmarsh, a Pete Dye concept. Look out for wind on Oceanside, alligators on Oysterbay and on Oakmarsh, beware of the 8th green perched on a peninsula jutting into a lagoon.

> *Student/teacher ratio: What does it mean? If the student/teacher ratio in your program is 4:1 and the total class is 12, you can expect one teacher for every four students on the range, in short game instruction and on-course training, with regular 1:1 consultations. Lectures will most likely be delivered to the entire group of 12.*

BOCA RATON

Dave Pelz Short Game School

Boca Raton Resort & Club
501 E. Camino Real, P.O. Box 5025, Boca Raton, FL 33431
800 327-0101   407 395-3000

Director: Jo Ann Pelz

3-day Executive, Premier and Alumni; March-June; Juniors (see page 131)*

Rates: $$$$

Info and reservations: Dave Pelz Short Game School, 1200 Lakeway Dr., Suite 21, Austin, TX 78734; 800 833-7370, 512 261-6493.

Golf scientist Dave Pelz maintains that the short game is the most misunderstood and neglected part of the game, yet these shots make up three out of every five swings. The curriculum is entirely devoted to improving students' putting, sand and wedge shots. The approach is highly scientific, calling on the latest research and teaching aids. Students internalize learning in classes with a 4:1 student/teacher ratio and the likes of "Wedgy, the mechanical wedge robot," "Perfy, the putting robot," slow motion replay and stop action photos, and laser alignment/position aids.

*Juniors, ages 13-17, accepted with an adult; Dave Pelz is personally involved in Executive sessions; Premier sessions are conducted by pros trained by Dave Pelz; Alumni programs are restricted to graduates of the school. Programs provide 8 hours daily instruction; includes lunch.

Includes three nights in The Cloister of the Boca Raton Resort and Club, rated by Golf Digest among the top golfing resorts in the country. The Mobil Five Star, AAA Five Diamond facility is set on 223 acres abounding with natural beauty, man-made comfort and unlimited activities. Convenient to Miami, Ft. Lauderdale and Palm Beach airports.

▶ Learning takes place on a newly constructed practice facility devoted entirely to the school. Two 18-hole, championship, Joe Lee-designed courses, one on the estate, a second nearby at Boca Country Club.

CAPE CORAL

Cape Coral Golf School

Cape Coral Golf & Tennis Resort
4003 Palm Tree Blvd., P.O. Box 150066, Cape Coral, FL 33915
800 648-1475   813 542-3191

Director: Todd Starane

4-day, begins Sun or Thu; year round

Rates: $$

Enjoy unregimented instruction while vacationing. At this school, students do not hit balls all day from driving stations. Instead, with a 4:1 student/teacher ratio, students' swings are videotaped and critiqued, correction is introduced and students and instructors take to the course to practice where it counts. Through clear and concise instruction, each student is encouraged to visualize his or her own optimal swing and to try to achieve it.

Includes complementary golf afternoon of arrival; 12 hours personalized instruction (4 mornings); unlimited daily afternoon golf, green fees and cart included; unlimited use of practice facility; graduation certificate. Provides 3 nights, 3 breakfasts and dinners, graduation luncheon.

A 100-room hotel in the tradition of Southern hospitality, with 8 tennis courts, oversized pool, 3 restaurants, spacious grounds; close to beaches, shopping and fishing charters. Convenient to Southwest Florida Regional Airport.

■ Dick Wilson-designed, 18-hole, championship course, 6,771 yards.

CLEARWATER

The Florida Golf School

Holiday Inn Surfside
400 Mandalay Ave., Clearwater Beach, FL 34630
800-HOLIDAY or 813 461-3222

Bardmoor Country Club, 7979 Bardmoor Blvd., Largo, FL 34647
813 397-0483

5-day; 3-day, M-W or Fri-Sun; Oct-May

Rates: $$

Info: The Florida Golf School, 800 365-6727. See page 36 for programs and methods.

Multi-story, 428-room, beachfront hotel features varied dining and lounges, concierge service, fitness center, nightly entertainment; 25 minutes from Tampa International Airport.

■ Par 72, 18 holes at Bardmoor Country Club, former home of the J.C. Penny Classic. Championship course characterized by small elevated greens, plays 6,960 from the blue tees, with water in play on 10 holes. Comprehensive, new Tom Fazio-designed practice facility.

CLEARWATER

United States Golf Schools

Belleview Mido Resort Hotel
25 Belleview Blvd., Clearwater, FL 34616
800 282-8072   813 442-6171

5-day, 3-day and 2-day weekend; year round

Rates: $-$$

Info: United States Golf Schools, 800 354-7415. See page 55 for programs and methods.

The Belleview Mido Resort Hotel is the largest occupied wooden structure in the world, with 292 spacious, renovated rooms, four restaurants, four all-weather clay tennis courts, six pools, Jacuzzis, a spa and fitness center. Up-to-the-minute amenities have not tarnished the grace and elegance of this charming period piece.

■ At Belleview Mido Country Club, a classic, 1925 Donald Ross-design, 18 holes, par 72, manicured and pampered. Plays 6,550 yards from the back tees.

CORAL GABLES

Heritage Golf Schools

The Biltmore Hotel
1200 Anastasia Ave., Coral Gables, FL 33134
800 727-1926

3-day, F-Sun or M-W; April and Nov

Rates: $$$$

Info: Heritage Golf Schools, 800 362-1469. See page 60 for programs and methods.

The Biltmore, opened in 1926, is listed on the National Historic Register. Restored to its original splendor and with every possible amenity for the discriminating guest, the tile-roofed, towered, grand dame of luxury affords a refined step back in time.

■ Course architect extraordinaire, Donald Ross, outdid himself on the 18-hole Biltmore course. The layout has been restored to its origins through drawings discovered in Ross's archives.

CRYSTAL RIVER

The Golf School

Plantation Inn and Golf Resort
Crystal River, FL 32629
800 632-6262   904 795-4211

Director: Jay Morelli

5-day, 2-day weekend; Oct-April

Rates: $$-$$$, rates at Plantation Inn adjusted for dates and accommodations.

Info and reservations (winter): The Golf School, P.O. Box 1116, Crystal River, FL 32629, 800 632-6262.

Other locations: West Dover, VT (Mt. Snow); Ocean City, MD

Director of Golf, Jay Morelli, 1988 New England PGA Teacher of the Year, has graduated 42,000 golfers. His Accelerated Method™ speeds the learning process and provides lasting improvement. Using motion as the foundation for developing a strong repeating swing, instructors stress timing, balance and rhythm. Videography reinforces correct grip, posture, alignment and target swing.

Five hours daily instruction, 4:1 student/teacher ratio, 40% of instruction on course (depending upon proficiency); use of clubs and all practice facilities, club fitting, after school and evening clinics. Unlimited complimentary green fees and carts. Five day program: 25 hours instruction, tournament, 5 nights; two-day program: 10 hours instruction, 2 nights. Programs at Plantation Inn include all meals, welcome cocktail party, banquet, social program. (Meals and accommodations vary site to site.)

Plantation Inn is a Mobil Four Star, ante-bellum style resort offering a marina and water sports on the Crystal River; pool, dining, lighted tennis courts. Lodging in the Inn, golf villas or condominiums. Located 70 minutes north of Tampa.

■ 27 holes, annual host of the Florida Women's Open; nine holes dedicated to the use of The Golf School.

> *If you do not own clubs, don't buy them before golf school. Chances are you can rent or borrow. Your school will likely offer an equipment clinic and club fitting for proper length, grip size and swing weight.*

Jimmy Ballard Golf Workshops

Jacaranda Golf Club
9200 W. Broward Blvd, Plantation FL 33324; 305 475-2250

2-day, Tu & W; 3 Half-Days, Thu-Sat; 3-day Mind/Body Connection, Thu-Sat; private VIP or staff lessons, Playing Lessons; Dec-Mar

Rates: staff $$-$$$, with Jimmy Ballard $$$, tuition only; school's private travel agency (800 284-9181) will arrange accommodations.

Info: Jimmy Ballard Golf Workshops, 305 475-2250 (winter); 803 837-3000 (April-Nov). See page 99 for programs and methods.

■ Complete practice facility at Jacaranda Golf Club, with two of South Florida's premier, semi-private courses.

John Jacobs Practical Golf Schools

Bonaventure Resort and Spa
250 Racquet Club Rd., Ft. Lauderdale, FL 33326; 800 327-8090

5-day, 2-day weekend; Oct-April

Rates: $$$; tuition only for weekend programs; ask John Jacobs Travel Desk for hotel rates.

Info: John Jacobs Practical Golf Schools, 800 472-5007. See page 6 for programs and methods.

Located on 1,250 acres of lush, tropical landscape, the 504-room hotel offers three freshwater pools, 23 tennis courts, squash and racquetball courts, cycling and jogging paths, a 51-stall equestrian center and an acclaimed spa.

■ Designed by Joe Lee, the championship East Course has been named one of Florida's "Top Ten" by GOLF Magazine. The 18-hole, West Course designed by Charlie Mahanna is pleasant and shorter.

Galvano International Golf Academy

Gateway Golf and Polo Club
11360 Championship Dr., Ft. Meyers, FL 33913; 813 561-1010

4-day, Tu-F, Jan-Mar; one 2-day program, Mar

Rates: $, tuition only; school arranges special rates at nearby hotels and resorts.

Info: Galvano International Golf Academy, 800 234-6121. See page 122 for programs and methods.

■ Rated among the top five semi-private courses in Florida, the 18-hole Gateway Golf and Polo Club, a Westinghouse property, is Titleist's testing center. The company's ball-striking robot is mesmerizing. A number of the country's big-name pros work on their game on Gateway's challenging Tom Fazio layout. Club has been host to the 1990 and 1991 Ben Hogan Gateway Open and the Southwest Florida Golf and Music Festival. Boasts a full training facility.

FORT PIERCE

The Florida Golf School - America's Favorite Golf Schools

P.O. Box 3325, Fort Pierce, FL 34948
800 365-6727   800 365-6640   407 464-3706
Director: Geoff Bryant
5-day; 3-day, M-W or F-Sun
Rates: $$
Locations: Florida Golf School holds programs at six Florida sites: Clearwater, Pompano Beach, Lehigh, Orlando, Naples and Palm Coast. America's Favorite Golf Schools operate at Santa Rosa, CA; Littleton, CO; Mystic, CT; Orlando and Pompano Beach, FL; Las Vegas, NV; Gettysburg, PA.

These two schools are administrated jointly. Their philosophy can be summed up in one word: "Simple." Methods are based on sound principles which have been simplified to help students easily grasp the mechanics of the golf swing. Instructors are selected not just for golfing expertise but for their ability to communicate. The vacation aspect of golf school is not lost, with ample "down" time to allow students to work on their game or take advantage of the niceties of each site.

Students are grouped according to ability, with the student/teacher ratio never exceeding 4:1, maximum 20 students in each session. Instructors deliver five hours instruction daily, including on-course play, frequent videotaping and critiques; complimentary green fees and carts during and after class. Florida Golf Schools provides lodging and all meals. America's Favorite Golf Schools provides lodging and no meals – on the premise that students wish to make their own choices.

JUPITER

Professional Golf Schools of America

103 U.S. Hwy. 1, Suite F5-150, Jupiter, FL 33477; 800 447-2744
Director: Mike Lucas
5-day; 3-day, M-W or F-Sun
Rates: $$
Locations: Mesa, AZ; Maggie Valley, NC; Mount Pocono, PA

Professional Golf Schools of America says K.I.S: Keep It Simple. In an uncomplicated, standardized approach, instructors stress the importance of the dynamically correct golf swing, thus providing consistency and accuracy.

Includes complimentary golf afternoon of arrival (subject to availability); 5 hours instruction daily, 4:1 student/teacher ratio, video analysis, on-course instruction,

01:52PM 28/10/93 367/460 4629 0152553

```
   1X 618 087299569456
TRADITIONAL SEPARATE            58.00
   1X 621 087296503156
TRADITIONAL CO-ORD.             58.00

       SUBTOTAL                116.00
       GST                       8.12
       PST                       9.28
       ** TOTAL **             133.40 T
EATON 060572100950/ 00
       CREDIT                  133.40
       CHANGE                    0.00 C
```

THANK YOU - TO EXCHANGE MERCHANDISE
PLEASE PRESENT THIS BILL

GST # R105254007

full use of practice facilities, daily green fees and carts. Programs provide lodging and all meals. Package rate may be applied to an extended stay. Efforts are made to pair unaccompanied golfers for double occupancy.

KISSIMMEE

Swing's The Thing Golf School

Orange Lake Country Club Resort
8505 W. Irlo Brondon Memorial Hwy, Kissimmee, FL 34747
800 877-6522   407 239-0000

3-day; year round

Rates $$-$$$

Info: Swing's The Thing Golf School, 800 221-6661 or 717 421-6666. See page 98 for programs and methods.

Includes three nights in fully appointed golf villas or clubhouse suites. Olympic-sized pool, hot tubs, kiddie facilities; 80-acre lake for water sports, 16 tennis courts with 7,000-seat stadium. The resort's 200,000 square foot clubhouse features shuffle-board, mini golf, health and fitness center, billiard and game room and general store. Numerous dining options. Convenient to Disney World and Orlando Airport.

■ Joe Lee-designed, 27-hole resort course with practice facilities. The three nines are Lake, Cypress and Orange.

LEHIGH

The Florida Golf School

Lehigh Resort and Country Club
225 E. Joel Blvd., Lehigh, FL 33936; 800 843-0971   813 369-2121

5-day; 3-day, M-W or F-Sun; Oct-May

Rates: $$

Info: The Florida Golf School, 800 365-6727. See page 36 for programs and methods.

A 121-room, full-amenity facility with motel-style accommodations and villas, just east of Ft. Meyers. Offers dining, a recreation area with volleyball and shuffleball, tennis, fresh and saltwater fishing.

■ Two scenic courses: the championship, 6,459-yard South course and the shorter North Course.

MARCO ISLAND

John Jacobs Practical Golf Schools

Marriott's Marco Island Resort & Golf Club
400 South Collier Blvd., Marco Island, FL 33937; 813 394-2511

5-day, Oct-May; 4-day, June-Sept; 2-day weekend, year round; Women's Golf Conference, Sept*

Rates: $$$, tuition only for weekend programs; ask John Jacobs Travel Desk for hotel rates.

Info: John Jacobs Practical Golf Schools, 800 472-5007. See page 6 for programs and methods.

*Women's Golf Conference: 4 days instruction, 3 nights, 2 rounds, continental breakfasts, dinners, networking, career seminars, women speakers.

Situated on a subtropical island on south Florida's West Coast where boats out-number cars and the beaches and shelling are legendary. Marriott's Marco Island Resort, the largest resort in the region, is a multi-story, beach-front hotel with 735 luxurious rooms, villas and lanais. Features tennis, three pools, health club, offshore and backwater fishing, jogging course, formal and casual dining and en-tertainment; 45 minutes from Ft. Meyer's Regional SouthWest Florida Airport; 15 minutes from Naples Municipal Airport.

A 6,925-yard, Joe Lee 18-hole course, named one of America's best new courses by Golf Digest. Water comes into play on 15 holes, relieved by wide fairways.

MELBOURNE
United States Senior Golf Academy

P.O. Box 410339, Melbourne, FL 32941
800 654-5752   407 253-5663
Holiday Inn, 2605 N. A1A, Indialantic, FL 32903; 407 777-4100
Indian River Colony Club, 6205 Murrell Rd.; Melbourne, FL; 407 255-6058
Director: Roy Smith
5-day (7 nights); Sept-June
Rates: $$

Don't let the "senior" in the name deceive you. It refers to the mature, seasoned, PGA and LPGA professionals who coach students of all ages and abilities, includ-ing juniors accompanied by an adult. Instruction is customized and professional with special emphasis on the mental side of the game to instill proper attitudes, habits and a sense of confidence. The pace of the program is dictated by students, with a flexible, accommodating schedule to insure learning. One-third of instruc-tion is on-course to promote transfer of skills from the range.

Guaranteed 3:1 student/teacher ratio with entire class size not exceeding 15. Forty+ hours instruction including daily on-course lessons, video monitoring and analy-sis. Includes 8-days, 7 nights (oceanfront), free lodging for up to four non-golfers, 7 breakfasts and lunches, 2 dinners.

Directly on the beach and a short drive from Disney World and the Kennedy Space Center, the 299-room, newly renovated Holiday Inn offers the Atlantic Ocean right on its doorstep; hot water spa, pool, tennis courts, varied dining and spacious rooms and suites. Located 15 minutes from the course.

18 holes at the semi-private, par 72, Indian River Colony Club, headquarters of United States Senior Golf Academy. A meticulously maintained, retired officer's club, the layout plays 6,647 from the champ tees.

> *Golf school can be an emotional roller coaster. One minute you're connecting with the ball. Next minute you've lost it and the fellow next to you is making consistent progress. Be assured, everyone's session will be filled with mood swings and performance lapses.*

M I A M I

Doral Golf Learning Center

Doral Resort and Country Club
4400 N.W. 87th Ave., Miami, FL 33178
800 22-DORAL   800 72-DORAL (Golf Learning Center)
Director: Jim McLean

3- and 5-day Players Schools, Jim McLean 1:1 Blue Monster Round, 2- and 3-day Instructional Schools, special programs (see below); year round

Rates: $$$-$$$$, tuition only; inquire about hotel rates and alternative accommodations.

Jim McLean, teacher of Tom Kite, Curtis Strange, Brad Faxon and many other luminaries, calls upon the latest innovations in golf learning, including state-of-the-art video, Golf Tek and Sportech swing computers, the SportsSense Swing Motion Trainer, and many others. A team of master professionals, selected and trained by McLean, concentrates on course management and communicates a winning frame of mind. Noting that the full swing is only 25% of the game, McLean's professional staff emphasizes the short game as the area in which to save strokes.

Five-day Player's School for 0-18 handicaps; 3:1 student/teacher ratio, limited to 12; 3-day Players School: 4:1 student/teacher ratio, limited to 16. Players Schools include 5-6 hours instuction daily, on-course training, lunch, green fees and carts. Blue Monster Round is a 1-day, 18-hole playing lesson with McLean on the Doral's nemesis, for 0-18 handicaps, followed by personal analysis. 2- and 3-day Instructional Schools provide 4 hours instruction, morning or afternoon, 4:1 student/teacher ratio (6:1 summer), video analysis. All schools include breakfast, gift videotape and workbook. Players School also include lunch and greens fees.

Special programs – Saturnia: 6 day, 48-hour personalized instruction program with McLean and a neuropsychologist, for 0-18 handicaps. Clinics: 1-day, half-day advanced (for pros, tournament and collegiate players), half-day, and 2-hour.

The Doral call itself "Florida's Ultimate Golf Resort." Indeed, the 2,400-acre, world-famous Doral is renown for endless activities, skillful service and bountiful pleasures. Provides 650 rooms in eight separate lodges, most with terraces, golf or tennis views, oversized baths, built-in refrigerators, hair dryers and mini-bars, numerous restaurants. The $28 million Saturnia International Spa is the last word in pampering and therapeutic offerings. Features the Arthur Ashe, Jr. Tennis Club, an equestrian center, pool, jogging trails, game rooms, the list goes on and on.

■ Five 18-hole courses: Silver, Gold, Red, White and Green, plus a par three beginner's course. Look out for Dick Wilson's fearsome, 18-hole Blue Monster course, loaded with sand and water, inspiring trepidation in those who would conquer it. Doral promotes its own line of golfwear, available in the tri-level Pro Shop and through catalogues.

How much will golf school cost? Turn to "How to use this Book," pages vi - vii, for the code to pricing.

Bill Skelley School of Golf

Main St., Miami Lakes, FL 33014
800 541-7707   305 828-9740

Director: Bill Skelley

5-day, 4-day*, 3-day; special programs

Rates: $$-$$$, rates vary according to accommodations; *4-day program at Miami Lakes only.

Locations: Apache Junction, AZ (Phoenix area); Copper Mountain, CO; Niceville, FL; Fairfield Glade, TN

Science replaces conjecture in this highly structured learning system with teaching delivered by year-round, full-time pros with two years of specialized training. Renown golf lecturer, Bill Skelley, has developed a curriculum which communicates the biomechanics of the golf swing in a step by step process. Students perfect their individual swing patterns through repetition of a correct sequence of body and arm movements. "Making the shot" is the inevitable result. If you don't learn to hit the ball longer and straighter, the school maintains an unconditional money back guarantee.

Five-six hours instruction daily, 4:1 student/teacher ratio, video analysis and feedback, high-tech learning devices and swing aids, lectures, stroke training, instruction manual. Corporate schools and clinics are often led by Tour winner Bruce Fleisher.

Five-day instructional program provides on-course training, green fees and cart during and after school, 5 nights (6 days, Sat-Thu), 5 breakfasts and lunches, 2 dinners, 2 receptions. Four-day program (F-M): green fees and cart, 3 nights, 3 breakfasts and lunches, 1 dinner, reception. Three-day program (F-Sun): green fees after school, 2 nights, 2 breakfasts and lunches, 1 dinner, reception (exceptions at various locations).

Bill Skelley School of Golf

Don Shula's Hotel and Golf Club
Miami Lakes, FL 33014
305 821-1150

5-, 4-, 3-day programs; Nov-May

Rates: $$

Info: Bill Skelley School of Golf, 800 541-7707. Refer to previous listing.

Planned from start to finish, the community of Miami Lakes is a beautifully planted, meticulously maintained area boasting 22 lakes. The resort is comprised of a 201-room hotel and 100-room Golf Club, offering fitness facilities, tennis, racquetball, aerobics, pool, varied dining, nearby shops and activities; 20 minutes from Miami International Airport.

■ Home of Don Shula and the Miami Dolphins, the par 72 course, 7,055 yards, is peaceful and serene, belying its formidable challenges. Water is nowhere to be seen on the front nine but everywhere on the back. Practice area and lighted driving range.

NAPLES

David Leadbetter Golf Academy

Quail West Golf and Country Club
6303 Burnham Rd., Naples, FL 33999
813 592-1444   813 592-1040

Director: David Leadbetter

2-day David Leadbetter Retreat, 2-day Academy Retreat, 3-day schools, 3-day Major Golf Schools, Half-Day Session; Personal Trainer Session, hourly instruction, Playing Lessons; special programs for Ladies Only, Juniors (see page 133) and Seniors

Rates: $$$$; David Leadbetter Retreat, $$$$$; tuition only

Info: David Leadbetter Golf Academy, 407 857-8276. See page 46, for programs and methods.

Quail West is a luxurious, private, residential golf community. Instruction is for members and guests of Quail West and Golf Academy commuter students (subject to confirmation). Students receive preferred rates at The Ritz Carlton, The Registry Resort and Enterprise Rent-a-Car; school will assist with alternative reservations.

■ An 18-hole course designed by Arthur Hills and Associates, set on more then 200 acres of lakes and natural preserves, opened in March 1992. A second course is planned. Lavish 70,000 square foot clubhouse with hot mineral spa, lap pool, leisure pool, steam rooms, private Jacuzzis, men's and ladies locker facilities, shops; all amenities and services available to students.

Inspired teaching notwithstanding, there is no substitute for faithful practice. Make a commitment to practice what you've been taught or run the risk of losing it.

Paradise Golf Schools

975 Imperial Golf Course Blvd., Naples, FL 33942
800 624-3543   813 592-0204

Director: Bill Beyer

5-day, 3-day; 3 or 5-day Masters Program*

Rates: $$-$$$; Masters Program $$$

Locations: Apache Junction, AZ; Carmel, CA; Naples and Kissimmee, FL

Instructors build on each golfer's natural ability, teaching fundamentals and concentrating on trouble areas. All fully qualified PGA professionals, the staff emphasizes the mental side of the game and the value of good course management, relating them to saving strokes. A take-home, follow-up program allows students to chart

progress as they relate to goals set with their instructor, thus continuing to learn.
Strict 3:1 student/teacher ratio, class limited to 21, on-course playing lessons emphasizing club selection, rules, etiquette and shot making. Video analysis, take-home tape, instruction manual, club fitting; no charge for golf and cart, club storage. Five-day program: 25 hours instruction, 3 playing lessons, 6 days green fees and cart; includes 6 nights (Sun-F), 2 receptions. Three-day program: 18 hours instruction, 2 playing lessons, 4 days green fees and cart, 3 nights lodging (Thu-Sat), 2 receptions. Inquire about meals at each site.

*Masters program at Apache Junction, AZ and Carmel, CA: same format as 3- and 5-day programs plus 1:1 instruction with sought-after golf teacher, Jim Wright.

N A P L E S

Paradise Golf School

Naples Beach Hotel & Golf Club
851 Gulf Shore Blvd., Naples, FL 33940
800 237-7600   813 261-2222

5-day; 3-day, Fri-Sun; Sept-May

Rates: $$$

Info: Paradise Golf Schools, 800 624-3543. See previous listing for programs and methods.

Family-owned, 315-room resort located on the Gulf of Mexico along a seven-mile stretch of sandy beach. The hotel is situated amidst 135 acres of natural foliage, affording tennis, swimming, sailing, windsurfing, paddle boating; supervised children's program (summer and holiday weeks). Backwater and deep sea fishing from nearby marinas, varied recreation, and shopping. Fine dining, including H.B.'s, the only Naples restaurant situated directly on the beach. Located 35 miles south of Southwest Florida Regional Airport; 5 minutes from Naples Airport.

■ A challenging 18-hole, PGA course, par 72, home of the Florida State PGA Seniors.

N A P L E S

The Florida Golf School

Quality Inn Golf & Country Club
4100 Golden Gate Pkwy, Naples, FL 33999
800 221-2222   813 455-1010

5-day; 3-day, M-W or F-Sun; Oct-May

Rates: $$

Info: The Florida Golf School, 800 365-6727. See page 36 for programs and methods.

A 153-room golf resort with 1- and 2-bedroom suites and efficiencies, located minutes from West Coast beaches; dining, heated pool.

■ Dick Wilson, 18-hole championship course on the grounds.

NICEVILLE

Bill Skelley School of Golf

Bluewater Bay Resort
1950 Bluewater Blvd., Niceville, FL 32578
800 874-2128   904 897-3613

3-day, 5-day; March-July, Sept-Nov*

Rates: $$

Info: Bill Skelley School of Golf, 800 541-7707. See page 40 for programs and methods.

A secluded residential resort community on 1,800 acres beside Choctawhatchee Bay on northwest Florida's Emerald Coast, with tennis, boating, bay cruising, fishing, deep water marina with 120 slips, five pools, nature and biking trails. Villa accommodations from efficiency to 2- and 3-bedroom homes. Located an hour from Pensacola Airport, 15 minutes from Ft. Walton Beach/Eglin Airport (daily flights via Atlanta).

*Five day program provides 4 nights, 4 breakfasts, 3 dinners, one cocktail party, unlimited golf carts. Three day program: 2 nights, 2 breakfasts, 1 dinner, 1 cocktail party, unlimited golf carts.

■ At Bluewater Bay Country Club, Northwest Florida's #1 rated course, 27 holes designed by Tom Fazio and Jerry Pate: Bay, Lake and Marsh. Choose from 30 challenging courses within an hour's drive.

> *Stretch, exercise, walk, practice, play golf, do something physical every day following golf school. After a week of vigorous exercise, you'll stiffen up terribly without activity.*
>
>

NICEVILLE

Golf Digest Instruction Schools

Bluewater Bay Resort
1950 Bluewater Blvd., Niceville, FL 32578
800 874-2128   904 897-3613

5-day; Sept-June

Rates: $$$$*

Info: Golf Digest Instruction Schools, 800 243-6121. See page 29 for programs and methods.

Refer to previous listing for resort and golf information.

*Includes 5 days instruction, 8 days, 7 nights accommodations, breakfast and lunch on school days, opening and closing dinners and cocktail parties.

NORTH PALM BEACH
Nicklaus Flick Golf School

11780 U.S. Highway #1, North Palm Beach, FL 33408
800 642-5528   407 626 3900

Head Pro: Jack Nicklaus; Golf Director: Jim Flick

Master Golf I (3-day); Master Golf II (5 day); Master Golf III (3 Half-Days); Master Golf IV (2½ days)

Rates: $$$$-$$$$$

Locations: Scottsdale, AZ; Pebble Beach, CA; Palm Beach Gardens, FL; Lihue, HI; Harbor Springs, MI; Santa Fe, NM.

Drawing on Jack Nicklaus' golfing prowess and Jim Flick's 40+ years as one of America's premier instructors, this school focuses on proven principles which have guided both masters throughout their careers. Their key to consistent distance and accuracy is in the hands and arms swinging the head of the club freely through the ball, with the feet and legs providing a foundation for support. According to Flick, this sensitivity to the clubhead governs a golfer's potential. A team of hand-picked instructors stresses precision in alignment, aim, grip and posture. They develop an agenda for students which attacks the biggest problems first and works toward an understanding of the cause and effect in the golf swing. School utilizes on-site video analysis via the 3-camera, mobile Jack Nicklaus Coaching Studio™, containing sophisticated multi-media tools for accelerated learning.

All programs: personal one-on-one instruction in small groups, total class limited to 18; detailed Master Golf Workbook, take-home videotape; instruction rounds, complimentary green fees and cart, unlimited use of facilities, equipment evaluation, gift, club cleaning and storage, optional custom golf fitness program, skill contest. Offers airport transportation, discounted car rental.

Master Golf I provides 3 days instruction, green fees and cart for one 9-hole round daily, 4 nights lodging, breakfast and lunch. Master Golf II: 5 days instruction, 3 days playing lessons, 6 nights, breakfast and lunch daily, welcome reception, mid-week dinner reception. Master Golf III: 3 half-days instruction, limited to 12, green fees and cart for 18-hole round daily, 4 nights, breakfast and lunch daily, welcome reception. Master Golf IV: 3 half-days instruction, limited to 15, two 18-hole playing lessons, 2 classroom sessions, 3 nights, orientation luncheon.

ORLANDO
Arnold Palmer Golf Academy

9000 Bay Hill Blvd.
Orlando, FL 32819-4899
800 523-5999   407 876-2429

President: Arnold Palmer; Academy Director: Brad Brewer
Teaching Director: Dick Tiddy

½-day, 1-, 2-, 3- and 5-day programs; 5-day Junior Advance (see page 134); 2-day Senior program; 2-day Parent/Child; Playing Lessons; individual lessons and assorted programs devoted exclusively to couples, women, advanced players, executive men and women, physically challenged golfers, future professionals.

Rates: $$$; all 2-, 3- and 5-day programs based at Bay Hill Club include accommodations; school will suggest lodging for programs based elsewhere.

Locations: Gulf Shores, AL; Tucson, AZ; Orlando, FL; Alton, IL; Lake Ozark, MO.

Arnold Palmer, "The Legend," has organized his own learning program for golfers of all ages and abilities. Palmer's powerful message is straightforward and grounded in basics. Specially trained instructors interpret the Palmer method, working with each individual, evaluating and building on his or her strengths, rather than forcing new techniques and styles. Four areas are emphasized: fundamentals, the scoring zone, practice techniques and course strategy. Through the Alumni Progress Program, students remain in touch with instructors and fine-tune their game back home.

2-, 3- and 5-day programs provide 7+ hours personalized instruction daily, 5:1 student/teacher ratio, daily playing lesson, unlimited golf, individual video analysis with take-home tape, Arnold Palmer instructional manual and tape, class photo, awards certificates. Includes 2, 3 or 5 nights resort accommodations (Bay Hill Club only), opening cocktail party.

Two-day Senior (55+) Academy: 6 hours instruction, unlimited golf and practice, video analysis, 2 nights. Two-day Parent/Child School: 16 hours instruction, daily playing lessons, video analysis, 2 nights. Half-Day Academy: 4-hours instruction, video analysis. One-day Academy: 8 hours instruction, 9-hole playing lesson.

Five-day Junior Advance: for commuting students, 20 hours instruction, lunch, organized competition daily, unlimited golf and practice. Physically challenged golfers: groups or individuals are mainstreamed whenever possible; instruction by specially trained teachers.

ORLANDO

Arnold Palmer Golf Academy

Arnold Palmer's Bay Hill Lodge and Golf Club
9000 Bay Hill Blvd., Orlando, FL 32819
800 523-5999   407 876-2429

Consult programs in previous listing; year round, check school for specific dates

Rates: $$$

Arnold Palmer's haunt when he's not on Tour is his own resort which furnishes all the thoughtful pampering of a private club. Seventy-room hotel, steps from the first tee, offers casual and formal dining, swimming, tennis, private marina on the Butler Chain of Lakes, water sports; 15 minutes from Disney World, 20 minutes from Orlando International Airport.

■ 27-hole private championship course sweeps across 270 acres, site of the nationally televised PGA Nestlé Invitational; ranked among the world's best. Designed by Dick Wilson in 1961, it was reworked in 1989 by the team of Arnold Palmer and Ed Seay, rendering it challenging and dramatic. Open only to members, guests and guests of the resort. Full practice facility.

David Leadbetter Golf Academy

Lake Nona
9100 Chiltern Dr., Orlando, FL 32827
407 857-8276
Director: David Leadbetter

2-day David Leadbetter Retreat; 2-day Academy Retreat, 3-day schools, 3-day Major Golf Schools, Half-day Session; Personal Trainer Session, hourly instruction, Playing Lessons; special programs for Ladies Only, Juniors (see page 133); Seniors

Rates: $$$$; David Leadbetter Retreat, $$$$$; tuition only*

Other location: Naples, FL

Leadbetter, called "instructor to the stars," has everyone talking about his swing theories which focus on movement of the big muscles of the torso and take the hands out of the action. Instruction here places great emphasis on the mechanics of the full swing, employing video technology and swing aids. Students gain a full understanding of their game and are taught to become their own best teacher.

David Leadbetter Retreat: 2-day, 14 hour intensive program led by Leadbetter, 2:1 student/teacher ratio, limited to 6, includes lunch, dinner party hosted by Leadbetter and gifts. Two-day Academy Retreat: same format led by Academy staff, includes lunch and gift. Three-day schools: 4:1 student/teacher ratio, video analysis, nine-hole playing lesson, green fees and cart, 2 free afternoons, lunch daily.

Half-day school: full swing instruction, limited to 5, tailored to ladies, seniors, low handicaps, etc.

Personal trainer: 7 hours Academy instruction, 1:1 student/teacher ratio, video analysis, lunch. Playing Lesson: 9 holes to reinforce skills. Major Golf Schools: less intense program combines on-course training, lesson tee instruction, video analysis, lunches, 2 free afternoons. Senior programs: four 2½ hour sessions scheduled over 2 weeks, 5:1 student/teacher ratio. Clinics customized to groups and individuals at Academy or local clubs.

*15-room lodge at Lake Nona. School arranges discounted rates at the Orlando Airport Marriott Hotel (7499 Augusta National Dr., Orlando 32822, 407 851-9000), 484-room, full destination resort with concierge level, suites, fitness trail, gym, two restaurants, pool; 10 minute drive to Lake Nona Golf Course.

■ Instruction at David Leadbetter's teaching facility at Lake Nona, a private club available to members, their guests and guests of the school. The course is an 18-hole, Tom Fazio-design.

Grand Cypress Academy of Golf

Hyatt Regency Grand Cypress Resort and Villas
One North Jacaranda, Orlando, FL 32836
800 835-7377   407 239-1975
Director: Fred Griffin

3-day Grand Cypress Series; 3-day Phil Rogers Series; Mini-School Series (3 half-days); year round

Rates: $$$-$$$$; Phil Rogers Series $$$$

Students draw upon a wealth of talent in the triumvirate of Director Fred Griffin, PGA Instructor Phil Rogers (both named among the nation's top 50 instructors by GOLF Magazine) and biomechanics expert Dr. Ralph Mann. A carefully crafted curriculum emphasizes close contact between teacher and student and provides comprehensive learning based on scientific principles. Dr. Mann brings a new dimension to golf learning with CompuSport, exclusively at Grand Cypress, in which the swings of 50 top professional golfers are combined and adjusted to tailor the perfect swing for each student. Computer models are superimposed on student's videotaped performance, from driving to putting, thus analyzing and instructing. Students return home with instructional tape for continued learning.

Classes limited to 8 per group, 2 groups maximum, 4:1 student/teacher ratio; includes on-course instruction (except Mini-Schools), take-home CompuSport computer video analysis with model overlay and instructor comments, CompuSport club fitting. Includes unlimited golf and use of practice facility, instruction manual, club storage, diploma, gift. Phil Rogers Series provides personal instruction by Rogers, himself. Selected dates feature Director Fred Griffin. Mini-School Series offers similar features, including lodging and unlimited golf, in half-day format. Corporate and custom tailored programs on request.

Includes 3 nights at the Villas or Hyatt Regency Grand Cypress, three lunches, opening reception.

A deluxe, busy, 1,500 acre resort comprised of the 750-room Hyatt Regency Grand Cypress, the Villas of Grand Cypress (1-4 bedrooms), Golf Club, Racquet Club, Equestrian Center, plus full fitness center, nature area, eleven restaurants and a vast array of leisure and active possibilities. Located 20 minutes from Orlando Airport.

■ The Academy's private, 21-acre instruction campus features three championship practice holes with teaching opportunities in every aspect of the game. Play centers on Jack Nicklaus signature courses: North, South and East, totaling 27 holes. The 18-hole, 6,181 yard, par 72, New Course is reminiscent of The Old Course at St. Andrews, Scotland.

> *The cost of golf school is indicated by $$$$$ symbols. We have based our Relative Pricing Scale on a $999, five-day, all inclusive model indicated by "$." An average price school, costing $1,500 for 5 days, is indicated "$$." If a school does not offer a 5-day program, we have extrapolated prices to reflect five days at the school's rate. For further details see page 71.*

John Jacobs Practical Golf Schools

Marriott's Orlando World Center Resort and Convention Center
8701 World Center Dr., Orlando, FL 32821
407 239-4200

5-day, 2-day weekend, year round; VIP schools, Feb and March*

Rates: $$-$$$ (VIP $$$-$$$$); tuition only for weekend programs; ask John Jacobs Travel Desk for hotel rates.

Info: John Jacobs Practical Schools, 800 472-5007. See page 6 for programs and methods.

*John Jacobs, himself, is on hand for these annual instruction sessions.

Florida's largest and most spectacular resort – and arguably the busiest – with 1,503 rooms. Offers 12 lighted tennis courts, four pools, six restaurants. Located 10 minutes from Disney World, 15 minutes from Orlando Airport.

■ A par-71, Joe Lee-designed, 18-hole course, 6,265-yards, boasting 14 lakes.

Ken Venturi Golf Training Centers

The Market Place
7600 Dr. Phillips Blvd, Suite 72, Orlando, FL 32819
800 735-3357 (ext. 100)   407 352-9669

Director: Ken Venturi

3-day programs, M-W or Thu-Sat; Traveling Schools*

Rates: $$$-$$$$

Locations: Tampa, FL; Hilton Head, SC; Dallas, TX

U.S. Open Champion, PGA Player of the Year, and for 25 years CBS Golf Teacher/ Analyst, Ken Venturi has a theory: gimmicks in golf instruction come and go – but the basic fundamentals stand the test of time. Rigorously trained, full-time instructors (and Ken, himself, when his CBS schedule permits) teach Venturi's "Fundamental Swing System," with meticulous attention to detail. The goal, in three days of intensive instruction, is to instill in every student a steady, consistent ability to walk onto the course and make every shot every time.

Three days instruction, 4 hours daily, on every aspect of the game, 4:1 student/ teacher ratio, same pro throughout to insure consistency, school limited to 20; daily 9-hole playing lesson with emphasis on course management and shot-making; complimentary green fees and cart for 18 holes daily; videotaping and analysis, take-home tape with drills; instruction book, equipment evaluation and recommendations; gift package, school photo, diploma. Includes three nights at an affiliated Hyatt, three breakfasts and lunches, opening reception, farewell cocktail party.

* Ken Venturi personally participates in 3-day Traveling Schools ($$$$) across the country, coinciding with the airing of Venturi/CBS-TV coverage of major tournaments. Schools scheduled around the MCI Heritage Classic, Hilton Head, SC (April); the Southwestern Bell Colonial Invitational, Dallas (late May), and others.

ORLANDO
The Florida Golf School - America's Favorite Golf Schools
Sheraton Plaza Hotel at the Florida Mall
1500 Sand Lake Rd., Orlando, FL 32809; 407 859-1500
Kissimmee Golf Club, 3103 Florida Coach Dr., Kissimmee, FL 34741
407 847-2816
5-day; 3-day, M-W or F-Sun; year round
Rates: $$
Info: The Florida Golf School, 800 365-6727 or 800 365-6640. See page **36** for programs and methods.

A multi-story, 496-room, self-contained, full-service resort located only minutes from Orlando Airport and Disney World and adjacent to Florida's largest shopping mall; two restaurants, pool, sauna, European spa, fitness center.

▪ An open, relaxed, 18-hole course at Kissimmee Golf Club, 20 minutes from the hotel. Called a "great warm-up course." Full practice and learning facilities.

ORLANDO
Vince Cali Golf School

925 Appleton Ave., Orlando, FL 32806; 407 857-4653
International Golf Course, Orlando, FL
Winter Pines Golf Course, Winter Park
Director: Vince Cali
Personalized programs, playing lessons
Rates: $$$, tuition only; students provide own lodging.

Calling itself "The Golf School With No Class," school provides one-on-one instruction at a choice of two golf courses. School stresses a positive, unmechanical approach, encouraging students to consider the golf swing analogous to tossing a ball. Vince Cali introduces the full range of shots and institutes measures to promote increased distance and control. Operational since 1976, the school accommodates students' vacations and business plans with flexible scheduling. Basic session furnishes $3^{1}/_{2}$ hours instruction and an optional playing lesson.

▪ The private, Joe-Lee designed International Golf Course plays 6,776 yards. Its Number #2 hole, 666 yards long, is dubbed "Mark of the Beast." The public, 18-hole Winter Pines course is located in nearby Winter Park.

ORLANDO   AREA
Exceller Programs Golf Schools
Mission Inn Golf & Tennis Resort
10400 County Road 48, Howey-In-The-Hills, FL 34737
800 874-9053   904 324-3101
5-day, 4-day, 2 day; Sept-May
Rates: $$-$$$
Info: Exceller Programs Golf Schools, 800 424-7438. See page 4 for programs and methods.

A family owned and operated, 204-room, Spanish style, Mobil Four Star Resort, offering fishing, boating, cruises on the resort's 1930's river yacht, three restaurants, tennis, full children's program. Situated in a country setting, 35 minutes north of Disney World, 50 minutes from Orlando Airport.

▶ Two 18-hole courses. Designed in 1926 by Scottish architect Captain Charles E. Clarke of Troon, the mature, hilly, El Campion (The Champion) boasts 85 feet of elevation change and water on 13 of 18 holes. It has long been among Florida's very best championship courses. The new Las Colinas (The Hills) designed by Gary Koch, demands accuracy.

ORLANDO AREA

Howie Barrow School of Golf at Grenelefe

Grenelefe Golf and Tennis Resort
3200 State Rd. 546, Haines City, FL 33844
800 422-5333 (ext. 6800)   813 422-7511
Director: Howie Barrow
Daily instructional programs, multi-day series, private lessons
Rates $$

Howie Barrow believes golf is an individual game and no two people will ever have the identical swing. Therefore, his instruction is geared to finding and producing the most effective swing for each person – and establishing consistency for every golfer. Students determine the length and intensity of their own programs. School day consists of three hours morning instruction at the school's own practice area, student/teacher ratio 4:1, followed by 9-hole on-course training. Provides before and after video analysis, unlimited use of practice facilities, bag storage and club cleaning. All programs include lodging in villa suites and all meals.

Grenelefe is a secluded, 950-unit, 1,000-acre, densely landscaped resort containing a 20-court Tennis Village, 6,400-acre recreational lake, four pools, miles of nature and fitness trails, restaurants and snack bars, nightclub, supervised children's program. Discounted car rentals. Located 30 minutes from Disney World, less than an hour from Orlando Airport.

▶ Three renown courses: The Ed Seay-designed East Course with multiple elevation changes in 6,802 yards. The South Course, designed by Ron Garl with Andy Bean, plays 6,869 yards from the back tees. The West Course, ranked Florida's #1 course for six years and repeatedly named among the nation's top 100, is a Robert Trent Jones design, par 72, 7,325 yards from the back tees.

ORLANDO AREA

Paradise Golf Schools

Poinciana Golf & Racquet Resort
500 E. Cypress Pkwy., Kissimmee, FL 34759;   800 331-7743
5-day; 3-day, F-Sun; Sept-May
Rates: $$-$$$; seasonal variations
Info: Paradise Golf Schools, 800 624-3543. See page 41 for programs and methods.

Located in the very heart of Central Florida, the 110-room Poinciana offers four lighted tennis courts, Olympic-size pool and a range of attractions, including nearby Disney World. Lodging in 1- and 2-bedroom fully-equipped villas. Clubhouse dining. A short drive from Orlando Airport.

 Designed by architects Bruce Devlin-Robert Von Hagge, the par 72, 18-hole, forested, championship layout plays 6,700 yards from the back tees. Called "a very serious affair" with threatening bunkers and water on 12 holes.

A school's home base is keyed with a "Headquarters" visor. Here you will discover methods and programs. Check the "Info" section of resort listings or the Index to find the Headquarters.

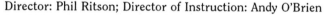

ORLANDO   AREA
The Phil Ritson Golf School

Windermere Country Club
2710 Butler Bay Dr., N., Windermere, FL 34786
407 876-6487

Director: Phil Ritson; Director of Instruction: Andy O'Brien

3 Half-Day program, Oct-May; Phil Ritson hourly private instruction, selected dates; shared or private lessons with staff, corporate programs

Rates: $$$; Phil Ritson private instruction $$$$$; tuition only. School will suggest area hotels.

Info: Phil Ritson Golf School, P.O. Box 1511, Windermere, FL 34786;
407 876-6487

Other locations: Overland Park, KS; Pawley's Island, SC (Myrtle Beach area); Oslo, Norway

Lauded as one of the world's finest golf coaches, Phil Ritson was awarded an unprecedented "Ten Stars" by Golf Magazine for his "Encyclopedia of Golf" video series. Thirty to forty percent of students at the Windermere site are professional golfers, testifying to Ritson's standing. Hand-picked and specially-trained teaching pros evaluate each student's natural abilities and level of performance and communicate the Ritson method, helping to build the right swing for every student, from beginner to pro. Instruction is made flexible through small classes. Emphasis is placed on fundamentals and on the mental approach in a curriculum designed by sports psychologist Carey Mumford. Director of Instruction, Andy O'Brien, is an expert left-handed golfer and a columnist on the subject.

Three Half-Days program provides 10½ hours instruction, 3:1 student/teacher ratio (Pawley's Island site: 4:1 student/teacher ratio). Includes video analysis, take-home video cassette with instructional voice-over and instructional videos, Phil Ritson drill tape for continued learning, unlimited use of practice facilities and clubhouse amenities. Afternoon golf at reduced rates.

 The private Windermere Country Club course is a compact Lloyd Clifton design, maintained to near perfection, year round. Characterized by undulating greens and manicured fairways, plays 6,700 yards from the back tees.

WEST   PALM   BEACH

Marlene Floyd's "For Women Only" Golf School

Palm Beach Polo & Country Club
13198 Forest Hill Blvd. WestPalm Beach, FL 33414
407 793-1113

2-day weekend; Jan

Rates: $$, tuition only. Contact school for assistance with accommodations.

Info: Marlene Floyd's "For Women Only" Golf School, 800 637-2694 or 919 323-9606. See page 88 for programs and methods.

PGA pro Marlene Floyd is on site and works with students for the entire session; limited to 15. Includes lunch.

▐ Extensive, up-to-the-minute practice facility. Layout comprises 45 outstanding holes of golf: the Jerry Pate-Ron Garl, Scottish links-style Dunes course; the Cypress Course by Pete and P.B. Dye, and nine Fazio holes.

PALM   BEACH   GARDENS

The Academy of Golf at PGA National

PGA National Golf Club, 1000 Avenue of Champions,
Palm Beach Gardens, FL 33418
800 832-6235   407 627-7593

Director: Mike Adams

3-day weekend (F-Sun); 3-day midweek (Tu-Thu); 3-day Short Game School; 3-day Players School (emphasis on course strategy); 3-day Parent-Child School (ages 8-19); 2-day Mini-Schools (Sat-Sun, summer only, instruction and 18 holes daily); clinics, special programs, year round; Junior and Advanced Junior Academies (see page 137)

Rates: $$$, tuition only*

Other locations: Colorado Springs, CO

Since 1983, the PGA's approach to golf learning has integrated fundamentals with the physical and mental aspects. Each student is evaluated biomechanically, optically, physically, mentally and fundamentally and an individualized program is developed. Director Mike Adams, known as "The Swing Doctor," hand-picks expert teachers to communicate in a unified, simple manner. Step-by-step, individualized teaching helps students build their own, personal, optimum golf swing based on each one's natural abilities.

Students grouped according to skill, 4:1 student/teacher ratio. Utilizes video, biomechanical and computer equipment for analysis. State of the art training devices enhance learning; personalized improvement program, fitness evaluation and take-home program, club fitting. Three-day schools provide morning instruction followed by complementary golf. Players School provides on-course training followed by on-range instruction. Students are invited to submit follow-up videotapes for critique.

*Suggested accommodations on the grounds at PGA National Resort and Spa (400 Ave. of the Champions, Palm Beach Gardens, FL 33418; 800 633-9150), home of the PGA. The ultra-busy, 2,340-acre, Mobil Four Star facility with an AAA Four

Diamond rating, boasts 335 rooms and suites; seven restaurants and lounges, two pools, Health and Racquet club with international spa and 19 tennis courts, five croquet lawns, 26-acre sailing lake, water sports, nature trails on 240 acre preserve, 17 miles from Palm Beach International Airport.

▇ Instruction at PGA's world-class practice facility. Golfers think they've gone to heaven with 90 holes of outstanding golf: five 18-hole courses – Champion, Haig, Squire, General, and Estate, bearing the signatures of Jack Nicklaus, Tom and George Fazio and Arnold Palmer.

PALM BEACH GARDENS

Nicklaus Flick Golf School

PGA National Golf Club
1000 Avenue of Champions, Palm Beach Gardens, FL 33418
800 832-6235   407 627-7593

PGA National Resort & Spa
400 Ave. of the Champions, Palm Beach Gardens, FL 33418
 800 633-9150 or 407 627-2000

Master Golf I (3-day); Master Golf IV (2½ day); Mar-May, Oct-Dec

Rates: $$$$-$$$$$

Info: Nicklaus Flick Golf School, 800 642-5528. See page 44 for programs and methods.

Includes deluxe accommodations at PGA National Resort and Spa. Consult previous listing for resort and golf.

PALM CITY

United States Golf Schools

Cutter Sound Golf & Yacht Club
2363 S.W. Carriage Hill Terrace, Palm City, FL 34990
407 221-1822
Holiday Inn Downtown* or Holiday Inn Oceanside**

5-day, 3-day, 2-day weekend; winter

Rates: $*, $$**

Info: United States Golf Schools, 800 354-7415. See page 55 programs and methods.

Lodging at either **Holiday Inn Oceanside (3793 N.E. Ocean Blvd., Jensen Beach, FL 34957; 407 225-3000), skirting the ocean on Hutchinson Island, 45 miles north of Palm Beach International Airport, midway between Miami and Orlando; 181 balconied rooms, oceanfront heated pool, dining, water sports, tennis, volleyball. Or *Holiday Inn Downtown (1209 South Federal Hwy., Stuart, FL 34994; 407 287-6200), ten minutes away and sharing all the amenities of the Holiday Inn Oceanside; 120-room, economical vacation retreat offers pool and patio, health club, dining and biking.

▇ The private Cutter Sound Golf & Yacht Club, with its 18-hole Gary Player-designed course, is the practice and playing site.

54   FLORIDA

PALM COAST

The Florida Golf School - America's Favorite Golf School

Sheraton Palm Coast Resort
300 Clubhouse Dr., Palm Coast, FL 32137; 800 654-6538   904 445-3000
5-day; 3-day, M-W or F-Sun; year round
Rates: $$
Info: The Florida Golf School, 800 365-6727. See page 36 for programs and methods.
Waterfront, 154-room resort features nearly every recreational pursuit known: an 18-court tennis center, two pools, exercise facilities, game room, racquetball, volleyball, shuffleboard, miniature golf, playground, an 80-slip marina. Located on Florida's Intracoastal Waterway between St. Augustine and Daytona Beach, an hour east of Orlando, 27 miles from Daytona Beach Airport.

■ Four championship courses: Hammock Dunes for members and guests of the resort, designed by Tom Fazio in the Scottish links style. On Palm Coast property are Pine Lakes, Palm Harbor, and the Arnold Palmer/Ed Seay-designed Matanzas Woods, named by Golf Digest as one of the best new courses in 1986.

PEMBROKE PINES

Roland Stafford Golf School

Grand Palms Golf and Country Club Resort,
110 Grand Palms Dr., Pembroke Pines, FL 33027; 305 431-8800   800 327-9246
5-day, 3-day, year round; 2-day weekend, summer only, (limited to 5 students)
Rates: $-$$
Info: Roland Stafford Golf School, 800 447-8894. See page 84 for programs and methods.
A 101-room resort with Olympic size pool, full exercise facilities, outdoor fitness course, lighted tennis courts and pavilion, assorted dining options. Located in the Hollywood area, 25 minutes from Miami and Ft. Lauderdale Airports.

■ New, 18-hole, championship, Ward Northup-designed course (additional nine holes under construction), two oversized practice greens, picturesque aquatic driving range.

POMPANO BEACH

The Florida Golf School - America's Favorite Golf Schools

Palm-Aire Spa Resort
2601 Palm Aire Dr. N., Pompano Beach 33069; 800 272-5624 305 972-3300
5-day; 3-day, M-W or F-Sun; year round
Rates: $$
Info: The Florida Golf School, 800 365-6727. See page 36 for programs and methods.
Palm-Aire is a 1,000+ acre, 215-room, deluxe resort with an acclaimed spa, 37 tennis courts, racquetball, jogging trail, dining, pools and nearby beach. Located between Palm Beach and Ft. Lauderdale.

■ Three courses, home to three Florida Opens and 1978's Florida PGA tournament. Two 18-hole courses: Pines and Palms, both William Mitchell designs; Sabals is a 3,401, nine-hole, executive course.

PORT ST. LUCIE
Club Med - Sandpiper

3500 Morningside Blvd, Port St. Lucie, FL 34952
407 335-4400   407 335-9497

5-day Golf Academy, M-F (segment of 7-day, 7-night, Sat-Sat, Club Med package); year round

Rates: $, plus golf school enrollment fee ($)

Info and reservations: Contact Club Med agents at 800-CLUB MED or your own travel agent.

Pick a sport – any sport – and Club Med will teach you how to do it. Golf is no exception. The Golf Academy at Sandpiper provides a full professional instruction program (4 hours daily teaching plus two days supervised on-course training). Students grouped according to skill, 4-5:1 student/teacher ratio. On-site video analysis, attentive coaching, midweek and final tournaments, driving and putting contests, awards. Includes unlimited practice and up to 36 complimentary holes of golf daily with shared cart; club storage, locker and gift. Optional nightly information sessions.

Includes all lodging, meals, amenities, and facilities at Sandpiper, a comfortable country-style resort on 500 acres fronting the mile-wide St. Lucie River, 20 minutes from Atlantic beaches. Terraced, air-conditioned rooms in 3-story lodges, three restaurants, 19 tennis courts, sailing, circus workshops, water-skiing, fitness center, exercise program, volleyball, basketball, soccer, bocce ball – in short, every participatory sport known. Nightly entertainment and dancing. Baby Club (including Baby Restaurant), Petit Club, Mini Clubs and Kids Club welcome young ones four months to 11 years with distractions and TLC. Located 45 miles from Palm Beach Airport.

■ Two championship 18-hole courses, Saint and Sinner, both par 72, plus a 9 hole pitch and put.

PORT ST. LUCIE
United States Golf Schools

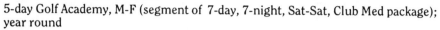

1631 S.W. Angelico Lane, Port St. Lucie, FL 34984
800 354-7415   407 871-6372

Directors: Mitchell Crum, Mike Mallon

5-day, 3-day and 2-day weekend

Rates: $-$$

Locations: Clearwater, Palm City, Sebring, FL; French Lick, IN; Biloxi, MI

U.S. Golf School treats each student as an individual, tailoring its program to complement strengths and concentrate on elements which need improving. Working with the same instructor throughout provides consistent learning. Because 50% of the game is played within 100 yards of the flag, instructors devote half the curriculum to the short game. Students transfer skills from the range to the course with on-course training daily.

All inclusive programs provide five hours instruction daily, maximum 4:1 student/teacher ratio, video analysis, two hours daily on-course instruction; unlimited golf, including green fees; equipment check, bag storage. Depending on duration of program, includes 5 nights (Sun-F), 3 nights (Sun-W or Thu-Sun), 2 nights (F & Sat); daily breakfast and dinner.

Sebring Golf School

Sebring Lake Golf & Tennis Resort
100 Club House Lane, Sebring, FL 33870
800 673-7686   813 655-0100
Director: Richard E. Cormier, Jr.
5-day; 2-day, M & Tu or Thu & F; year round

Rates: $$

Shunning the band-aid approach to golf instruction, Sebring Golf School teaches solid fundamentals and employs extensive videotaping and split screen, role model tapes to help students chart their own progress. Each student has his or her own pro throughout, insuring continuity. Proven principles of sports psychology are taught, along with relaxation methods – including wearing stereo headphones on the practice range. Students take home a personal videotape, written and audio instructional manual (great listening while commuting to work) and are encouraged to take advantage a a of free follow-up critique on videotape. Money back guarantee on instruction if not completely satisfied.

Maximum 1:1 student/teacher ratio, limited to 11 students; 30 hours instruction (5-day program); all sessions include on-course playing lessons, green fees and cart for after-class play, high speed videotaping, personalized drills and exercises, club fitting.

Five-day program includes 6 nights; 2-day program includes 3 nights; all programs include breakfast and lunch.

The resort provides 2-bedroom, 2-bath villas with private screened porches. Offers full fitness center, tennis courts, boating and fishing on Lake Istokpoga, clubhouse dining. Located in south central Florida, 80 miles from Disney World, 85 miles to Atlantic and Gulf coasts.

▶ Spring Lake, a par 72, 6621-yard, championship, 18-hole course. Features a 45,000 square foot green, the largest in the nation. Nine-hole executive course; indoor and outdoor practice facilities.

United States Golf Schools

Sebring Lake Golf & Tennis Resort
100 Club House Lane, Sebring, FL 33870
800 673-7686   813 655-0100
5-day, 3-day; March-May

Rates: $

Info: U. S. Golf Schools, 800 354-7415. See page 55 for programs and methods.

Accommodations and golf at Spring Lake Golf and Country Club. Consult previous listing for description.

SUN   CITY

Ben Sutton Golf School

Sun City Hotel
1335 Rickenbacker Dr., Sun City Center, FL 33573; 813 634-3331.
Director: Dick Sutton
8-day (Sun-Sun), year round; 3-day (F-Sun), Oct-Dec & June-Sept
Rates: $$-$$$
Info and reservations: P.O. Box 9199, Canton, OH 44711
800 225-6923   216-453-4350

In 1968, the late Ben Sutton pioneered the concept of personalized golf instruction in a vacation setting. Under the direction of his son, the school continues to deliver quality instruction and enjoyment. Emphasis is placed on reinforcing and strengthening fundamentals, developing finesse, adopting a pre-shot routine. Students are taught a proper turn, how to cock their wrists for maximum distance and the elements of a dependable short game. And they are encouraged to enjoy every minute while learning.

Six hours personalized daily instruction, 6:1 or 7:1 student/teacher ratio, on-course playing lessons. Utilizes before and after video analysis with instant replay and graph-check sequence photographs and instructional films. Includes daily golf and cart fees; no charge for golf and cart for non-school spouse. Eight day program provides tournaments with prizes, 7 nights lodging, breakfast and dinner daily, cocktail parties. Three-day program: 3 nights, full board.

Forty courtside rooms are reserved for the golf school at the 100-room, full-amenity resort located 45 minutes south of Tampa International Airport (inquire about airport transfers).

■ Six courses available, 108 holes in all; 27 holes at Sun City Center Country Club. The school's 9-hole, 40-acre training facility simulates all playing conditions and includes a lake, trees, sand and grass bunkers; multiple tees allow each practice hole to be played as a par 3, 4 or 5; 360° grass tee driving range with target greens.

T A M P A

Al Frazzini's Golf Course

Quail Hollow Country Club, 6225 Old Pasco Rd.,
Wesley Chapel, FL 33544
800 598-8127   904 532-1112
Holiday Inn, Busch Gardens
2701 East Fowler Ave., Tampa, FL 33612; 800 99-BUSCH
Director: Al Frazzini
5-day; Oct-May
Rates: $$
Other locations: Lake Geneva, WI

A teaching professional for 34 years, Al Frazzini makes an appearance on the Senior Tour whenever time permits. He can more often be found teaching golf; he estimates he's conducted over 12,000 golf lessons with students ages 2½ to 90. Frazzini's proven method stresses small classes (3:1 student/teacher ratio), high quality instruction, direct communication, on-course playing lessons to transfer learning to the game itself, and the correct mental attitude. His school sharpens each student's own ability and techniques to reach maximum potential.

Forty hours instruction, personalized video analysis, 9-hole playing lesson; includes golf cart and green fees, club storage, equipment check, unlimited use of practice facilities, school gift. Provides 6 nights, 5 breakfasts, cocktail party, lunch daily at Quail Hollow.

A short ride from the course and next door to the popular Busch Gardens, the Holiday Inn offers executive king guest rooms, dining, a French Bakery, pool, exercise room and an inviting array of nearby attractions.

■ Instruction and play on Quail Hollow's par 72, 18-hole course; plays 6,761 from the blue tees.

T A M P A

Ken Venturi Golf Training Centers

Hyatt Regency Westshore
6200 Courtney Campbell Causeway, Tampa, FL 33607; 813 268-9814
Lansbrook Golf Club, 2500 Village Center Dr., Palm Harbor, FL; 813 784-7333
3-day; year round
Rates: $$$-$$$$
Info: Ken Venturi Training Centers, 407 352-9669. See page 48 for programs and methods.

A 14-story, 445-room resort on a 35-acre wildlife preserve on the shores of Tampa Bay. Features four restaurants, pools, private beach, yacht charter, nature walks; shuttles to airport, golf and shopping. Located five minutes from Tampa International Airport.

■ Thirty minutes northwest of Tampa, near Tarpon Spings, Lansbrook Golf Club is the site of a permanent Ken Venturi Golf Training Center, one of the most complete and up-to-date golf teaching facilities anywhere. The course, a par 72, playing 6,018 from the middle markers, is noted for its challenges, its abundance of wildlife and perhaps the most lush and plush fairways in Florida.

T A M P A

S.E.A. Experts Only Golf School

Bloomingdale Golfers Club
1802 Natures Way Blvd., Valrico, FL 33594; 813 685-4105
3½ day Experts Only School (0-10 handicaps and collegiate players), Thu-Sun; Feb
Rates: $$-$$$, tuition only*
Info: Sports Enhancement Associates, 800 345-4245 or 602 284-9000. See page 10 for programs and methods.

*Discounted accommodations at Sheraton Inn and Conference Center (7401 East Hillsborough Ave., Tampa, FL 33610; 813 626-0999), a full destination, 276-room hotel with exercise facilities, pool, restaurant and lounges, 13 miles from Tampa International Airport; complimentary airport service.

■ Nearby Bloomingdale Golfers Club provides its comprehensive practice facilities to S.E.A. For those remaining after the program, Bloomingdale's Ron Garl layout is a test. Golfweek rated it number one in the Tampa area and ninth best in the state. Attesting to its wiles, the club numbers 200 single digit handicappers among its members, including a number of PGA and LPGA pros.

TARPON SPRINGS
Innisbrook Golf Institute

Innisbrook Resort and Country Club
P.O. Drawer 1088, Tarpon Springs, FL 34286; 813 942-2000
Host Pro: Jay Overton; Director: Lew Smither, III
Institutes: 5-day (W-Sun), and 4-day (Thu-Sun), Jan-May, Oct-Dec; 5-day Playing School (Sat-W), Feb-May, Oct & Nov; regular and low handicap programs; Junior Institute (see page 137)
Rates: $$$-$$$$
Other locations: Durango, CO

Established in 1979 by Host Pro Jay Overton, Innisbrook's Golf Institute has seen more than 1,000 golfers a year return home with improved skills and new confidence. Teaching professionals combine the latest technology with what still remains the most effective method: 1:1 instruction. On-line and on-course, Innisbrook's method can be summed up: P-G-A — posture, grip and alignment. Innisbrook is all about exceptional instruction in an exceptional resort setting where golf is the #1 activity.

Four and 5-day Institutes: 4:1 student/teacher ratio, 4 hours daily instruction, video taping with analysis for at-home follow-up, includes all related golf fees and golf services, gift pack. Provides 4 nights on 5-day program, 3 nights on 4-day program, breakfast and lunch daily, social functions. Tampa International Airport transfers. Playing School: 2 mornings on-course playing lessons with Jay Overton, 3 afternoons on-line instruction, daily golf; 4-nights, 3 meals daily, all related golf fees and services, gift pack, social events.

Located on 1,000 heavily wooded acres in the rolling hills of Pinellas County. Lodging in 1,000 suites in 28 lodges, each named for a famous golf course; 6 pools, tennis, fitness center, supervised children's programs; assorted restaurants and pro shops, every comfort.

■ 63 holes. Copperhead, the school's instruction site, is rated Florida's #1 course by GolfWeek and one of "America's Greatest" by Golf Digest. It is home to the televised JC Penney Classic; Sandpiper, a shotmaker's course, recently has been reconfigured to 27 holes; the Island course, voted "Most Interesting" by a panel of writers and pros, is a hilly par 72, 7,000 yards from championship tees.

TARPON SPRINGS
Golf Digest Instruction Schools
Innisbrook Resort and Country Club
P.O. Drawer 1088, Tarpon Springs, FL 34286; 813 942-2000
3-day regular, Short Game School, Ladies program; Oct-Nov, Jan-April, selected dates
Rates: $$$$

Info: Golf Digest Instruction Schools, 800 243-6121. See page **29** for programs and methods.

Golf Digest Instruction Schools brings its own instructional staff to Innisbrook. See previous listing for resort and golf course information.

VERO BEACH

John Jacobs Practical Golf Schools

Grand Harbor Golf and Beach Club
2121 Grand Harbor Blvd., Vero Beach, FL 32967; 407 562-9000
4-day, Oct; 2-day weekend, Jan-March and Oct
Rates: $$-$$$, tuition only
Info: John Jacobs Practical Golf Schools; 800 472-5007. See page **6** for programs and methods.

Hotel welcomes inquiries concerning accommodations. Grand Harbor Resort comprises 878 acres of subtropical islands along the Intracoastal Waterways. On its own private channel, the luxurious Grand Harbor features tennis, boating, pool, beach, informal and formal dining. One hour from Palm Beach Airport; one hour and 30 minutes from Orlando Airport on Florida's East coast.

■ Two waterfront championship courses by the world's greatest names in golf: Pete Dye and Joe Lee. In the tradition of the old courses in Scotland, Dye's 18-hole design unites the player with the environment, in this case: lush salt marshes, waterways and teeming native wildlife.

WINTER PARK

Heritage Golf Schools

1089 W. Morse Blvd., Suite C
Winter Park, FL 32789; 800 362-1469   407 628-5818
Director: Jay Edgar; Director of Instruction: Rina Ritson
3-day, M-W or F-Sun
Locations: La Quinta and Napa, CA; Coral Gables, FL; Kiawah Island, SC; The Woodlands, TX, Hot Springs, VA
Rates: $$$$

Instruction centers on personal attention by director of instruction, Rina Ritson, and the Heritage staff of top notch professional teachers, including members of the Hall of Fame and instructors named among the Top 50 in America by GOLF Magazine. Discriminating students benefit from the same instruction lavished on the pros. The message is: "What's Right for You," as the staff covers every facet of the game: full swing, chipping, pitching, putting, sand play, as well a the mental approach and course strategies. The school travels to America's premier resorts with outstanding golf courses, a different setting each month, varying its venue but not the quality of instruction.

Three days personalized teaching; 8 hours daily; 6:1 maximum student/teacher ratio, limited to 40; students grouped according to handicap. Includes nine-hole scramble with pro on final morning, green fees and cart on play day, on-site videotaped analysis and take-home videocassette. Includes 4 nights (Sun-W or Thu-Sun), breakfast and lunch daily.

GEORGIA

ATLANTA
Mazda Golf Clinics for Executive Women
Druid Hills Golf Course, April
Info: 800 262-7888. See page 73 for programs and methods.

ATLANTA AREA
Golf Digest Instruction Schools
Chateau Elan Golf Club
6060 Golf Club Dr., Braselton, GA 30517; 404 339-9838
2-day weekend and Mini-Schools; April-July, Sept & Oct
Rates: $$$$, tuition only; school will recommend lodging.
Information: Golf Digest Instruction Schools, 800 243-6121. See page 29 for programs and methods,
◼ Chateau Elan Golf Club: Tournament quality course designed by Denis Griffith and Associates, sharing 2,400 acres in northeast Georgia with its sister vineyard and winery by the same name. Plays 7,030 yards from the champ tees, par 71, with water coming into play on 10 of 18 holes. A private second course is under construction. Training center boasts 40 natural turf tee stations with a variety of elevated and bunkered target greens; Wee Links is a 3-hole loop inviting finesse shots. Located 45 minutes north of Atlanta.

SEA ISLAND
Golf Digest Instruction Schools
The Cloister
Sea Island, GA 31561; 800 732-4752
Sea Island Golf Club
100 Retreat Ave., St. Simons Island, GA 31522; 912 638-5118
3-day, 5-day and Mini-Schools; year round; 5-day Parent-Child program (July); Women's Only session (Sept)
Rates: $$$$
Information: Golf Digest Instruction Schools, 800 243-6121. See page 29 for programs and methods.
Opened in 1928, the 264-room Cloister holds Mobil's coveted Five Star award and AAA's Five Diamond rating. It is legendary for luxury, striking Spanish-style decor, traditional Southern hospitality, and the last word in comfort and service. Provides Sea Island Beach Club and Spa, 18 tennis courts, outstanding grounds for hiking or strolling.
◼ 36 holes of links-style golf at The Sea Island Golf Club, located on the grounds of the Retreat Plantation, a former cotton operation on the south end of Sea Island. The courses are comprised of four nines: Seaside, Plantation, Retreat and Marshside. The first two are the work of English designers H.S. Colt and Charles Allison in 1929. Number 4 at Seaside is named the world's greatest hole by GOLF Magazine. Retreat is the creation of Dick Wilson. Joe Lee's Marshside is a shot-maker's course demanding accuracy. Instruction is centered at Golf Digest's own Learning Center.

HAWAII

KAPALUA

Kapalua Golf Club

300 Kapalua Dr., Kapalua, Maui, Lahaina, HI 96761; 808 669-8044

Director: Gary Planos; Touring pro: Gary Player

1-day program; private lessons (with or without video), one hour clinics daily (M-F) on various aspects, 9-hole Playing Lessons; year round

Rates: $$$, tuition only; inquire about accommodations.

Class A, PGA teaching professionals introduce newcomers to golf or reinforce the game for advanced golfers in a one-day comprehensive course touching on all aspects of play. Student/teacher ration 4:1, personalized instruction, drills, customized advice and video analysis. Includes a 9-hole pro-am scramble with instruction.

Kapalua, on the glorious northwest shore of Maui, is a master-planned resort with a hotel and groupings of fully equipped, one- and two-bedroom rental villas in scenic enclaves overlooking Oneloa Bay, high atop a ridge and fronting the fairways. Each area has its own recreation facilities: pools, outdoor barbecues and private gardens. Inquire about rentals and golf packages, including golf school.

▪ Two Arnold Palmer designs: the seaside 6,600-yard, par 72, Bay Course and the 6,632-yard, par 71, Village Course which climbs from the foot of the West Maui mountains to mingle with pineapple fields and eucalyptus groves. The Plantation Course, a Coore & Crenshaw creation opened in 1991, offers the most dramatic vistas in all Maui. Steep and hilly, it is a par 73, playing 7,263 from the championship tees.

LIHUE

Nicklaus Flick Golf School

Westin Kauai at Kauai Lagoons
Kalapaki Beach, Lihue, HI 96766; 800 228-3000   808 245-5050

Kauai Lagoons Golf Club, P.O. Box 3330, Lihue, HI 96766
800 634-6400   808 246-5078

Master Golf III (3 Half-Days); May & Oct

Rates: $$$$-$$$$$

Info: Nicklaus Flick Golf School, 800 642-5528. See page 44 for programs and methods.

A world unto itself, the 846-room, ocean-front Westin Kauai surrounds a gargantuan 26,000 square foot pool bordered by five jacuzzis, perhaps the world's largest. World-famous for its lush plantings, exotic surroundings and lavish decor, the resort features tennis, a European Spa and Wellness Center, 12 restaurants, a splendid beach offering every known water sport (or none at all for confirmed sunbathers), 40 shops, a nature preserve, even a 40-acre lagoon for cruising.

▪ Two picturesque, Nicklaus signature courses opened in 1989: the 7,070-yard, par 72, Kiele layout, selected by Golf Digest as the "Best New Resort Course of 1990," and the more forgiving, traditional, links-style Lagoons course, ranked in 1990 among America's "Top 10 Best New Courses."

WAIKOLOA

John Jacobs Practical Golf Schools

Royal Waikoloan Hotel
Queen Kaahumanu Hwy., Waikoloa, Big Island of Hawaii, 96743
800 464-6262   808 885-6789

Waikoloa Beach Golf Club, 808 885-4647

5-day, Jan-March, Oct-Nov

Rates: $$$

Info: John Jacobs Practical Golf Schools, 800 472-5007. See page 6 for programs and methods.

Overlooking a tropical lagoon on the Kahala coast of the Big Island of Hawaii, the resort brings together Hawaiian traditions – luaus, paniolo-style barbeques and hukilau beach parties – plus all the amenities travelers seek: deluxe service, state of the art fitness facilities, imaginative dining in seven restaurants and lounges, 546 spacious rooms and suites.

■ Adjacent to the hotel, Waikoloa's two courses are carved out of a 5,000-year-old lava flow on the slopes of the Mauna Kea volcano. The 18-hole, 1981, Waikoloa Beach Course bears the signature of Robert Trent Jones, Jr. The 18-hole, 1990, King's Course is the work of Tom Weiskopf and Jay Morrish. The latter has been named among the top five courses in Hawaii.

WAIKOLOA

The Golf Clinic, Pebble Beach California

Royal Waikoloan Hotel
Queen Kaahumanu Hwy., Waikoloa, Big Island of Hawaii, 96743; 800 464-6262
808 885-6789

Waikoloa Beach Golf Club, 808 885-4647

5-day Golf Clinic; March & Nov

Info: The Golf Clinic, Pebble Beach, California, 800 321-9401. See page 20 for programs and methods. See hotel details in prior listing.

Includes round-trip air fare, luxury accommodations at Royal Waikoloan Hotel (see description above) or Hyatt Regency, three meals daily, personalized Pebble Beach Golf Clinic instructional program with take-home, videotaped, one-on-one swing instruction and analysis.

■ Unlimited instructional golf with cart at the Robert Trent Jones Beach course and the Tom Weiskopf and Jay Morrish King's Course at the Waikoloan Beach Golf Club, adjoining the hotel.

According to GOLF Magazine, 90% of teachers believe in the value of video as an instructional tool. Expect to have your swing videotaped and played back for analysis. Most schools send students home with their own instructional tape for continued learning.

IDAHO

Floating Green Golf School

Coeur d'Alene Resort
900 Floating Green Dr., Coeur d'Alene, ID 83814
800 688-5253   208 765-4000

Coeur d'Alene Resort Golf Club, 208 667-4653

Director of Golf: Mary DeLong-Nuttelman

4 and 3-day programs exclusively for beginners, intermediates and advanced intermediates; 2-day Short Game School; April-Sept

Rates: $-$$

Golf-building techniques are communicated through easy-to-understand instruction and visual references. Instructors identify students' strengths through video technology and institute drills, supervised practice and on-course training. Attention devoted to mental strategies for performance at the highest level. Includes four hours personalized daily instruction, class limited to five, on-course training (depending upon proficiency), optional club fitting, unlimited use of practice facilities. Includes one, two or three nights lodging according to duration of program, daily lunch.

National Geographic calls Lake Coeur d'Alene one of the five most beautiful lakes in the world. Star attraction is the ultra-contemporary resort, ranked America's Number One Mainland Resort by Condé Nast Traveler Magazine. The 338-room tower provides postcard-perfect views and every diversion: two waterfront restaurants, outdoor and indoor pools, tennis, racquetball, fitness center, spas, bowling, hiking, lake cruises, on-site marina with world's longest floating boardwalk, horseback riding, wilderness program, children's program. Located 45 minutes from Spokane, WA International Airport.

■ Architect Scott Miller has designed a layout to take advantage of Coeur d'Alene's forested slopes and magnificent lake views. Mahogany launches ferry players to the course, the only one in the world with a floating island green. On pontoons, the 15,000 square-foot #14 can be towed from 75 to 175 yards offshore. Players have two attempts to hit the green and then a chauffeured launch transports them – ingloriously – to the drop zone.

Golf Digest Instruction Schools

Sun Valley Resort
Sun Valley Rd. Sun Valley, ID 83353
800 635-8261   208 622-4111

3-day and Mini-Schools; June-Aug

Rates: $$$$, tuition only; inquire about resort accommodations.

Info: Golf Digest Instruction Schools, 800 243-6121. See page 29 for programs and methods.

An impressive family resort with a romantic past. (among former regulars were the likes of Ernest Hemingway and friends). Offers health and fitness facilities, spa, pool, equestrian sports, tennis, adjoining shopping, and weekly professional ice shows on the resort's outdoor rink. Stay in the lodge or condos. Situated minutes from Ketchum.

■ William Bell's 1937 course has been reworked by Robert Trent Jones, Jr. It is an 18-hole, hilly layout with impressive mountain views, host to the Idaho Governor's Cup and numerous others. Plays 6,057 yards, par 71.

ILLINOIS

ALTON

Arnold Palmer Golf Academy

Spencer T. Olin Community Golf Course
4701 College Ave., Alton, IL, 62002; 618 465-3111

2-day and 3-day; July & Aug

Rates: $$$, tuition only; school will suggest area accommodations.

Info: Arnold Palmer Golf Academy, 800 523-5999. See page 44 for programs and methods.

■ In Illinois, just across the Mississippi River from St. Louis, the course is an 18-hole Arnold Palmer-design opened in 1988. For two years voted the favorite public course in the St. Louis area. Built on hills and deep ravines, it is wide, spacious and gently hilly; plays 6,941 yards from the champ tees.

CHICAGO AREA

Golf Digest Instruction Schools

Three Chicago area sites:

Cog Hill Golf and Country Club, 119th and Archer Ave., Lemont, IL 60439
708 257-5872 ; 2-day weekend and Mini-Schools.

■ A teaching facility southwest of Chicago, with four courses. With a towering 75.4 rating, its No. 4 course, dubbed Dubsdread, has been named among America's 100 Greatest Courses by Golf Digest magazine.

Pine Meadow Golf and Country Club, Pine Meadow Lane, Mundelein, IL 60060; 708 566-4653; 3-day, 2-day weekend, and Mini-Schools

■ A teaching facility located 22 miles north of Chicago's O'Hare Airport, the Pine Meadows course is ranked among Golf Digests Top 25 Public Courses. It is exciting and long, 7,141 from the back tees.

St. Andrews Golf Club, 3 North 441 Rte. 59, West Chicago, IL 60185; 708 231-3100
2-day weekend and Mini-Schools.

■ A practice facility with acres of grass tees aimed at a target fairway and greens; plus two 18-hole courses. Situated within an hour of downtown Chicago.

Rates: $$$$, tuition only; contact school for area accommodations.

Info: Golf Digest Instruction Schools, 800 243-6121. See page 29 for programs and methods. Programs scheduled May-Aug.

Mazda Golf Clinics for Executive Women
White Eagle Golf Course, June
Info: 800 262-7888. See page 73 for programs and methods.

GALENA

Eagle Ridge Golf Academy
Eagle Ridge Inn and Resort
U.S. Route 20, Box 777, Galena, IL 61036
800 892-2269   815 777-2444
Director: Laura Schlaman

2-day and 3-day Academies: Standard Academy, Playing Academy, Advanced Academy (low handicap), Mini Academy, Alumni Academy, Junior Academy (ages 8-16, see page140); coed and Women Only programs; April to Oct.

Rates: $

PGA instructors help students build a solid swing to last a lifetime. Program combines personalized instruction in classes with a student/teacher ratio of 4:1 and play on the resort's three courses; daily videotaping on a personalized take-home tape to measure progress; includes daily green fees and carts during and after classes, gift pack and club storage.

Programs includes lodging and all meals. Standard Academy: five hours instruction daily, on-course playing lesson, videotaping; co-ed and Women Only. Playing Academy stresses course management in a daily 18-hole playing lesson, plus instruction. Advanced Academy for 0-12 handicaps includes instruction and 18-hole playing lesson daily. Two-day, weekend, Mini-Academy (arrive Fri) provides eight hours instruction and instructional play daily. One-day Alumni Academy for former students: five hours instruction and 9-hole playing lesson.

Located on a cliff overlooking 6,800, rolling, wooded acres in the northwest corner of Illinois, Eagle Ridge Inn has been named among the top family resorts in the country by Better Homes & Gardens magazine. Area offers a field day to bird watchers, fishermen, cyclists and equestrians. Resort provides tennis, a complete fitness center including massage, pool, sun deck; recreational staff, children's and youth programs, entertainment, casual and formal dining – even an ice cream parlor.

■ 45 holes. Eagle Ridge's South Course, laid out in 1984 by Larry Packard, was named "Best New Resort Course" by Golf Digest. It combines cliffs and creeks, creating a stiff test. The North course, a 1977 Roger Packard design, is scenic and hilly. The pair has repeatedly been named among the top resort courses in the country. The new 9-hole East Course is scenic and challenging.

> *Stock up on Band Aids, first aid cream, your favorite brands of aspirin or anti-inflammatories. You'll be engaged in serious, repetitive exercise. Stretch out before you begin in order to head off trouble.*

INDIANA

FRENCH LICK

United States Golf Schools

French Lick Springs Golf and Tennis Resort
8670 West State Rd. 56, French Lick, IN 47432
800 457-4042   812 936-9300

5-day, 3-day and 2-day weekend; summer

Rates: $

Info: U.S. Golf Schools, 800 354-7415. See page 55 for programs and methods.

For over a century, French Lick Springs Resort has welcomed the rich and famous and ordinary to its healthful mineral springs set in opulent surroundings. Its European Mineral Spa presents a complete menu for health and coddling. Rich in tradition and recently brought up-to-the-minute in comfort, the 485-room grand hotel is situated on 2,600 acres. Offers croquet, indoor and outdoor swimming, tennis, skeet and trap shooting, horseback riding, bowling, billiards, and an arcade room. Dine royally in five full-service dining rooms. Located 108 miles south of Indianapolis.

■ 36 holes designed by Donald Ross, architect of Pinehurst No. 2. French Lick's woodland Country Club course, par 70, playing 6,625 from the championship tees, has rolling hills with large undulating greens. The Valley Course, par 70, playing 6,003 yards, is player-friendly and level.

MONTICELLO

Indiana Golf Academy

Pine View Golf Resort
905 W. Norway Rd., Monticello, IN 47960
800 972-9636   219 583-7733

Director: Steve Bonnell

3-day (M-W), April-June, Aug-Sept; 2-day weekend, April-June

Rates: $

Improved performance lies in learning sound fundamentals and principles, according to Indiana Golf Academy's PGA pros who utilize simplified methods and call on refined communication skills to help students grasp the mechanics of a solid, reproducible swing. Classes limited to 4:1 student/teacher ratio, on-course training, video analysis, unlimited practice; includes golf on day of arrival plus 9-hole green fees after class (carts additional). Includes three (Sun-Tu) or two nights (F & Sat) and all meals.

Situated in northwest Indiana, a half mile from Indiana Beach, the state's largest amusement park. Motel lodging on the course with pool, restaurant, lounge; boating and fishing on Lake Shafer.

■ 45 holes: two championship courses and a 9-hole, lighted, par 3 course for all-night play. Access to nine courses in uncrowded Indiana "where golfers can walk on without a tee time and play 18 holes for less money than they pay for lunch."

PLYMOUTH

United States Golf Academy

Swan Lake Golf Resort
5203 Plymouth-LaPorte Trail, Plymouth, ID 46563
800 582-7539   219 935-5680
Director: Roger Swanson
3-day, M-W or F-Sun*; April-Sept
Rates $

Special attention is paid to teaching every technique properly. Personalized videotaped instruction allows each student to study his or her own swing, to visualize improvement and make the necessary corrective adjustments – all under the eyes of concerned, experienced instructors. Provides 3 hours instruction, plus 3 hours on-course teaching daily, 5:1 student/teacher ratio; classes for beginners, intermediates and advanced golfers (men and women separate); evening instructional films. Complimentary greens fees (carts additional); unlimited practice. Juniors under 16 accepted with an adult.

*Arrive Sun or Thu; make advance tee times for day of arrival. Lodging (double occupancy) in the Academy Motel, just off the 17th fairway, or dorm-style in carpeted, air-conditioned comfort. Three meals daily. Located two hours from Chicago, north of Indianapolis. South Bend's Michiana Airport is 30 minutes from the first tee.

■ 36 holes of championship play. The West course, par 72, 6,942 yards, is characterized by large greens and wide fairways. Lakes and streams wind their way through seven of the back nine holes of the 6,854-yard East course, offering errant shots a watery grave.

KANSAS

OVERLAND PARK

The Phil Ritson Golf School

Deer Creek Golf Club
7000 West 133rd St., Overland Park, KS 66209; 913 681-3100
1-, 3- and 5 Half-Day programs, April-Oct; shared or private lessons; Juniors accepted with an adult

Rates: $$$, tuition only; additional charges for lodging* and golf.

Information: The Phil Ritson Golf School, 407 876-6487. See page 51 for programs and methods.

Provides 3 ½ hour sessions, morning or afternoon; 5 Half-Day programs begin Mon and include two 9-hole playing lessons; 3 Half-Day programs begin Mon or Thurs. *Accommodations arranged at nearby Marriott (913 451-8000), Devil Tree (913 451-6100) or Ramada (913 888-8440) resorts. Five miles west of Kansas City.

■ Deer Creek Golf Club, designed by Robert Trent Jones Jr., was recognized by Golf Digest in 1990 as one of the three best new courses in America. Plays 6,870 from the back tees, tight and demanding, packed with 85 bunkers.

Schools seldom (read: almost never) cancel classes. Therefore, all-weather gear is essential. In the best of circumstances, you'll need full-strength sun block and a hat with a deep visor. Worst case scenario: rain jacket and pants and waterproof golf shoes. Bring all of them and you won't be sorry.

MAINE

BETHEL

Guaranteed Performance™ School of Golf

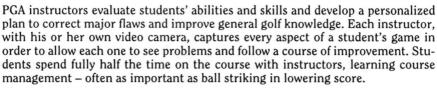

Bethel Inn and Country Club
Bethel, ME 04217; 800 654-0125   207 824-2175
Director: Allen Connors
5-day, 3-day programs; May-Sept
Rates: $

PGA instructors evaluate students' abilities and skills and develop a personalized plan to correct major flaws and improve general golf knowledge. Each instructor, with his or her own video camera, captures every aspect of a student's game in order to allow each one to see problems and follow a course of improvement. Students spend fully half the time on the course with instructors, learning course management – often as important as ball striking in lowering score.

Includes complimentary golf on day of arrival and on check-out afternoon (make tee times in advance). Maximum 4:1 student/teacher ratio, class limited to 16. Includes video analysis, unlimited golf and use of practice facilities, green fees and carts, club storage. Five-day program provides 20 hours instruction, four nights lodging. Three-day program, arrive M, W, or F; 10 hours instruction, two nights lodging. Provides all meals and welcome cocktail party.

Elegant AAA Three Diamond country resort comprised of five colonial guest houses, a recreation center and lake house on 202 acres in Maine's White Mountains. Health club, heated pool, poolside lounge, lake swimming, sailing, canoeing. Celebrated cuisine, year-round veranda dining. Fly to Portland (70 miles), Augusta (50 miles); located 22 miles from the nearest McDonald's.

■ Geoffrey Cornish-Brian Silva, championship, 18-hole course incorporates the 150-year old Mill Brook dam and takes advantage of the natural mountain topography.

*How much will golf school cost? Turn to page **71** for the code to pricing*

KINGFIELD
Sugarloaf Golf Club & School

The Sugarloaf Inn
Route 27, Box 5000, Carrabassett Valley, ME 04947
1 800 THE-LOAF
Director: Scott Hoisington

5-day programs for Juniors (see page 148), Women Only, Couples, Seniors; 2-day weekends; 1-day session (Tu or Thu); Peak Performance Golf Focus Week for Women*; June-Sept

Rates: $

A PGA professional staff guarantees students five hours personalized instruction daily in classes with 4:1 student/teacher ratio and limited to 12. Instruction builds on students' strengths and bases its success on improving existing skills. Newcomers to golf receive patient, step-by-step instruction in fundamentals. Instructors utilize instant feedback video analysis and frame-by-frame visualization and, teaching devices. Includes green fees and cart, preferred tee times, health and fitness club privileges. Multi-day programs include on-course instruction.

Five-day midweek program provides tournament, 5 nights, breakfast and lunch, welcome cocktail party and awards banquet. Two-day weekend: 2 nights, breakfast and lunch, cocktail party. One-day school: 1 night lodging, breakfast and golf fees for day prior or following program.

*Peak Performance Golf Focus Week for Women: a spa/health club program composed of exercise, massage, facials, diet, and includes 15-20 hours on-course golf instruction in classes limited to 4:1 student/teacher ratio.

A 105-room, relaxed mountain resort with lodging in the Inn or, for multi-night stays, in a choice of hundreds of condos. Offers tennis, pool, scenic hiking, varied dining. Provides vacation packages in instructional and recreational mountain biking, wilderness excursions and white water rafting adventures, a teen sports camp and full children's program for vacationing families. Less than a four hours drive from Montreal or Boston.

■ Literally carved out of the Maine woods by Robert Trent Jones, Jr., Sugarloaf Golf Course has been rated by Golf Digest as the #1 course in Maine for four years in a row and one of the top 75 resort courses in the U.S. Called superb, a gem and one of the most scenic links in America by those who know. Plays 6,900 yards from the championship tees.

ROCKPORT
Samoset Golf School

Samoset Resort, Rockport, ME 04856
800 341-1650   207 594-2511
Director: Bob O'Brien

3-day (Sun-Tu or Tu-Thu), May-June (sessions may be combined for an extended program)

Rates: $

Recognizing that three days does not permit time to rebuild a student's golf swing, this school concentrates on instituting minor changes to bring about results. Working within student's capabilities and level of performance, PGA pros emphasize sound mechanics and leave students with two or three swing keys for continued improvement. Provides five hours instruction over three days; includes green fees and cart (with advance reserved tee times) for two rounds; putting contest. Two nights lodging, daily breakfasts, one dinner, one clubhouse lunch.

AAAA Four Diamond resort located on 230 oceanside acres in the rugged mid-coast area of Maine. Accommodations in 150 luxurious rooms, suites and townhome residences, plus the new Flume Cottage, a two-bedroom villa adjacent to the fourth fairway, situating it literally at sea. Provides indoor and outdoor pool, sauna, croquet, racquetball, fitness center with aerobic classes, tennis courts, basketball, cycling, and children's day camp. The elegant Marcel's Restaurant is an area favorite. Down East attractions include the charming towns of Camden, Rockport and Rockland; museums, boating, lighthouses, antiquing, theater, and much more. Located 10 minutes from Knox County Airport, with commuter service from most major Northeast cities.

▶ With ocean vistas on 13 of 18 holes, Samoset has been described as the Pebble Beach of the East. Designed by Robert Elder in 1972, the course plays 6,384 from the back tees. Beware of stiff sea breezes, distracting seascapes, and the 7/8-mile jetty straight off the seventh green with the area's oldest lighthouse perched at the tip. Finishing your round in regulation four hours earns you a 15 percent discount in Samoset's pro shop.

RELATIVE PRICING SCALE

(Based on a 5-day program)

$ – *Less than $999 for 5 days instruction, 5 nights lodging, all meals and unlimited golf.*

$$ – *$1,000 to $1,499 for the same 5-day package; this is in the low-average range.*

$$-$$$ – *$1,500-$2,999. Costs creep up to high-average due to seasonal variations, fewer nights or meals, or add-ons (green fees, amenities, tips).*

$$$-$$$$ or $$$$– *$3,000-$4,999 range for 5-day programs (or the equivalent) situated at luxurious resorts or headed by a well-known pro. Or perhaps with smaller classes or sophisticated technology. Many special programs such as Low Handicap, VIP, or Playing Schools are in this category.*

$$$$$ – *$5,000 to $10,000/week–usually those with world-class teachers, private or semi-private instruction, located at the finest resorts.*

MARYLAND

BETHESDA - WASHINGTON, D.C. AREA

Mazda Golf Clinics for Executive Women
Bethesda Country Club, May
Info: 800 262-7888. See page 73 for programs and methods.

OCEAN CITY

Swing's The Thing Golf Schools
Comfort Inn Gold Coast
11201 Coastal Hwy, Ocean City, MD 21842
800 228-5151   410 524-3000

Ocean Pines Golf and County Club, 1449 Ocean Pines, Berlin, MD 21811
410 641-8653

3-day; April-Oct

Rates $$-$$$, adjustments for 2 or 3 nights

Info: Swing's The Thing Golf School, 800 221-6661. See page 98 for programs and methods.

This 202-room, five-story, interior-corridor Inn features a microwave, wet bar and refrigerator in every room; Jacuzzis, enclosed pool, direct access to the beach, dining. Adjoins 45-store mall and theater complex; 15 minutes from the course.

■ Learning center at the Clubs of Ocean Pines, a 3,500-acre residential community featuring Yacht and Beach Clubs, a Swim and Racquet Club and a Country Club featuring a Robert Trent Jones, 18-hole course. Ample practice areas with a double-ended driving range.

OCEAN CITY

The Golf School
Comfort Inn Gold Coast
11201 Coastal Hwy, Ocean City, MD
800 228-5150   410 524-3000

River Run Golf Club, 11433 Beauchamp Rd., Berlin, MD 21811
800 733-RRUN or 410 641-7200

5-day, 2-day weekend; April & May, Sept & Oct

Rates: $-$$

Info: The Golf School, 800 632-6262 or 904 795-4211. See page 34 for programs and methods.

Includes breakfasts and lunches. See Comfort Inn details in previous listing.

■ Skills are honed at the Peninsula Golf Center, a professional, 16-acre practice facility with covered hitting stations and an abundance of situations simulating actual course conditions. Afternoon on-course training and up to 18 holes free play at River Run, a Gary Player signature course which takes full advantage of its gently rolling, idyllic setting on Maryland's Eastern Shore. Plays 6,705 yards, par 71.

MASSACHUSETTS

BERNARDSTON

Crumpin-Fox Club Adult Golf Institute

Crumpin-Fox Golf Club
Parmenter Rd., Bernardston, MA 01337
413 648-9101   413 648-9107

Director: Ron Beck

3-day Institute, May & June; group and individual lessons, outings; Junior camps (see page 150)

Rates: $, tuition only*

Other locations: Tampa, FL (sister course, Fox Hollow, a Robert Trent Jones, Jr. design, under construction)

The objective of instruction is to help students clearly understand and implement the fundamentals of setting up and swinging the club to produce all the shots to lower scores. Each golfer is evaluated, strengths are identified, and correction is instituted to make each one more effective. Golfers of all ages and abilities receive attentive, perceptive instruction. The staff employs a full range of innovative learning and practice aids, as well as video replay with take-home tape for continued learning. Three-day program includes 15 hours on-line instruction, 4:1 student/teacher ratio, class size limited to 12; includes green fees and carts, unlimited use of facility, welcome dinner party, lunch.

*Located along the Massachusetts/Vermont border near historic Old Deerfield, a few miles from Brattleboro, VT. School refers students to a full range of area hotels, country inns and motels. Crumpin-Fox is set to open its own lodge, The Fox Inn; full service restaurant at the course.

◼ Roger Rulewich and Robert Trent Jones Jr. have designed a course lauded by Golf Magazine in 1991 as one of the "Top Ten New Courses You Can Play." Awarded honorable mention by Golf Digest as "Best New Public Course in America." Learning/practice center simulates playing situations; enclosed fully-equipped learning center shed.

BOSTON

Mazda Golf Clinics for Executive Women

Nine one-day clinics at golf clubs across the country to benefit
Susan G. Komen Breast Cancer Foundation; Feb-Oct

Locations: Phoenix, Los Angeles, Atlanta, Washington DC, Chicago, Boston, NYC, San Francisco, Dallas. See individual listings for courses and dates.

Boston area location: Spring Valley Country Club, Sharon, MA, July

Rates: $200; luncheon-only, $75

Info: To reserve, call 800 262-7888 or FAX 617 723-8230

Executive women with median incomes of $100,000 learn about the personal and professional benefits of golf while networking and benefiting breast cancer research. Full day program, 7:30 am to 6 pm. Experienced golfers play a 9-hole scramble under the supervision of LPGA teaching pros, followed by instruction. Less experienced golfers receive instruction from LPGA teaching pros and LPGA celebrities including Beth Daniel, Patty Sheehan, Pat Bradley, Shelley Hamlin, Meg Mallon and Jane Blalock. Nine-hole scramble follows instruction. Opening and closing receptions and lunch.

CAPE COD - BREWSTER
Golf Digest Instruction Schools

Ocean Edge Resort and Golf Club
Route 6A, Brewster, MA 02631
800 343-6074   508 896-9000

3-day, June-Aug

Rates: $$$$

Info: Golf Digest Instruction Schools, 800 243-6121. See page 29 for programs and methods.

See following entry for details of resort and golf.

CAPE COD - BREWSTER
Ocean Edge Golf School

Ocean Edge Resort and Golf Club
Route 6A, Brewster, MA 02631
800 343-6074   508 896-9000

Director: Ron Hallett

3-day weekend, F-Sun; April-June; Memorial Day Weekend, Sat-M

Rates: $-$$

Info and to reserve: Call Golf School, 508 896- 5911

Teaching emphasizes fundamentals, grip, posture, balance, and pre-shot routines – all the components of a competent golf swing. Provides five hours highly individualized daily instruction with PGA staff, maximum 6:1 student/teacher ratio, personalized video analysis, complimentary golf following school. Provides three nights accommodations in 1-, 2- and 3-bedroom villas bordering the course; includes welcome reception, daily breakfast and lunch and one dinner.

On a magnificent site overlooking Cape Cod Bay, a secluded conference center/resort with memorable dining, a health club, private beach, indoor and outdoor pools, tennis – on the beautifully restored Victorian estate once frequented by President Grover Cleveland. The resort is home to the Tim Gullikson World Class Tennis School. Located 12 minutes from Barnstable Municipal Airport at Hyannis, 85 miles from Boston.

■ A scenic, 18-hole 6,665-yard, par 72, Geoffrey Cornish and Brian Silva design, host of the New England PGA Championship, 1986-'91. Traverses ponds and skirts cranberry bogs. Named among the Top 10 Resort/Conference Center Courses by Golf Illustrated magazine.

CAPE COD - BREWSTER
S.E.A. Nice Shot! Golf Schools

Ocean Edge Resort and Golf Club
Route 6A, Brewster, MA 02631; 800 343-6074   508 896-9000

3½ day Golfers School; July

Rates: $$-$$$, tuition only; accommodations package arranged at Ocean Edge Resort.
Info: Sports Enhancement Associates, 800 345-4245 or 602 284-9000. See page 10
for programs and methods. See previous entry for details of resort and golf.

CAPE COD - SOUTH YARMOUTH

Cape Cod Golf School

Blue Rock Motor Inn and Golf Course
Todd Rd., Off Highbank Rd.
South Yarmouth, MA 02664
800 23-PUTTS

Director: Robert V. Miller

4-day, April-Sept; 3-day weekend and mid-week Mini-Golf School, April-Oct; 3-day
Playing School; April-June

Rates: $

Director Robert Miller, 1990 New England PGA teacher of the year and author of
the first large-print golf book, "Golf the Ageless Game," encourages golfers of all
ages to improve their game and make golf more fun. PGA and LPGA professionals
tailor the program to their students, covering all aspects and employing the latest drills and video equipment. On tape or in instantly printed, 9-frame, still photos, students are able to visualize their swing. Corrections are made under the careful
eye of instructors in classes not exceeding 4:1 student/teacher ratio.

Four-day program provides 10 hours instruction, four days unlimited play; 3 nights,
3 breakfasts and lunches. Two-day Mini-School program provides 4 hours instruction,
3 days unlimited play, 2 nights, 2 breakfasts, 1 lunch. Three-day Playing school: 4
hours instruction, 4:1 student/teacher ratio, 9-hole on-course training, 3 days complimentary golf, 2 nights, 2 breakfasts and lunches.

The Inn offers a friendly atmosphere, private ocean beach, pool, tennis, bicycling,
homey restaurant. All rooms with balcony and golf course view.

■ Sports Illustrated named the 9-hole, 3,000-yard, Geoffrey Cornish-designed Blue
Rock Golf Course, the nation's finest par 3. Students need all the clubs in their
bag for holes ranging from 103 to 249 yards, four with water. Instruction centers
on practice range, two putting greens; pro shop with repair and club building.
Numerous regulation courses nearby.

NORTON

Bob Toski Golf School

Golf Learning Center of New England, 19 Leonhard St.,
Norton, MA 02766; 508 285-4540

Norton Country Club, 188 Oak St., Norton, MA; 508 285-2400

Instructional team: Bob Toski and Gary Battersby

4-day, W-Sat; June - Aug, selected dates

Rates: $$$-$$$$, tuition only*

Info and registration: Bob Toski Golf School, Senior Tour Players, Inc., 264 Bea-
con St., Boston, MA 02116, 800 888-4656.

Bob Toski, for four decades one of America's most respected teachers, founder and dean of the world famous Golf Digest Instruction Schools, winner of 10 tour championships, and Golf Digest contributing writer, conducts programs based on the traditional, hand-on model. His students, Tom Kite, Sam Snead and Tom Shaw, attest to his effectiveness. Ignoring gimmicks and high tech learning devices, Toski and his teaching staff "diagnose" each player and institute a corrective practice plan which will lead to their playing better golf. Stressing fundamentals, the Toski method concentrates on posture, grip, swing path, timing, mental aspects, as the essentials that contribute to consistancy and success.

Provides 26 hours closely supervised instruction by PGA pros and Toski, himself, in classes limited to 24, with a 6:1 student/teacher ratio. Combines range and on-course training. Includes lunch. Located 35 miles from Boston, 25 miles from Providence and Cape Cod.

*Lodging and meal package available at nearby Holiday Inn (700 Miles Standish Blvd., Taunton, MA 02780, 508 823-0430), 150-room hotel, ten minutes from Norton; offers indoor pool, fitness club, squash and racquetball; restaurant.

■ Golf Learning Center of New England provides a comprehensive learning environment including covered hitting area for inclement weather. Nearby Norton Country Club course is compact and challenging, plays 6,505 from the blue tees, par 71.

SEEKONK

Bob DiPadua Golf School at Firefly

Firefly Golf Course
320 Fall River Ave. (Rte 114A), Seekonk, MA 02771
508 336-6622

Director: Bob DiPadua

1-day schools, 4-lesson series; private and group instruction; April-July

Rates: $, commuter-only programs

Bob DiPadua, teaching pro certified by the U.S. Golf Teachers Association and the National Golf Educators Foundation, imparts the basics to get golfers started or to correct bad habits. Classes limited to 6:1 student/teacher ratio. Provides six hours instruction in one day school or in four 1½-hour sessions scheduled over four consecutive weeks.

■ Turf practice range with practice bunker, target and putting greens at 18-hole Firefly executive course.

The majority of schools provide daily club storage and cleaning, unlimited use of practice facilities and send you home with mementos: towels, bag tags, visors, a class photo, diploma or the like.

STOW

Stow Acres Country Club

58 Randall Rd., Stow, MA 01775; 508 568-9090

Director: Sal Ruggiero

4-day, May-Aug; 2-day weekday and 2-day weekend, April-Oct; Junior clinic, June-Aug (see page 150)

Rates: $, tuition only; school will suggest nearby lodging.

Director Sal Ruggiero brings 23 years of experience to teaching. A born communicator, he stresses the enjoyment of the game and the importance of sound fundamentals. "Simplicity" is the hallmark of Ruggiero's method which is delivered by PGA pros in a relaxed atmosphere.

Provides five hours instruction daily, maximum 5:1 student/teacher ratio, students grouped according to skill; includes video analysis, instruction manual, gift; unlimited use of practice facility, complimentary golf after school, club fitting. Four-day program includes on-course instruction. All programs include breakfast and lunch.

■ 36 holes designed by Geoffrey Cornish, voted "Best" by Boston Magazine and one of the "Top 50 Public Courses in the Nation" by Golf Digest. The North course stretches nearly 7,000 yards. The shorter, sportier South course is equally challenging at 6,600 yards. Complete practice facility reserved for the school includes covered hitting area, driving range with target greens, lighted driving area and short game site.

MICHIGAN

BOYNE FALLS

Boyne Super 5™ Golf Week

Boyne Mountain Resort
Boyne Mountain Rd., Boyne Falls, MI 49713; 800 GO BOYNE

5-days, Sun-F; June-Aug

Rates: $

Info: Refer to following listing for details of the resorts and golf.

Experienced PGA and LPGA instructors provide as much or as little instruction as students require in an unregimented, unrestricted, play-and-learn experience. Group lessons – as many or as few as students desire – are available day-in-day-out, from 9 am to noon and 1-4 pm, on all aspects of the game. Students are urged to work on any aspect of their game which needs clarification or improvement and to fit their golfing and recreational plans around classes which include video analysis, a putting contest and a mixed scramble tournament.

Super 5™ Golf Week includes unlimited golf with cart, unlimited instruction, five nights lodging in condos or hotel, breakfast and dinner daily and a host of activities.

■ Two top-ranked courses at Boyne Mountain: Monument and Alpine. Boyne Highlands Resort, 26 miles south, offers Heather, Donald Ross, and Moor courses. Guests regularly shuttle between the sister resorts, taking advantage of the amenties of both. Refer to following listing for further golf information.

HARBOR SPRINGS

Nicklaus Flick Golf School

Boyne Highlands Resort/Heather Highlands Inn
Harbor Springs, MI 49740; 800 GO-BOYNE   616 526-2171

Master Golf I (3-day); July

Rates: $$$$-$$$$$

Information: Nicklaus Flick Golf School, 800 642-5528. See page 44 for programs and methods.

Situated in the hills of northwest Michigan, Heather Island Inn is set amidst 6,000 private acres a few miles from the shores of Lake Michigan. Guests enjoy evening entertainment, tennis, hiking, biking, swimming, fishing and water sports from SCUBA diving to water skiing. Villa accommodations. Sister resort, Boyne Mountain, 26 miles away, offers an equally wide variety of activities. Located 185 miles from Lansing; resort has its own jet strip or fly to Traverse City or Pellston.

■ With five world class golf courses, the twin resorts are ranked by Golf Digest among the first 25 of "America's 75 Best Resort Courses." GOLF magazine names them Silver Medal Resorts. At Boyne Mountain are the high, scenic Alpine and Monument courses, the latter named for the plaques mounted on boulders at every tee, commemorating golf legends. At Boyne Highlands: Heather, a Robert Trent Jones, Jr.-design, ranked among the nation's top 100; the tough Moor Course, and the new Donald Ross Memorial Course which recreates the 18 finest holes designed by the father of American golf architecture. The latest addition to the Boyne golf family is Hemlock, a newly remodeled, par 30, executive.

TRAVERSE CITY

John Jacobs Practical Golf Schools

Grand Traverse Resort
6300 North U.S. 31, Grand Traverse Village, Acme MI 49610
800 678-1308   616 938-2100

5-day and weekend; June-Aug.

Rates: $$

Information: John Jacobs Practical Golf Schools, 800 472-5007. See page 6.

On the shores of Lake Michigan, six miles northeast of Traverse City, the 750-room Grand Traverse Resort has carried Family Circle magazine's "Family Resort of the Year" designation for three years in a row. Provides sailing at its Shores Beach and Sailing Club, plus a spa, indoor sports complex, indoor and outdoor tennis, aerobics, racquetball, ten restaurants for ethnic and regional American dining. Accommodations in hotel or 17 story-tower. One- two- and three-bedroom rental condominiums line the golf courses and face the lake. Ten minutes from Cherry Capitol Traverse City Airport.

■ Two courses, including the fearsome, 18-hole Bear, designed by Jack Nicklaus, "The Bear," himself. Features heather-covered mounding, cavernous pot bunkers and tiered fairways. Named among the "Top 50 Courses in the Nation" by GOLF Magazine, The Bear plays 7,177 from the champ tees and nearly 1,000 yards shorter from the whites. The Resort course, a 1978 Bill Newcomb-design, plays 6,176 yards and can only be tamer.

MINNESOTA

BREEZY POINT

Proper Swing Golf School

Breezy Point Resort Golf Club, Breezy Point, MN 56472
800 328-2284   218 562-7811

Director: Jim McElhaney

3-day (M-W or Thu-Sun), 1-day, May-Sept; Junior Institute (see page 152)

Rates: $; rates vary according to accommodations

Instruction is directed at building a solid foundation for a lifetime of enjoyable golfing. Program is designed to introduce beginners to the game and to assist more experienced players to be more proficient. Provides a total of 16 hours range instruction plus daily playing lessons, in classes not exceeding 4:1 student/teacher ratio. Includes personalized teaching and supervised practice, videotaping with analysis for at home review and all golf fees. Provides three nights lodging, breakfasts and dinners.

Situated on 3,000 acrea of unspoiled, deep woods and lakes, Breezy Point offers a range of activities and numerous, rustic lodging choices from efficiency cabins to VIP accommodations in your own 10-bedroom, 8-bath log mansion. Offers varied dining, indoor and outdoor pools, tennis, fishing, boating, childrens program, game room, volleyball, bocce ball, hiking, horseshoes and the High Village Spa with whirlpool, sauna and sun deck. Located in Central Minnesota, 140 miles from the Twin Cities.

▪ Two 18-hole courses, the older, par 68 Traditional and the challenging Championship, with complete learning facilities.

MISSISSIPPI

BILOXI

United States Golf Schools

Broadwater Beach Resort & President Casino
2110 Beach Blvd., Biloxi, MS 39531; 800 647-3964   601 388-2211

5-day, 3-day and 2-day weekend; fall-spring

Rates: $$

Info: United States Golf Schools, 800 354-7415. See page 55 for programs and methods.

Hospitable sportsman's paradise with 360 spacious guest rooms, suites or private cottages set in lush, tropical gardens. Offers a complete marina and a wide variety of water sports, fishing charters, pool, shuffleboard, lighted tennis, sandy beach and gambling; dining in five specialty restaurants featuring an array of Mississippi's signature seafoods. Many area attractions, including NASA's Space Technology Labs. Includes breakfast and dinner.

▪ The Gulf of Mexico constitutes a water hazard on the forested, tight, 18-hole Sea Course, measuring 7,190 from the back tees. A block away, the par-72, 18-hole Sun Course is not without water – in fact, 14 holes can lure you into the drink.

MISSOURI

LAKE OZARK

Arnold Palmer Golf Academy

North Port National Golf Club
Business Hwy. 54, Lake of the Ozarks, MO 65049; 314 365-1100

2-day and 3-day; July & Aug

Rates: $$$, tuition only; ask school about accommodations

Info: Arnold Palmer Golf Academy, 800 523-5999. See page **44** for programs and methods.

On the site of a proposed residential development, hotel and conference center. Club House with dining available to students. Limited accommodations in newly built condos or at area hotels and resorts. Located in central Missouri, three hours from St. Louis; fly to nearby commuter airport at Osage.

■ The Osage Course was unveiled with the Michelob Skins Classic in August, 1992. It is the first of three courses planned for this complex. Instruction at North Port's state of the art, 3-hole, lighted practice facility and putting green.

OSAGE BEACH

John Jacobs Practical Golf Schools

Marriott's Tan-Tar-A Resort and Golf Club
State Rd. K.K., Osage Beach, MO 65065; 800 826-8272   314 348-3131

4-day and weekend; May-Sept

Rates: $$

Info: John Jacobs Practical Golf Schools, 800 472-5007. See page **6** for programs and methods.

A 1,000-room, Mobil Four Star, AAA Four Diamond resort situated on 420 wooded acres overlooking Lake of the Ozarks in central Missouri. Water sports and golf are king here. Also horseback riding, scenic hiking, bowling, mini golf, sailing, fishing, indoor and outdoor tennis, parasailing, swimming, sauna and spa. Organized recreational programs for teens and children over five. Accommodations in the hotel or in 200 individual guest houses divided into rooms or suites. Located midway between St. Louis and Kansas City.

■ 27 holes; the 18-hole Oaks course, designed by Bruce Devlin and Robert Von Hagge, calls on intelligence and shot-making. Hidden Lakes course is a hilly, challenging nine-holer. The resort hosts numerous regional tournaments.

> *Write it all down. Most schools provide an instruction manual with lots of room for personal notes. Take the time to jot down the fine points of what you are told. Trust us, your notes will come in handy when you get home.*

NEVADA

LAS VEGAS

America's Favorite Golf Schools

Riviera Hotel
2901 Las Vegas Blvd South., Las Vegas, NV 89109
800 634-3420   702 734-5110

Sahara Country Club, 1911 East Desert Inn Rd., Las Vegas, NV 89109
702 796-0013

5-day; 3-day, M-W or F-Sun; year round

Rates: $-$$

Info: America's Favorite Golf Schools, 800 365-6640. See page 36 for programs and methods.

Located right on the famous Las Vegas Strip and boasting the world's largest casino, the 2,100-room Riviera is a full-amenity resort, featuring dazzling live entertainment, pool, men's and women's health clubs, numerous restaurants, a food court and a game room for kids. Casino and shops – even a wedding chapel. Within walking distance of many major attractions; five miles from McCarren International Airport.

▶ Seven minutes from the hotel, an 18-hole championship course at Sahara Country Club, with every green bunkered by sand or water; plays 6,815 yards from the back tees; home of Tournament of Champions and others.

NEW HAMPSHIRE

AMHERST

Exceller Programs Golf Schools

Ponemah Green Learning Center
55 Ponemah Rd., Amherst, NH 03031
603-672-4732

2-day weekends, Mini-Schools (5-lesson series for 1-5 students); Clinics (series for beginners and intermediates); private instruction (single lessons or series); Playing Lessons; Junior programs (see page 126), May-Aug
1-day Business Women's Seminars, July

Rates: $, tuition only*

Info and registration: Exceller Programs Golf Schools, 800 424-7438. See page 4 for programs and methods.

*Commuter-only programs at this learning center which is an extention of Exceller's regular resort sites. Obtain information from school on nearby accommodations in this popular vacation area. Located one hour north of Boston, 15 minutes from Nashua, NH.

▶ Practice facilities at Ponemah Green Golf Course include a 20-station driving range with measured targets and full chipping and putting areas. Ponemah Golf Course is a 9-hole Scottish Links, Goeffrey Cornish design. Adjoining Amherst Country Club offers an 18-hole championship course.

World Cup Golf School

World Cup Driving Range
9 River Rd., Hudson, NH 03051; 603 598-3838

Director: Bob Griswald

1-day, 2-day, 3-day for adults, Juniors (see page 155), seniors; lesson packages; spring-fall

Rates: $, tuition; commuters only

School provides a comprehensive introduction to golf for beginners, giving them the satisfaction of hitting a ball crisply and effectively on their very first lesson. More advanced players benefit from perceptive instruction and supervised practice, with on-course training promoting concepts of course management and club selection. Orientation to all shots and situations in five hours of daily instruction plus a nine-hole playing lesson (9am-6pm). Utilizes drills, video swing analysis and reinforcing practice.

Includes personal videotape and instruction manual, custom club fitting, unlimited use of practice facility, daily lunch. Provides green fees (cart additional). Senior program (55+): flexible scheduling, 1-2 hours weekly instruction for a total of five hours.

■ One mile away, the Green Meadow Golf Club provides practice areas and 36 holes to accomodate golfers of all abilities.

NEW JERSEY

John Jacobs Practical Golf Schools

Marriott's Seaview Golf Resort
401 South New York Rd., Absecon, NJ 08201
609 652-1800

4-day and weekend, May-Sept; Women's Golf Conference, June*

Rates: $$

Information: John Jacobs Practical Golf Schools, 800 472-5007. See page 6 for programs and methods.

*Women's Golf Conference: 4 days instruction, 3 nights, 2 rounds, breakfasts, dinners, networking, career seminars, women speakers.

Situated on 670 acres, Marriott's 298-room, historic and elegant Seaview Resort offers varied dining, game room, tennis, indoor and outdoor pools, sauna, steam room. Minutes from Atlantic City's entertainment and gambling casinos and easily accessible to deep-sea fishing, water sports and sun bathing on the New Jersey shore. Privileges extended at nearby Health and Racquet Club.

■ Two 18-hole championship courses. Pines Course, designed by William Flynn and Howard Toomey, is noteworthy for its nearly 110 bunkers. The Donald Ross Bay Course is a challenging veteran, dating from 1915. In the links style, it is windswept, with small greens, rolling character and pot bunkers.

BLACKWOOD
Great Golf Learning Centers

1001 Lower Landing Rd., Suite 303
Blackwood, N.J. 08012
800 TEE-OFF-9   609 227-1600
Director of Golf: Bob Freer

Half-hour individual sessions or prepaid subscription plan

Rate: NA

Locations: 18 franchised Learning Centers in CT, DE, GA, NJ, PA, OH; call NJ central office (above) for center closest to you.

The key to this scientific learning system is the Pathfinder Club®, a self-teaching aid recommended by Golf Digest, which provides feedback by way of a laser beam. Swing patterns are captured on videotape to facilitate further training. Pupils are supplied with a Pathfinder Club for at-home practice. They receive supervised practice, regular private lessons and a personal videotaped library of progress. Initial one-hour, videotaped swing analysis is followed by a program of half-hour lessons and practice sessions. Prepaid lesson packages range from the "Par" program of analysis and three 30-minute sessions to the "Training Program," a year of regularly scheduled sessions.

NEW MEXICO

SANTA FE

Nicklaus Flick Golf School,
Las Campanas
218 Camino La Tierra, Santa Fe, NM 87501
Master Golf I (3 half-days); Aug

Rates: $$$$-$$$$$, tuition only; school will suggest accommodations*

Information: Nicklaus Flick Golf School, 800 642-5528. See page 44 for programs and methods.

*Hotels range from economical Days Inn and High Mesa Inn to the luxurious Inn of the Anasazi and Eldorado resort. Las Campanas, the area's newest residential community, is located 10 miles from the Plaza in Santa Fe, one of the most compelling vacation spots in the Southwest. The property encompasses 4,800 acres of rolling hills and, once completed, will incorporate homes, shops, a clubhouse, pool, equestrian and tennis center.

▶ Just completed, the East Course at Las Campanas (the first of two) is Jack Nicklaus's 100th design. He forecasts "it will knock your socks off." In keeping with the new more gentle direction of his latest creations, it incorporates sloping greens, bunkers with long, swooping fingers and a close relationship with the land.

Reserve well in advance. Golf school is a popular destination.

NEW YORK

Roland Stafford Golf School

P.O. Box 81
Arkville, NY 12406; 800 447-8894   914 586-3187
Director: Roland Stafford

5-day, 3-day midweek, 2- and 3-day weekends, 3-day holiday weekends (Memorial, Labor, Columbus Day weekends, at selected sites)

Rates: $-$$, meal plans vary resort-to-resort.

Locations: Pembroke Pines, FL; Clymer and Windham, NY; Stowe, VT; Quebec, Canada·

A former Tour and Senior Tour winner, Roland Stafford offers a personalized, step-by-step program of comprehensive instruction and supervised practice. Stafford emphasizes a full grasp of fundamentals to build the proper swing. He encourages students to develop a few basic thoughts and to avoid over-analysis. School welcomes beginners to low handicappers.

Students are grouped according to ability and experience slow-motion, stop-action video, grid board photography and analysis in classroom and TV studio. All sites have grass tee areas, oversized putting and chipping greens, multiple bunkers for teaching problem lies and covered hitting areas. Includes green fees during and after class, unlimited use of practice facilities, equipment clinics. Instruction covers rules and etiquette. Clubs supplied for beginners. Fitting for Roland Stafford's own equipment, the Stafford Legato (musical parlance for "connected").

Five-day program (arrive Sun): 23 hours instruction with on-course playing lessons, 4:1 student/teacher ratio, final day tournament, 5 nights. Three-day midweek (arrive Sun): 15 hours instruction, 5:1 student/teacher ratio, 3 nights. Two-day weekend (arrive F): 10 hours instruction, 5:1 student/teacher ratio, 2 nights. Three-day holiday weekends (Sat-M, arrive F): 15 hours instruction, 5:1 student/teacher ratio, 3 nights. Sessions begin with a welcoming reception.

CLYMER

Roland Stafford Golf School

Peek'n Peak Resort
RD 2, Box 135, Ye Olde Rd., Clymer, NY 14724; 716 355-4141

5- and 3-day midweek (arrive Sun), 2-day weekend, 3-day holiday weekends (Memorial, Labor, Columbus Day, arrive Fri); May-Oct

Rates: $; includes all meals

Info: Roland Stafford Golf School, 800 447-8894. Refer to previous listing for programs and methods.

A 1,000-acre charming Old World-style resort with natural beauty, Edwardian elegance and modern amenities: 109 rooms and 51 condominiums, indoor pool, saunas, indoor and outdoor tennis, fitness center, biking and hiking, varied dining. Located in southwest New York State, at the center of the Tri-State intersection.

▪ 18-hole, par 72 course, playing 6,260 from the back tees; another nine holes under construction. Professionally designed practice area next to the course, with covered tee area, video station and school building.

KIAMESHA LAKE
The Concord Golf School

The Concord Resort Hotel, Rte. 17, Kiamesha Lake, NY 12751
800 431-3850   914-4000

Director: Bill Burke; Teaching Director: Leo Tabick

4-day, May-Sept; 4-day Women Only program; Juniors (age 12+ with an adult)

Rates: $$

Teaching the concepts of Carl Lohren's "One Move to Better Golf," Bill Burke and a cadre of specially trained pros work with students to maximize the use of their bodies in an athletic motion. They promote the development of a technically correct, accurate and efficient swing through free motion – without over-analysis and intrusive swing thoughts. According to Burke, this action-oriented approach coupled with a positive mind-set gets results quickly and leads to a game which can meet even the stiffest challenges.

Four-day program: 18 hours of professional instruction, 5:1 student/teacher ratio, class limited to 16; daily on-course instruction, all green and cart fees, club fitting, before and after video analysis with take-home personal tape and Carl Lohren's book (and tape), "One Move to Better Golf." Includes 3 nights accommodations, all meals, arrival and graduation cocktail receptions.

The Concord has built an international reputation as a total destination resort abounding with friendliness, unlimited activities, good food, top entertainment, and superb sports facilities. Vacationers from all over the world are drawn to this 3,000-acre, 1,200-room resort where anything is possible.

■ The Monster lives up to its name – 7,650 from the championship tees, called the Northeast's most difficult course. Certainly Joe Finger's design is the most exhausting. Plus the 6,800-yard International, no slouch on its own, and a 9-hole challenger named, what else? – Challenger. Indoor instruction area for inclement weather.

LONG ISLAND
John Jacobs Practical Golf Schools

Marriott's Wind Watch Golf Club
1717 Vanderbilt Motor Pkwy, Hauppauge, NY 11788; 516 232-9850

4-day, 2-day weekend; June-Sept

Rates: $$, tuition only; request rates for Marriott's Wind Watch Hotel.

Info: John Jacobs Practical Golf Schools, 800 472-5007. See page 6 for programs and methods.

The ten-story Wind Watch is set amidst rolling farmland, quaint ferry ports and nearby antique shops and wineries. The resort offers tennis, a health spa and indoor swimming. Ten minutes from MacArthur Airport in Islip and 45 minutes from La Guardia Airport, 45 miles east of Manhattan.

■ On Long Island's second highest point, 6,405-yard, 18-hole, Joe Lee-designed course encompasses 15 acres of water hazards on eleven holes. Three-acre practice and learning center.

MARGARETVILLE

John Jacobs Practical Golf Schools

Hanah Country Inn and Golf Resort
Rte. 30, Margaretville, N.Y. 12455; 800 752-6494   914 586-2100

4-day, 2-day weekend, 3-day holiday weekends (Memorial, Independence, Labor and Veteran's days); May-Oct

Rates: $

Info: John Jacobs Practical Schools, 800 472-5007. See page 6 for programs and methods.

Located in the scenic Catskill Mountains in New York State, the Inn is a relaxed, country retreat from the hectic pace of city life. Offers every amenity on 900 unspoiled acres, including a fine restaurant and spa. Two-and-a-half hours from Albany Airport.

◼ The recently redesigned, challenging 7,000 yard, 18-hole course offers winding waterways and ponds flowing through manicured fairways.

NEW YORK CITY

Mazda Golf Clinics for Executive Women

Wykagyl Country Club, August
Info: 800 262-7888. See page 73 for programs and methods.

ROSCOE

Exceller Programs Golf Schools

Huff House Resort
R.F.D. #2, Roscoe, NY 12776; 800 358 5012   914 482-4579   607 498-9953

2-, 3-, 4- and 5-day sessions, 3-day holiday weekends (Memorial, Independence, Labor and Veteran's days); May-Oct

5-day summer Junior commuter program (see page 126); Women's Only school, July; Business Women's Conference, Sept

Rates: $-$$

Info: Exceller Programs Golf Schools, 800 424-7438. See page 4 for programs and methods.

A 188-acre, family-owned, mountain estate overlooking the Catskills, with a four-generation history of fine service. Lodging in outlying cottages and in the 47-room, Victorian Inn established in 1886, with updated amenities. Refined dining with fresh produce from the inn's own gardens; glass-walled restaurant overlooking the Catskills. Pool, indoor and outdoor recreation areas. Located one mile from Roscoe, the birthplace of American fly fishing, known also as "Trout Town, USA."

◼ The school makes use of the resort's extensive practice facilities, including a video station and nine-hole course. Students play neighboring 18-hole courses.

WINDHAM

Roland Stafford Golf School

Christman's Windham House
Windham, NY 12496; 518 734-4230

5-day and 2-day weekend, 3-day holiday weekends (Memorial, Labor, Columbus Day); May-Oct

Rates: $

Info: Roland Stafford Golf School, 800 447-8894. See page 84 for programs and methods.

A 200-year-old Greek Revival country inn in the Catskill Mountains, set on 260 acres. Sing-alongs, country dances, boating pond, pool, tennis courts, hiking trails. Modern lodging in five Colonial-style buildings. Includes home-cooked breakfasts and dinners daily. Two-and-a-half hours from NYC, via New York Thruway.

■ Full-sized, nine-hole course manicured by Dan and Patch, the inn's team of draft horses; 18-hole Windham Public Course, five minutes drive.

NORTH CAROLINA

BLOWING ROCK

Resort to Better Golf

Chetola Resort at Blowing Rock
North Main St., Blowing Rock, NC 28605
1 800 CHETOLA   704 295-9301

Director: Joyce Ann Jackson

5-day, M-F; May-June

Rates: $$

Info and reservations: Resort to Better Golf, P.O. Box 360323, Birmingham AL 35236, 205 988-0978

LPGA Master Professional Joyce Ann Jackson and her fellow teachers help students unlock the key to reaching and maintaining a better level of play. Their simple approach focuses on fundamentals and cause/effect relationships in the swing. Taking into consideration the unique characteristics of each student (build, flexibility, gender, strength, etc.), instructors help fashion a swing which is correct for each person. Avoiding over-analysis and governed by simple truths, the school helps students achieve the satisfying, repeatable "click," which signals a correct swing and a successful shot.

This is a school on the go. Provides five days instruction and supervised play at five different mountain courses within 25 miles of the lodge; maximum 18 students, 6:1 student/teacher ratio (playing lessons 3:1); includes daily green and cart fees, swing analysis, educational materials, club care, scenic drive to various courses (8 am to 6 pm, transportation provided). Provides six nights Meadow View or Deluxe Lake View rooms in the lodge, 6 breakfasts and dinners, cocktail parties.

Located in North Carolina High Country, Chetola was once a summer resort for wealthy visitors from the "flatlands." Tasteful modernization has proceeded with regard for its history, charm and unique architecture. The resort's McCauley Recreation Center provides indoor pool, racquetball, fitness center, whirlpool, sauna. Classic dining. Served by Piedmont shuttle flights from Charlotte.

Bonnie Randolph, Mason Rudolph Golf Instruction

High Hampton Inn and Country Club
P.O. Box 338, 262 Hampton Rd., Cashiers, NC 28717
800 334-2551   704 743-2411

Pros: Bonnie Randolph and Mason Rudolph

4-day Bonnie Randolph Mini-Schools, Sun-Thu, April-Sept
5-day Mason Rudolph Houseparty, Sun-F, May

Rates: $; all programs include lodging, three meals daily.

Bonnie Randolph Mini-Schools: 4-day sessions by the resort's resident pro, former
LPGA Tour winner and instructor at Ben Sutton Golf Schools in winter. Includes
green fee and cart on arrival afternoon. Morning personalized instruction for
golfers of all levels, small classes, followed by daily 18-holes of golf.

Mason Rudolph Golf School and Houseparty: Host and teacher Mason Rudolph
is a former National Junior Amateur Champion, All-Army champ and winner of
six Tour championships. Five-day Houseparty includes daily instruction and 18-
holes of golf, including green fees and cart, use of practice facility, clinics, social hours, movies and congenial golf talk.

"Where time stands still and very little changes except the seasons," the cen-
tury-old, 130-room High Hampton Inn is listed in the National Register of Historic Places. At 3,600 feet in the Blue Ridge Mountains, 49 miles from Ashville
Airport, the Inn offers accommodations in the rustic lodge or in cottages, all with
mountain crafted furniture and up-to-the-minute comforts. American cuisine,
daily afternoon tea; seven tennis courts with pro; sailing, renown fly-fishing and
boating on Hampton Lake, nature walks and hiking on the 1,200 acre former
estate; fitness trail. Planned activities every evening, summer children's program.
The Inn has a no-tipping policy; bring your own alcoholic beverages, coats and
ties required at dinner.

■ Adjacent to the Inn, 18-hole, par 71 course designed by George W. Cobb, with
bent grass greens. The course has no sand bunkers – good news for many – and
provides unparalleled scenic beauty.

Marlene Floyd's "For Women Only" Golf School

5350 Club House Lane, Hope Mills, NC 28348
800 637-2694   919 323-9606.

Director: Marlene Floyd

2-day weekends, 2-day graduate schools

Rates: $$, tuition only, contact school for assistance with accommodations.

Other locations: Palm Beach, FL, Hilton Head, SC

Marlene Floyd is an integral part of 1988's "Golf Family of the Year," with father,
L.B., a renown teacher, and brother, Ray, a star on the PGA and Senior Tours. In
her own right, Marlene is a 17-year veteran on the LPGA Tour and for 16 years
has been a TV golf commentator. Women teaching women makes sense, she says.
By first internalizing a mental picture of the correct golf swing, women overcome

disadvantages of anatomy and lesser strength. Her program accentuates understanding and visualizing the golf swing and covers all aspects of the game. Students are taught how to properly coil and "load up" and how to release the larger
muscles and hands for greater advantage.

Provides 6 hours classroom and range instruction daily, 5:1 student/teacher ratio,
class limited to 15, guaranteed personalized 1:1 attention by LPGA teaching professionals; video analysis. PGA pro Marilyn Floyd is on site and works with students for the entire session. Includes lunch.

Cypress Lakes Golf Course, Hope Mills, NC hosts the school in Nov. See other locations and dates.

Complete learning Center at Cypress Lakes.

MAGGIE VALLEY

Professional Golf Schools of America

Maggie Valley Resort and Country Club
340 Country Club Dr., Maggie Valley, NC 28751
800 438-3861   704 926-1616

5-day; 3-day, begins M or F; May-Nov

Rates: $$

Info: Professional Golf Schools of America, 800 447-2744. See page 36 for pro-
grams and methods.

Nestled in pastoral meadows against a backdrop of the Blue Ridge and Great Smoky
mountains, the relaxed Maggie Valley Resort offers tennis, swimming, glorious gardens
and panoramic mountain views from balconied guest lodges or villas; features lo-
cal cuisine, Thursday evening clogging show and regular evening entertainment.
Located 35 miles west of Ashville, 100 miles southeast of Knoxville.

18-hole, par-71, championship course winds its way from the valley floor to
the mountains in a gradual ascent of 1,100 feet. Water comes into play on 13 of 18
holes. Scenically beautiful and naturally challenging.

NEW LONDON

Golf Digest Instruction Schools

Old North State Club at Uwharrie Point
1520 Uwharrie Point Pkwy., New London, NC 28127
800 252-1005

2-day weekend and 3 half-day Mini-Schools; June-Aug

Rates: $$$$, tuition only; school will suggest area lodging; eight rooms on-site at
the Lodge at Uwharrie Point.

Info: Golf Digest Instruction Schools, 800 243-6121. See page 29 for programs
and methods.

A new, 18-hole Tom Fazio design on the shores of Badin Lake, within 1¼ hours'
drive of Winston-Salem, Greensboro, Ashville and Charlotte.

➜   Pinehurst: Regular flights to Moore County/Pinehurst Jet Center via USAir or fly to Raleigh/Durham (60 miles away), Charlotte, Greensboro, Fayetteville or Southern Pines, NC. Many resorts provide airport transfers.

PINEHURST

Pinehurst Golf Advantage School

Pinehurst Resort and Country Club
P.O. Box 4000, Pinehurst, NC 28374
800 927-4653

Director of Golf: Don Padgett; School Director: Wayne Nooe

4-day, 3-day weekend; Junior program (see page 161); March-Oct

Rates: $$$

A select group of teaching pros under the supervision of former PGA President, Don Padgett, trains golfers of all abilities who are ready to make a serious commitment to their game. Pinehurst's program teaches fundamentals through instruction, drills, and exercises. Includes playing lessons. The school emphasizes rules and proper etiquette. State of the art facilities include on-course classrooms, a 4,500 sq. ft. enclosed instruction site, the latest in teaching technology and methods, covered hitting area, a video room and classrooms.

Provides 5:1 student/teacher ratio, five hours daily personalized instruction; includes green fees, cart, club storage, personalized video analysis and take-home tape, Pinehurst instructional video and club fitting. Four-day program provides 5 nights; 3-day includes 4 nights. Includes all meals, graduation cocktail party and awards ceremony.

Golf is king at the august, 354-room Pinehurst Hotel, where the Roosevelts, Rockefellers, DuPonts and Morgans came to play. Offers 28 tennis courts, five outdoor pools, three croquet courts, a 200 acre lake for sailing and boating; equestrian sports, gun club with skeet, trap and sporting clays; jogging trails, health club, refined dining.

■ Seven regulation courses –The Donald Ross Number One; the legendary Number 2 with small, sloping greens and deep bunkers; the short, eclectic Number 3; the Donald Ross Number 4, renovated in 1983 to make it even more challenging; the Number 5, a 1928, Ellis Maples design, boasting new bunkers, tees and water hazards; Number 6, opened in 1979, a George and Tom Fazio design located three miles from the main club house. Number 7, the newest addition, is a rolling, par 72, fringed with marshes and dotted with water.

PINEHURST

The Golf Group of the Carolinas

P.O. Box 3246. Pinehurst, NC 28374; 800 845-3402

Director: Bob Burwell

Playing lessons, custom programs

Rates: $, tuition only*

A unique program in place since 1977. Each session is entirely based on the needs and desires of students and on information garnered from a detailed, advance questionnaire. Extensive use of video technology, sports psychology, and reinforcement of fundamentals. Students are encouraged to develop muscle memory and thus feel the correct swing – and reproduce it every time. Students receive 1½ hours instruction and video analysis followed by 9-hole, on-course training at your choice of 15 area courses. Includes unlimited green fees and cart. Students return home with a personalized instruction tape, reference materials and an invitation to consult anytime following the school. Individual enrollment or in small groups.

*Accommodations arranged at area motels and resorts at affordable prices, including Holiday Inn, Hampton Inn, Villas at Beacon Ridge and EconoLodge. Includes complimentary breakfast and free admission to the PGA/World Hall of Fame.

PINEHURST   AREA

Bertholy-Method Golf Schools

Wedgewood Drive I, Foxfire Village, Jackson Springs, NC 27281
919 281-3093

Director: Paul Bertholy

3-days private* or group**, M-W; Junior instruction (see page 161); March-Nov and year-round by appointment

Rates: $$$$*- $$$**, tuition only; the school will suggest area hotels and condos; program requires Bertholy-Method Book II and swing pipe teaching tool.

Paul Bertholy, a teaching editor of GOLF Magazine, is known as a teacher's teacher. Since 1947, he has been building golf swings through P.P.I.C. — Progressive, Precise, Intensified Conditioning. His method is the ultimate in programming muscle memory. Highly trained instructors (and Bertholy, himself, Dec and Jan) teach isometric techniques and positions, using a weighted iron bar. Through faithful practice of a series of static holds and slow motion swings, students create a fail-safe, repeating swing.

Classes 1:1 or 4:1 student/teacher ratio; total of 16 hours instruction at the school's privately owned, six-acre, indoor and outdoor practice areas adjacent to the 36-hole Foxfire Country Club, "three crow miles" from Pinehurst. First two days are spent in the 900-square foot indoor teaching studio at mirrored practice stations, sensitizing and training muscles before a single ball is hit. Students return home with a regimen of practice routines.

> *Nearly every golf school provides a "commuter" option whereby students pay tuition and select their own accommodations. The commuter rate usually includes lunch. Commuter students may be invited to buy a discounted meal or banquet plan to share festivities with fellow students.*

Mid Pines Resort Golf Instructional Package

1010 Midland Rd, Southern Pines, NC 28387
800 323-2114   919 692-2114

Pro: Chip King

Daily instruction/play, 2 night minimum; Mar-Sept

Rates $

PGA professionals deliver beginner or brush-up instruction in a program which provides one hour daily teaching of fundamentals, proven swing improvement methods and course management. Includes unlimited golf, superior room, breakfast and dinner daily. Extra charge for videography and carts.

Discover the peaceful world of the MidPines resort, nestled on 250 acres in the beautiful Sandhills area of North Carolina. Built in 1921, the stately brick and white-frame hotel provides 118 guest rooms, a friendly dining room, a fully equipped game room. Tennis and pool.

■ The hotel's own Donald Ross-designed, 18-hole, par 72, championship course. Practice range and 18-hole putting green. Numerous area courses.

> *Please let us know how you fared at Golf School. Complete the form at the back of the book with your frank comments.*

Pine Needles Golfari ™*
Pine Needles Learning Center**

Pine Needles Lodges and Country Club
600 Midland Rd, Southern Pines, NC 28388
919 692-7111

Professionals: Peggy Kirk Bell and Dr. Jim Suttie

Peggy Kirk Bell, 5-day, May-Sept; 5-day Women Only, Feb & May
Dr. Jim Suttie, 3-day Learning Center program**

Rates: $-$$, $$$**

*Golfari™ is the trademarked name for Peggy Kirk Bell's 5-day, golf saturation programs for men and women, Women Only, youth (ages 10-18) and families.

Owner Peggy Kirk Bell, recognized as one of the five most influential women in golf, is a former LPGA Teacher of the Year and author of "Women's Way to Better Golf." Dr. Jim Suttie, a Ph. D. in biomechanics, is an instructor at a number of highly respected golf schools and instructional editor of Golf World magazine. Teaching at Pine Needles is tailored to the strengths, weaknesses and needs of individual students, rather than molding each one to a given method of swinging the golf club. The school stresses the visual mode of learning, utilizing high speed video cameras and feedback. Graduates are taught to understand why they hit the ball the way they do and what is necessary to correct problems. All programs include lodging, meals, green and cart fees.

Five-day Golfari™ provides two hours individualized instruction daily on all aspects of the game; playing lessons, video swing analysis, tournaments. Complimentary green fees and carts following instruction, club storage. Evening golf films, lectures, socializing.

3-day Learning Center Golf School stresses hi-tech, visual imaging with computer graphic overlay of each student's swing and personalized corrective instruction. Includes full swing, short game, course management, psychology, equipment clinic and follow-up to encourage continued learning.

Pine Needles is an intimate, family-owned vacation spot, serving 140 guests. Accommodations in individual lodges. Sauna, whirlpool, heated pool, tennis, congenial dining. Airport transfers.

■ Site of upcoming 1996, 51st U.S. Women's Open. A 6,603 yard, Par 71, Donald Ross design, a 1927 classic. Named one of the leading resort courses in the U.S. by Golf Digest. Indoor driving/teaching facility.

SUNSET BEACH

Carl Tyner School of Golf

Oyster Bay Golf Links/The Colony at Oyster Bay
900 Shoreline Dr., Sunset Beach, NC 28468
800 222-1524

Director: Carl Tyner

3-day; May-Sept

Rates: $$

As a former teaching associate with famed instructor, Jimmy Ballard, Carl Tyner taught the best: Curtis Strange, John Schroder, Janie Blalock and Betsy King. At his own school, Tyner emphasizes that the quality of a superior teacher is to incorporate basic and important fundamentals into an individual's unique physical characteristics and to enhance his or her ability to feel the correct motion. Using videography to analyze each student's swing, Tyner institutes changes and supervises practice to make perfect. Programs provide 4:1 student/teacher ratio, 3¹/₂ hours morning instruction daily, on-course playing lessons, three nights at the Colony at Oyster Bay, daily breakfasts and lunches, cocktail party, and unlimited golf.

Located in serene, coastal Carolina surroundings just over the line from South Carolina. Offers spacious 1- or 2-bedroom, fully equipped villas lining the fairway of the renown Oyster Bay Golf Links. Outdoor heated pool, Jacuzzi, nature walks; situated minutes from the tees of a half-dozen championship courses.

■ The Dan Maples-designed Oyster Bay Links plays 5,970 yards from the white tees. Named by Golf Digest in 1983 "Best New Resort Course in America" and again designated by the magazine in 1990 as one of the "Best 50 Courses in America." After class, play Oyster Bay or other first class courses: Marsh Harbour, The Legends (3 courses) and The Highlands.

Woodlake Total Performance Golf Schools

Woodlake Country Club
150 Woodlake Blvd., P.O. Box 648. Vass, NC 28934
800 334-1126   919 245-4031

Director: Tom Ream

3-day, Feb-Nov; Junior program (see page 162)

Rates: $$

Based on a new concept that improved performance on the course depends on more than just an improved swing, this school presents a plan which includes golf specific exercises and sports nutrition to enhance strength and flexibility and enable students to "play better, feel better and live longer." A series of physical performance tests determines the starting level for each student. Daily instruction tailored to students' ability builds a solid foundation in golf fundamentals.

Individualized classes limited to 12, 4:1 student/teacher ratio, three hours instruction, on-course playing lessons, manual and take-home before and after video analysis, personal fitness and nutritional evaluation (additional fee); includes green fees, carts, two nights, breakfast and lunch daily.

Condominium accommodations at Woodlake Country Club, situated in the Sandhills of North Carolina, 20 minutes from Pinehurst and Southern Pines. Offers swimming boating and fishing on the resort's 1,130 acre lake; tennis, jogging, hiking and refined dining.

■ 18-hole original Ellis and Dan Maples design. Nine-hole Dan Maples-designed teaching course and private, covered, practice areas.

O H I O

Paul Tessler's Golf Schools

Paul Tessler's Westgate Golf Center
3781 State Route 5, Newton Falls, OH 44444
800 553-7285   216 872-7984

Director: Paul Tessler

1-day; Half-Day, Day-and-a-Half; April-Aug

Rates: $-$$, tuition only; nearby accommodations available for students in One-and-a-Half-Day school

Certified PGA teaching pro Paul Tessler works his students through every club in their bags in six hours comprehensive instruction in a thorough one-day school. The goal is to groove a smoother, crisper, more powerful swing and to promote greater accuracy and confidence. Includes videotaping, equipment analysis, lunch, and golf fees after school. Half-day school (afternoon or evening) provides three hours instruction; 1½-day school (½ day Fri, all day Sat) furnishes 12 hours teaching.

■ Practice and play at the school's nine-hole, par 28, executive course.

OKLAHOMA

A F T O N

K.I.S.S. Golf Clinics

Shangri-La Resort
Rte. 3, Hwy 125 South, Monkey Island, Afton, OK 74331
800 331-4060   918 257-4204
Director: Marshall Smith

3-day programs, May; Junior school, June and Aug (see page 164); customized group clinics and private lessons; year round

Rates: $-$$

Marshall Smith emphasizes that simple, straightforward teaching of a simple, uncomplicated swing is the key to playing better golf. In his words: "Your thumbs look up to God at the top of your backswing and again at the top of your finish. Forget your lower body. Just go along for the ride, passive like. You wind up like throwing a man out at second base. Same motion. Same finish." Shangri-La's 3-day program provides 20 hours instruction, 4-5:1 student/teacher ratio, videotaping and analysis, personal drills for individual learning, on-course training and early evening scramble.

Under the proprietorship of Club Resorts, the people who own Pinehurst, Barton Creek and Quail Hollow, the 650-acre Shangri-La Resort is winding up a $7 million facelift, centered on service, amenities and accommodations. The natural setting of Shangri La, on the banks of Oklahoma's Grand Lake o' the Cherokees, could not be improved upon. Guest select from among 450 lodge rooms, suites, condos and estate homes. Golden Leaf Recreation Center on the grounds offers indoor/outdoor swimming and tennis, bowling, racquetball, volleyball, game room, fishing guide service, and a full-service spa offering the works: wraps, massage, toning, exercise and more. The Hogan is special: a pavilion for the two-steppin', barbecue-chowin', country music-lovin' cowpoke in everyone. Situated in the extreme northest corner of the state, 75 miles north of Tulsa; private airfield.

■ Two Don Sechrest courses, tree-lined, hilly, and recently upgraded to championship tournament standards. The Blue course is only the second in the state to be overseeded with winter rye grass for winter play. It is long and rolling and plays 7,012 from the back tees. The Gold course is shorter, more open, and wetter.

OREGON

K L A M A T H   F A L L S

Craft-Zavichas Golf School

Shield Crest Golf Course, 3151 Shield Crest Dr., Klamath Falls, OR 97603
503 884-1493
Red Lion Inn
3612 South Sixth, Klamath Falls, OR 97601; 503 882-8864
5-day; June-July*
Rates: $

Info: Craft-Zavichas Golf School, 800 858-9633. See page 26 for programs/methods.

*Program differs somewhat from other school locales. Provides 22+ hours instruction, separate men's and women's classes, on-course strategy session, green fees and cart for unlimited play after class, unlimited use of practice facility, 5 nights, 2 banquet receptions, 4 lunches, green fees and cart for unlimited play after class; separate men's and women's classes.

Located in beautiful southern Oregon near Crater Lake and historic lava beds, the Red Lion Inn offers 108 guest rooms, pool and airport courtesy service.

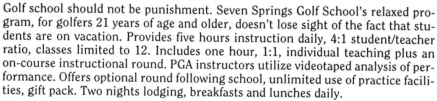 The 18-hole Shield Crest Golf Course, 7,005 yards from the back tees, is flat and forgiving. Provides spacious, versatile practice facilities.

PORTLAND

S.E.A. Nice Shot! Golf Schools

Oregon Golf Club
25700 South West Pete's Mountain Rd., West Linn, OR 97068; 503 650-6900

3¹/₂ day Golfers School; Sept

Rates: $$-$$$, tuition only*

Info: Sports Enhancement Associates, 800 345-4245 or 602 284-9000. See page 10 for programs and methods.

*Discounted accommodations are available at Sunny Side Inn, a 137-room, Best Western hotel, fifteen minutes from Portland Airport.

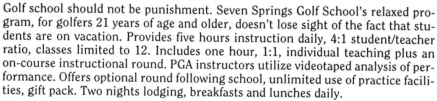 Oregon Golf Club provides its complete practice facilities.

PENNSYLVANIA

CHAMPION

Seven Springs Golf School

Seven Springs Mountain Resort
RD 1, Champion, PA 15622; 800 452-2223   814 352-7777

Head pro: Fred Haddick; Director: Matt Trimbur

3-day mid-week and weekend programs, May-Aug;

Rates: $$, early arrival and extended stay available

Golf school should not be punishment. Seven Springs Golf School's relaxed program, for golfers 21 years of age and older, doesn't lose sight of the fact that students are on vacation. Provides five hours instruction daily, 4:1 student/teacher ratio, classes limited to 12. Includes one hour, 1:1, individual teaching plus an on-course instructional round. PGA instructors utilize videotaped analysis of performance. Offers optional round following school, unlimited use of practice facilities, gift pack. Two nights lodging, breakfasts and lunches daily.

Cozy, rustic, 300-room family resort on 4,000 mountain-top acres. Accommodations in main lodge or nearby apartments and townhouses. Area is a boon to hunters and fishermen; offers tennis, pools, varied dining, biking, jogging and a spectacular vista of two states from the Tee Top Lounge.

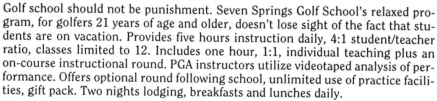 18-hole Seven Springs course plays 6,360 yards from the back tees, fairly flat with outstanding mountain views. Recently redesigned by Ron Forrest.

Invest in waterproof golf shoes — and break them in. Bring sneakers or a second pair of golf shoes to change off. And consider cushioned socks. You'll be on your feet interminable hours.

FARMINGTON

The Woodlands Golf Academy

Nemacolin Woodlands Resort
Route 40 East, Farmington, PA 15437
800 422-2736   412 329-8555
Director: Greg Ortman

Alternating 2-day programs (Thu & F or Sat & Sun), April-Sept: Fundamental School (beginners), Basics School (intermediates), 2-day Progressive School (experts), General School (mixed levels), 1-day Refresher School (Tu or W); clinics, lessons and special programs

Rates: $$, tuition only; $ lodging and meals at Nemacolin Woodlands

Instruction by PGA pros is geared toward helping students feel the effortless power of correct golf techniques through concentrated instruction, video feedback, and close personal attention. Special emphasis is placed on teaching aids and props, on the assumption that experiencing the correct swing promotes a high degree of retention. Customized Personal Practice Plan to insure progress.

School assures a 4:1 student/teacher ratio, classes limited to 12. Five hours daily instruction (1-day Refresher School: 5½ hours), video and computer swing analysis with take-home tape, unlimited use of practice facilities, equipment evaluation, instruction manual.

Pennsylvania's only AAA Four Star-rated resort features hotel or villa accommodations with whirlpool baths, a three-story, 20,000 square foot world-class spa with every health and beauty treatment including spa cuisine. (Hotel guests enjoy spas, steam, sauna, whirlpool, weight room and lap pool at no extra charge.) Choose from canoeing, tennis, fishing, equestrian sports, billiards, swimming, the list goes on and on.

◪ PGA recognized driving range with sheltered areas for wet weather, short game practice facilities and classroom. Woodlands Golf Links is a 6,900, par 72, 18-hole course showcasing surrounding mountains and meadows.

GETTYSBURG AREA

America's Favorite Golf Schools

Penn National Inn Resort Hotel
3809 Anthony Hwy., Fayetteville, PA 17222;   800 231-0080   717 352-2400
Penn National Golf Club
3720 Clubhouse Dr., Fayetteville, PA 17222;   800 211-7366   717 352-3000
5-day; 3-day (M-W or F-Sun); May-mid-Oct

Information: America's Favorite Golf Schools, 800 365-6640. See page 36 for programs and methods.

Set among the fertile Appalachian Mountains, the area offers natural and historic attractions rich in Americana. The colonial-style, 36-room Penn National Inn Resort Hotel is located within Penn National Estates, an 1,100-acre planned recreational community, 55 miles from Baltimore and 65 miles from Washington, D.C. Offers swimming and tennis in a rustic setting.

■ A sportsman's challenge with greens up to 11,000 square feet, the Ed Ault, 7,000-yard course boasts 4,000 new plantings and a 7½ acre, man-made lake. Lighted driving range with 40 practice tees and covered hitting area.

MT. POCONO

Professional Golf Schools of America

Mount Airy Lodge
Woodland Rd., Mt. Pocono, PA 18344; 800 441-4410   717 839-8811

5-day; 3-day, begins M or F

Rates: $-$$

Information: Professional Golf Schools of America, 800 447-2744. See page 36 for programs and methods.

Mt. Airy's vast Sports Palace features six tennis courts, ice skating, a regulation basketball court, handball, volleyball, archery, a health club and an Olympic size pool – all indoors. There is no end to outdoor activities, as well, at this year-round recreational paradise in the Poconos. Plus nightly entertainment, a wide choice of dining, and accommodations. Located 90 miles from Manhattan.

■ Eleven years in the making, the "18 Best" course is patterned after Sports Illustrated magazine's 18 best holes in America. Designed by Hal Prudy and beautifully situated among tall stately trees, stone bridges, with sparkling lakes and brooks, it is both classic and extravagant. Plays 7,123 from the back tees, par 72.

SHAWNEE-ON-DELAWARE

Swing's The Thing Golf Schools

Box 200, Shawnee-on-Delaware, PA 18356
800-221-6661   717 421-6666

Co-directors: Dick Farley, Rick McCord

3-day, 3 night schools; 3-day, 2 night schools; 1-day refresher, VIP schools (limited to 12)

Rates: $$-$$$

Other locations: Scottsdale, AZ; Palm Springs area, CA; Orlando, FL; Oceanside, MD; Myrtle Beach, SC; and British Columbia, Canada

The school's directors, Dick Farley and Rick McCord, were selected by GOLF Magazine among the "50 Best Teachers in America." The foundation of their system is "the one correct swing which will be yours on every shot." This 24-year-old school teaches students to swing in a free, relaxed manner, without fear, by empowering them to trust their swings. Through the use of uncomplicated, step-by-step personal instruction, drills, training aids and high-speed video analysis, instructors make golf learning crystal clear. So clear, in fact, that Swing's The Thing brought their method to Japanese Public TV in a 5-part series.

Includes daily instruction on private practice ranges, stop-action video, instructional and personalized take-home tape, textbook; includes golf (restrictions apply at some sites). Three-day programs provides 18 hours instruction, 3 lunches and 2 or 3 nights; 1-day refresher scheduled at most sites is an intensive 7-hour review for former students, includes lunch.

SHAWNEE-ON-DELAWARE

Swing's The Thing Golf School

Shawnee Inn
Shawnee-on-Delaware, PA 18356
1 800-SHAWNEE; 717 421-1500

3-day (2 or 3 nights); May-Oct

Rates: $$

Former home of Fred Waring and his Pennsylvanians, the Inn is situated on the banks of the Delaware River, putting guests at the heart of a host of vacation activities. Resort offers indoor and outdoor pool, tennis, boating and water sports, professional theater, fitness center, horseback riding, varied dining. Located 45 miles north of Allentown.

■ Situated on an island in the middle of the Delaware River, the Shawnee Inn golf course dates from a 1906 A.W. Tillinghast design. It was reworked in 1960 to three nines: Red, White and Blue. Course hosts PGA and NCAA championships. The Guinness Book of World Records says there is trouble for those who fail to carry the river. One golfer's ball was swept so far by the current that it took her 166 strokes to play it back.

SOUTH CAROLINA

✈ Hilton Head is served by direct flights by U.S. Air Express, American Airlines Eagle and GP Express from Charlotte, Raleigh/Durham and Atlanta. Hilton Head is a 45 minute drive from Savannah (GA) Airport.

HILTON HEAD

Jimmy Ballard Golf Workshops

Hilton Head National Golf Club
Hwy. 278, Bluffton, SC 29910; 803 837-3000

2-day (Tu & W), 3 Half-Days (Thu-Sat), 3-day Mind/Body Connection (Thu-Sat); private VIP or staff lessons, playing lessons; April-Nov

Rates $$-$$$, tuition only; school's private travel agency arranges accommodations.

Info and registration: Jimmy Ballard Golf Workshops, P.O. Box 22686, Hilton Head, SC 29925; 803-837-3000

Other locations: Ft. Lauderdale, FL

GOLF Magazine's "Teacher of the Decade," Jimmy Ballard, goes back 30 years, when he first gained national attention coaching the pros. He's still at it, with students the likes of Curtis Strange, Seve Ballesteros and Gary Player. A pioneer in many of the teaching methods taken for granted today, Ballard subscribes to theories of "feeling" the correct swing and imprinting "muscle memory." The Jimmy Ballard Swing Machine™, a patented simulator, enables students to experience striking the ball like the masters of the game. It is combined with drills in fundamentals, mental aspects, extensive videotaping and analysis and lots of practice under the eyes of specially trained professionals and Jimmy himself.

Two-day and three Half-Day programs provide 10 hours concentrated instruction, 5:1 student/teacher ratio, class limited to 15. Three-day Mind/Body Connection, for serious golfers, provides nine hours intensive instruction and nine hours personalized mental conditioning in consultation with psychologist and author, Dr. Ron Cruickshank. Private on-course playing lessons available to transfer skills to the course.

■ Hilton Head National Golf Course is an acclaimed Gary Player-design on 300 acres of low country terrain with towering pines and oaks. Located on the mainland, a minute's drive to the bridge to Hilton Head Island, it is the home of the 1991 Amoco-Centel Championship. Complete practice facility with classroom and videography facilities.

H I L T O N   H E A D

Ken Venturi Golf Training Centers

Old South Golf Links
50 Buckingham Plantation Dr., Bluffton, SC
803 785-5353

Hyatt Regency, Palmetto Dunes Plantation, Hilton Head Island, SC 29938
803 785-1234

3-day, M-W or Thu-Sat; year round; Traveling School, April*

Rates: $$$$

Info: Ken Venturi Golf Training Centers, 800 753-3357, ext. 100. See page 48 for programs, methods and other Traveling Schools.

With over 500 balconied guest rooms and suites, the Hyatt Regency Hilton Head is situated directly on the Atlantic, five minutes from Hilton Head Airport. The resort offers unspoiled beachfront, indoor and outdoor pools, 25 courts at the Rod Laver Tennis Center, a complete spa and health club, water sports, nightly live entertainment, varied dining and all the attractions of a first class full destination resort.

■ The school's dedicated training center at Old South offers a 300-yard practice range, a brand new 1,500 square foot teaching studio, short game learning stations and a 5,000 square foot putting green. The course, a par 72, Clyde B. Johnson-design on 400 acres, connects four different islands and merges oak forest, open pasture and silvery, tidal marsh.

*Ken Venturi himself is on hand for three 3-day schools in April which coincide with Venturi/CBS-TV coverage of the MCI Heritage Classic.

HILTON HEAD

Marlene Floyd's "For Women Only" Golf School

Port Royal Golf Club
10 A Grasslawn, Port Royal Plantation,
Hilton Head Island, SC 29926; 803 686-8801

2-day weekend; March and May

Rates: $$, tuition only; contact school for lodging information.

Info and registration: Marlene Floyd, Hope Mills, NC, 800 637-2694 or
919 323-9606. See page 88 for programs and methods.

PGA pro Marlene Floyd is on site and works with students for the entire session.
Includes lunch.

🚩 Port Royal Golf Club provides classroom and complete golf learning facility.

HILTON HEAD

Palmetto Dunes Golf

P.O. Box 5849, Hilton Head Island, SC 29938; 803 785-1136

Director: Chip Pellerin

3 Half-Day School, Tu-Thu; clinics, private lessons, supervised practice, playing
lessons, corporate and Ladies-Only programs; year round (by request in winter)

Rates: $, tuition only; arrange lodging at a wide range of hotels and villas through
Sand Dollar Management, 803 785-1162.

Three-day school provides comprehensive personalized instruction on all phases
of the game; includes video analysis. Two hours morning instruction daily, 6:1
student /teacher ratio, maximum 12 students. Make reservations for afternoon playing
lessons at an additional fee.

🚩 The Plantation incorporates five courses, three at Palmetto Dunes and two at
nearby Palmetto Hall Plantation. At Palmetto Dunes: Arthur Hills at Palmetto Dunes;
Palmetto Dunes' George Fazio course, rated among Golf Digest's "100 Best," and
Palmetto's original Robert Trent Jones course. At Palmetto Hall: the Arthur Hills
course is rated among the nation's "Top Ten New Resort Courses" by Golf Maga-
zine, and the unique and highly touted, geometric Robert Cupp Course with square
greens and pyramidal mounding.

HILTON HEAD

Royal Golf Academy

95 Mathews Dr. E7, Suite 306, Hilton Head Island, SC 29926
800 925-0467   803 686-8801

Port Royal Golf Club
10A Grasslawn, Port Royal Plantation, Hilton Head, SC 29926

Director: Keith Marks II

3-day, 1-day workshop; private lessons, corporate programs; year round

Rates: $$$, tuition only; 4-night lodging packages available*

Second generation teaching pro, Keith Marks II, places special emphasis on swing
essentials: posture, balance, plane of swing and head position. With a goal of perma-

nent improvement, Marks and Port Royal PGA pros establish the root cause of their students' swing problems and develop an agenda of corrective measures. Programs are tailored to golfers of all levels. Each student receives a written improvement program daily and returns home with a personal videotape for continued learning.

Provides 5 hours instruction daily, 4:1 student/teacher ratio, 8 students per class; full swing video analysis, daily on-course play with pro; includes green fees and carts, continental breakfast and lunch. (One-day workshop: 3 hours instruction, limited to 8)

*Accommodations packages at:

Players Club (35 DeAllyon Ave.; 800 497-7529 or 803 785-8000): economical, newly renovated rooms with balcony, refrigerator and wet bar. Spa, Nautilus equipment, 50-ft. indoor lap pool, sauna, whirlpools, racquetball courts; outdoor pool, tennis.

The Westin Resort (Port Royal Plantation, 2 Grasslawn Ave; 800 228-3000 or 803 681-4000) is the Carolina's only AAA Five-Diamond-rated grand hotel; 410 luxurious balconied guest rooms or 2 and 3-bedroom villas; refined dining, racquet club, indoor heated pool, 2 outdoor pools, health club, directly on the beach.

▌ 54 holes at Port Royal Golf Club. The 6,188-yard Robber's Row course is rich in Civil War history. The Barony Course, 6,038 yards, requires accurate approach shots to small protected greens. The newest addition is Planter's Row, site of the 1985 Hilton Head Seniors International.

HILTON HEAD

Sea Pines Academy of Golf

Sea Pines Sports & Convention Center
Box 7000, Sea Pines Plantation, Hilton Head Island, SC 29938
800 845-6131

Director: Don Trahan; Head Teaching Pro: Rick Barry,

4-day Academy of Beginner Golf (M-Thurs), 1-day Academy (Wed), Half-Day School/Half-Day Golf (Tu or Thurs); Set Up and Shot Clinics, playing lessons, private instruction; selected dates March through Nov

Rates: $$, tuition only, inquire about accommodations.

PGA Master Professional, GOLF Magazine teaching editor and ranked one of America's 50 Best Teachers, Don Trahan believes in going "back to basics." Stressing a methodical approach to achieving consistency, Trahan's instructors evaluate students and provide a written proposal for improvement, touching upon all aspects of the game. Instruction is personalized, intense and corrective.

One-day Academy: 7 hours instruction, video analysis, drills, practice, exercises, full-swing thoughts, short game instruction; continental breakfast and lunch. Four-day Beginner Academy: 2½ hours daily instruction covering all aspects of golf; Half-Day School/Half-Day Golf: 4 hours morning instruction followed by 18-holes at either Ocean or Sea Marsh courses; limited to 8, includes green fees and cart. Clinics: one-hour sessions, scheduled twice daily, on various aspects of the game.

Sea Pines Plantation encompasses miles of beaches, a forest preserve, more than 500 rooms in villas and hotels and home rentals; bicycling, Stan Smith's Tennis Academy, water sports, bird watching, deep sea fishing, numerous restaurants, shopping.

Multiple golf opportunities, including Harbor Town Golf Links, site of the annual MCI Heritage Classic, with a towering 74 course rating from the championship tees; the Ocean and Sea Marsh courses, both George Cobb designs; three additional courses at nearby Port Royal Golf Club; 25+ courses in the immediate area.

HILTON HEAD

Skip Malek's Golf School

Country Club of Hilton Head
70 Skull Creek Dr., Hilton Head Plantation
Hilton Head, SC 29926; 803 681-4653

Director: Skip Malek

Three Half-Day Schools (M,W and Fri); year round (2 Half-Day sessions in fall)

Rates: $, lessons only; additional package ($) provides two 18-hole rounds, one at Country Club of Hilton Head, one at Indigo Run and lunch. No lodging.

Fundamentals are presented in the simplest terms to foster a clear understanding of the golf swing. Instructors strip away the blitz of often conflicting information students garner from TV, magazines, and fellow golfers, to enable each one to develop his or her own reliable, effective repeating swing. The object, Skip Malek stresses, is not to "mass produce" golf swings or copy the famous players, but instead to find the key to reaching each person's potential. Presents three separate mornings personalized instruction, 8:30 am-12:30 pm, covering every aspect of the game; video analysis, personal written improvement plan.

■ Hilton Head CC's course is a challenging, scenic Rees Jones-design with training facility, including driving range, putting and chipping areas and practice bunker. Indigo Run, one of the island's newest courses, is by Golden Bear Design Associates, a Nicklaus Company. Stretching 7,014 yards, it plays at par 72.

KIAWAH ISLAND

Heritage Golf Schools

Kiawah Island Inn & Villas
Kiawah Island, SC 29455; 800 654-2924   803 768-2121

3-day, F-Sun or M-W; Oct

Rates: $$$$

Info: Heritage Golf Schools, 800 362-1469. See page 60 for programs and methods.

Occupying an unspoiled barrier reef island, 45 minutes south of Charleston, Kiawah Inn and Villas present world class accommodations fronting 10 miles of beach. Three pool complexes, four restaurants, tennis facilities, paved scenic biking paths and assorted nature programs, including canoeing excursions, ocean seining expeditions, marsh and nature talks. Accommodations in fully equipped, spacious villas.

■ Three top courses: Marsh Point designed by Gary Player, 6,203 yards, par 71; Turtle Point designed by Jack Nicklaus, 6,919 yards, par 72; and the stunning Pete Dye Ocean Course, a world class links course, host to the 1991 Ryder Cup matches at which the U.S. regained possession of the famous prize. It meanders along two and a half miles of beach with every hole overlooking the ocean and ten in intimate contact with it.

MYRTLE BEACH
Grand Strand Golf Instructions

River Oaks Golf Plantation
831 River Oaks Dr., Myrtle Beach, SC 29577; 800-453-6488
Director: Glen Davis

2-day weekend; 3-day (M-W or W-Sat), 5-day (M-F); 1-Day and Half-Day series; year round

Rates: $-$$, tuition only*

Teaching is entirely flexible and personalized with no set program or style. Instead, the goal is to build a simple powerful swing for each individual. Golfers of all levels are taught to understand their own swing tendencies in order to continue improvement after leaving the school. Course assures a 3:1 student/teacher ratio, 5 hours daily instruction on every aspect of the game; high-speed, stop-action video analysis; optional complimentary on-course playing lesson daily; includes green fees, cart and unlimited use of practice facility.

*Students are encouraged to make their own reservations. Instruction is discounted for guests at nearby economical Holiday Inn Oceanfront (800 845-0313) or Holiday Inn West (800-847-2707); hotel rates include breakfast and 18-hole round daily

⬛ Instruction centered at River Oaks Golf Plantation, 27-hole, scenic Gene Hamm-design, 6,791 yards, stretching along the Intracoastal Waterway.

MYRTLE BEACH
Image Golf, The Instructional School

Rt. 2, Box 142-B, Ocean Isle Beach, NC 28469
800 424-7947   919 579-1690

Myrtle Beach West Golf Club, Hwy. 9, North Myrtle Beach 29582; 800 842-8390
Pro: Ben Hunt

3-day, 5-day; private instruction; year round

Rates: $, tuition only*

PGA Teaching Professional Ben Hunt's approach is "Learn, See and Feel." He has enabled hundreds of golfers at all levels to understand their own swing. Building on his students' strengths, he stresses the fundamental laws of the golf swing, proper techniques, the mental aspects of the game, short game skills and course management. Program provides 4:1 student/teacher ratio, high speed video swing analysis, equipment check, on-course instruction, unlimited use of practice facility, instruction manual, diploma.

Five-day program provides 17½ hours instruction, 5 rounds of golf with cart, 18-hole playing lesson, 6 nights lodging. Three-day program: 10½ hours instruction, 3 round of golf with cart, 4 nights.

*Students may select their own accommodations or take advantage of vacation package at the 57-acre oceanfront Ocean Creek Resort (10600 North Kings Hwy., Myrtle Beach, SC 29572; 800-845-0353 or 803 272-7724). Provides indoor, outdoor and ocean swimming; Jacuzzis, tennis, and restaurants. Accommodations in ocean-front towers with upgrades to villas or townhomes. Neighboring Barefoot Landing offers 113 shops; restaurants line the area.

■ Myrtle Beach West Golf Club: an 18-hole, Tom Jackson design, par 72, located in North Myrtle Beach. Extensive practice facility. Grand Strand offers a choice of 70 courses.

MYRTLE BEACH

Myrtle Beach Golf Academy

701 Hilton Rd., Myrtle Beach, SC 29577
800 882-5121   803 449-4146

Arcadian Shores Golf Club, 701 Hilton, Rd.,
Arcadian Section, Myrtle Beach, 29577; 803 449-5217

Pro: Matt Leslie

3-day, 5-day; year round

Rates: $$, includes lodging at your choice of a range of hotels or condos.

Matt Leslie is dedicated to producing lasting improvement with a program tailored to each student. Covers all aspects of the game, using the latest high speed video technology for analysis of both long and short game. Take-home instructional video for continued learning. Close attention to accuracy and finesse around the green.

Programs include green fees and cart and all meals (where applicable). Five-days: 17½ hours instruction, 6 nights, 5 rounds of golf, $50 gift certificate. Three-days: 10½ hours instruction, 3 rounds, 4 nights, $30 gift certificate.

■ Arcadian Shores is rated one of the "Top 20 Courses in the Southeastern U.S." by Golf Digest. Designed by Rees Jones, it is a par 72; plays 6,567 yards. Modern clubhouse and complete practice area. Access to numerous area courses.

MYRTLE BEACH

Myrtle Beach Golf School

P.O. Box 1484, N. Myrtle Beach, SC 29598
800 94-SWING

Brick Landing Golf Club, Brick Landing Plantation, Rt. 2, Ocean Isle Beach, NC 28459; 800 222-9938

Sands Ocean Club, Dept. 60, 9550 Shore Dr., Myrtle Beach, SC 29572
803 449-6461

Director: Peter Anderson

7-day (Sun-Sat), 5-day (Sun-Thu), 4-day weekend (Thu-Sun); year round; 3-day winter sessions (begin M, W or F)

Rates: $-$$, students may purchase rain insurance for lodging from Sands Ocean Club.

Recognizing that many golfers have perfectly adequate "raw" swings, Peter Anderson promotes improvement through teaching the concepts of proper mechanics and inducing minor changes in approach angle, swing path or clubhead rotation. The result is immediate and lasting proficiency. The school utilizes four steps to a lifetime of better golf by enabling student to visualize their performance on video, by creating a personal regimen of drills and swing aids, through improving on-course management and by sending students home with a personalized video for continued progress.

Provides 5 hours daily instruction, 4:1 student/teacher ratio, on-course training with pro, personalized video; complimentary golf, greens fee and cart. Seven-day program: 27 hours (6 days) instruction, 6 nights lodging. Five-day program: 20 hours instruction, 4 nights. Four-day program: 15 hours instruction, 3 nights.

The twin towers of the Sands Ocean Club rest directly on South Carolina's Grand Strand. Offers a Health and Fitness Center, pool and tennis; basketball and volleyball on the hotel's sport deck. Varied dining, summer supervised Kid's Club and video game room. All rooms with kitchenette. Optional lodging at Brick Landing Plantation villas, offering clubhouse dining, pool, tennis and fitness complex.

■ An H. Michael Brazeal course designed to respect the natural elements of the Intracoastal Waterway, par 72, 6,482 yards. Constructed on the site of a landing used to unload bricks during the 17th century.

MYRTLE BEACH

Riley School of Golf

River Hills Golf Club
Hwy. 17, Little River, SC 29566; 800 264-3810

Ocean Creek Plantation Resort
10600 North Kings Hwy., Myrtle Beach, SC 29572; 800-845-0353   803 272-7724

3-day, 4-day, 5-day, 2-day weekend commuter*; year round

Rates: $$-$$$

Info: Riley School of Golf, 800 847-4539. See page 16 for programs and methods.

*Two-day weekend commuter program, Myrtle Beach only; Sat afternoon and Sun morning; 5:1 student/teacher ratio, includes golf fees and cart after Sun instruction.

Ocean Creek Resort, a 10-minute drive from River Hills course, is a 57-acre oceanfront plantation providing indoor, outdoor and ocean swimming; Jacuzzis, tennis, and restaurants. Accommodations with kitchenettes with upgrades to villas or townhomes. Neighboring Barefoot Landing offers 113 shops; restaurants line the area.

■ The 18-hole, Tom Jackson-designed course occupies a densely wooded setting with frequent 40-foot elevation changes. River Hills, opened in 1988, was nominated in 1989 by Golf Digest magazine as Best New Course and by Golf Week as one of the top 25 new courses in South Carolina for 1990.

MYRTLE BEACH

Swing's The Thing Golf School

Colonial Charters Golf and Country Club
301 Charter Dr., Longs, SC 29568; 803 249-8809

3-day V.I.P; March & April

Rates $$-$$$, Instruction limited to 12. Includes 3 nights lodging, choice of accommodations; arrange with Condominium Rental Services, 800 772-6636.

Info: Swing's The Thing Golf School, 800 221-6661. See page 98 for programs and methods.

■ Opened in 1988, the 18-hole, par 72 Colonial Charters course is designed by John Simpson. Plays 6,734 yards from gold tees. Boasts "fastest Bermuda greens on the Strand."

MYRTLE BEACH AREA

Favorite 5 Golf School

9480 Indigo Club Dr., Murrells Inlet, SC 29576
800 397-2678   803 650-2678

Indigo Creek Golf Plantation
U.S. 17 Bypass, Garden City, SC 29587; 803 650-0381

Indian Wells Golf Club
U.S. 17 Bypass, Garden City, SC 29587; 800 833-6337

Pros: Steve Dresser, Billy Delk

3-day (M-W or Thurs-Sat), 5-day (M-F); private instruction, playing lessons, daily clinics; year round

Rates: $, tuition only; ask school about discounted lodging at a selection of Grand Strand resorts and condos.

With a total of 8 students in the entire school at any one time, instructors Steve Dresser and Billy Delk lavish attention on each golfer, starting with the short game and working up to the full swing. In a relaxed, casual atmosphere, students maximize their own capabilities to develop a solid, repeating swing. Instruction does away with myths and long-held hurtful advice. Instructors employ visual references, understandable terminology and stop-action video replay to help students learn and improve quickly. Two hours concentrated instruction daily.

■ Discounted afternoon golf at Indigo Creek, a 1990, Willard Byrd-design, par 72, 6,745 yards, or at Indian Wells, a Gene Hamm-design, par 72, 6,624 yards. The area offers more than 70 courses for afternoon play. Complete custom club and repair facilities on the premises at Indian Wells. Students may demo clubs with no obligation.

MYRTLE BEACH AREA

The Phil Ritson Golf School

Pawleys Plantation Golf and Country Club
Hwy. 17, P.O. Box 2580, Pawleys Island, SC 29585
800 624-4653   803 237-4993

Pro: Phil Ritson; Director: Mel Sole

2-day, 3-day (begins M or Th), 5 Half-Day programs; Juniors (accompanied by an adult), private and semi-private sessions, corporate outings; year round

Rates: $$; special programs $$$; additional fees for afternoon green fees and cart

Info: See page 51 for programs and methods.

One of America's oldest and most unspoiled beach resorts, Pawleys Island is a picturesque barrier island where nature is one's nearest neighbor. The Pawleys Plantation Golf and Country Club plays host to the school, providing deluxe accommodations in two or three-bedroom villas. Club House with pool and grill room for lunches and fine evening dining. Located 30 minutes from Myrtle Beach, one hour from Charleston. Serviced by nearby Myrtle Beach Jetport.

Programs vary from site to site. At Pawleys Island: five Half-Day program (M-F) provides 10½ hours instruction, two 9-hole playing lessons, six nights and breakfasts. Three half-day program (begins M or Thu): 10½ hours instruction, three nights and breakfasts. Classes 4:1 student/teacher ratio; 2:1 Classic program available. Playing privileges at Pawleys Island Plantation at reduced fees.

■ Pawleys Island Course is an 18-hole, Jack Nicklaus Signature course, ranked among the top ten in South Carolina by Golf Digest. Traverses natural wetlands, providing 13 water hazards on ten holes. Less challenging golf can be arranged for beginners.

TENNESSEE

FAIRFIELD GLADE

Bill Skelley School of Golf

Fairfield Glade
101 Pea Vine Rd., Fairfield Glade, TN 38557; 615 484-7521

5-day and 3-day; June-Sept

Rates: $$

Info: Bill Skelley School of Golf, 800 541-7707. See page 40 for programs and methods.

Slow down and relish the lush surroundings of the Cumberland Plateau. Fairfield Glade is a 97-room resort plus rental condominiums, situated on 12,000 wide-open acres overflowing with recreational options. Offers indoor and outdoor tennis and pools, full service marina, fishing and boating on eleven lakes; an equestrian center, children's playground, dining and dancing, and entertainment. Located 120 miles from Opryland, 105 miles from Dollywood; one hour drive from Knoxville.

5-day program provides 4 nights, 4 breakfasts, 3 dinners, 1 cocktail party. Three-day program: 2 nights, 2 breakfasts, 1 dinner, 1 cocktail party.

■ With room to spare, the resort features four courses boasting bent grass tees, greens and fairways throughout. Learning takes place on an 18-hole course with driving range and practice facility.

TEXAS

AUSTIN

Academy of Golf Dynamics

The Hills of Lakeway
45 Club Estates Parkway, Austin, TX 78738
800 879-2008   512 261-3300

President: Bill Moretti; Head instructor: Jay Bowden

3-day midweek, March-June, Sept and Oct; 3-day weekend, Feb-Nov; Parent-Youth, July and Aug (see page 171)

Rates: $$-$$$, tuition only, inquire about area lodging.

Other locations: Colorado Springs, CO (includes accommodations)

Golf standout Tom Kite, in GOLF Magazine, ranked this unusual school the number one training and practice facility in the country. The Academy has been named among the nation's top golf schools in Money Magazine, Changing Times and Golf Lifestyles. Bill Moretti and Jay Bowden, both Class A, PGA pros, personally teach. Each golfer is evaluated for the mode by which he or she learns most effectively. Working as a team, student and instructor concentrate on fundamentals to elevate each student's swing to the point at which dramatic improvement occurs. Concentrated instruction underscores the correct mental attitude necessary to play well and enjoy the game.

Guaranteed 3:1 student/teacher ratio; high speed video swing analysis, specialized swing enhancement devices and training aids; swing drills for continued improvement. Includes opening breakfast and graduation lunch. Located 30 minutes from Austin.

▌ A total learning center designed by Jack Nicklaus: a 500-yard driving range, 7,500 square foot putting green and three complete holes, pars 3, 4, and 5, created to provide a wide range of challenging course simulations. Afternoon play at leisure at two courses in the Lakeway area. Graduates have privileges for one year at the practice course.

A U S T I N
Barton Creek Golf Advantage School

Barton Creek Resort
8212 Barton Club Dr., Austin, TX 78735
800 336-6157   512 329-4000

Director: Chuck Cook; Head Instructor: Joe Beck

3-day and 5-day; specialized programs for beginners and Women Only; intensive Player's Club and Short Game School; customized instruction; Mar-June and Sept
Rates: $$$

Under the supervision of Chuck Cook, mentor of touring pros Payne Stewart and Tom Kite and one of GOLF magazine's Top 50 golf teachers, instructors at Barton Creek offer students a competitive edge through expert trouble-spotting, comprehensive customized instruction and state-of-the-art teaching tools, including computer graphics videotaping, modeling tapes, video prints, and audio tapes on the mental aspects of the game. Barton Creek's program follows students home with free analysis of mail-in videos and continued contact. Includes master club fitting and consultation with Dr. Dick Coop, educational/sports psychologist.

Provides 5:1 student/teacher ratio, limited to 15 students; reserved tee times for on-course instruction, complimentary green fees, instruction notebook, at-home fitness program, two free mail-in video lessons. Fun closing competition. Includes 5 or 3 nights lodging, all meals, transportation to/from Austin Airport.

Barton Creek is a 4,000 acre convention center and resort community in Texas hill-country, with a luxurious 150-room hotel and a renown European-style spa with every health and beauty treatment; indoor pool and health club, tennis courts, billiards and game room, memorable dining.

▌ 54 holes. The original Tom Fazio course is ranked second best in Texas by Golf Digest. The Crenshaw & Coore course, designed by Barton Creek's touring pro, Ben Crenshaw, affords broad, rolling fairways and varied greens. The Arnold Palmer Lakeside Course showcases spectacular views of Lake Travis. Teaching is enhanced by a covered teaching area, a dedicated range for students, and a new short-game facility.

John Jacobs Practical Golf Schools
Rancho Viejo Resort
1 Rancho Viego Rd., Brownsville, TX 78520; 800 531-7400   210 350-4000
5-day and weekend; Jan-Mar
Rates: $$
Info: John Jacobs Practical Golf Schools, 800 472-5007. See page 6 for programs and methods.

Twelve miles from Mexico and 30 minutes from the beaches of the Gulf, the south-western-style, 89-room, 1,400-acre Ranch Viejo Resort boasts a 6,000 square foot landscaped pool complete with cascading waterfall and swim-up bar. Luxury suites, renown Casa Grande Supper Club. Twenty minutes from Valley International Airport, Harlington, TX.

▌ Two 18-hole courses: The devilish 6,899-yard El Diablo with frequent "resacas," otherwise known as water hazards, and El Angel, challenging, with plentiful water and subtle troubles, it belies its name.

Mazda Golf Clinics for Executive Women
Bent Tree Country Club, October
Info: 800 262-7888. See page 73 for programs and methods.

John Jacobs Practical Golf Schools
Marriott's Fossil Creek Golf Club
3401 Clubgate Dr., Fort Worth, TX 76137
817 847-1900
3-day (M-W or F-Sun); May & June
Rates: $$, tuition only; call golf club directly for help with accommodations.
Info: John Jacobs Practical Schools, 800 472-5007. See page 6 for programs and methods.

▌ Located 15 miles north of Dallas-Forth Worth Airport, Arnold Palmer-designed, 18-hole Fossil Creek Golf Course combines bent grass greens, crystal clear lakes, contoured bluffs, rocky ledged creeks and towering trees, amidst 1,150 acres of Texas greeenbelt. Plays 6,865 yards from the championship tees.

S.E.A. Experts Only Golf School
Hyatt Bear Creek Golf and Racquet Club
W. Airfield Dr. at Bear Creek Ct., Dallas/Ft. Worth Airport, TX 75261
214 615-6801
3¹/₂ day Experts Only School (0-10 handicap and collegiate players), Thu-Sun; April
Rates: $$-$$$, tuition only*
Info: Sports Enhancement Associates, 800 345-4245 or 602 284-9000. See page 10

for programs and methods.

■ Instruction centers on the advanced practice facilities at Hyatt Bear Creek Golf and Racquet Club, a 335-acre resort with two 18-hole courses, on the grounds of the D/FW Airport.

*Discounted accommodations at Hyatt Regency D/FW Hotel (P.O. Box 619014, International Pkwy - DFW Airport, Dallas, TX 75261; 800 228-9000 or 214 453-1234), a full-destination, 1,390-room, modern hotel at the airport.

H O U S T O N   A R E A

Heritage Golf Schools

Woodlands Resort - TPC at The Woodlands
2301 No. Millbend Dr., The Woodlands, TX 77380
800 433-2624   713 367-7285

3-day, F-Sun or M-W; Sept

Rates: $$$$

Info: Heritage Golf Schools, 800 362-1469. See page 60 for programs and methods.

Not far from Houston lies a world of quiet wonder, ringed with lush forests and dotted with tranquil lakes brimming with wildlife. Woodlands Resort affords accommodations for 268 guests in 13 lodges scattered about the property. Provides indoor and outdoor pools and tennis courts, men's and women's health spas, refined dining in five dining rooms and complete privacy.

■ Serious golf is played on The Woodland's two premier courses, both designed by Robert Van Hagge and Bruce Devlin. The Tournament Players Course, with substantial mounding surrounding the greens and an island green on #13, hosts the PGA Tour's Shell Houston Open and others. TPC is selected often for finals of the PGA Tour Qualifying School. The North Course, first host to the Houston Open, is a semi-private facility available to guests of The Woodlands.

J U N C T I O N

Texas Tech University Graduate Golf Workshop

Texas Tech University, Junction TX

Instructor: Dr. Danny Mason

3-week program for graduate credit; July

Rates: $, in-state or out-of-state college tuition, plus surcharge; includes dorm-style housing, meals, and golf fees.

Info: Texas Tech University, Box 43011, Lubbock, TX 79409; 806 742-3335

Limited to 15 students and open to college graduates who teach, coach or wish to learn to teach golf. Designed to enable teachers to improve their teaching skills and to learn the latest teaching concepts and methods in all phases of the game, including the principles of building a sound golf swing and how to present these principles by progression. Final week includes teaching junior golfers. Includes minor club repair. Workshop carries 1, 2 or 3 college credits and may be taken in full or in one or two-week increments.

Columbia Lakes Golf School

Columbia Lakes Resort and Conference Center
188 Freeman Blvd., West Columbia, TX 77486
409 345-5151, ext. 532

Directors: Mark Steinbauer and Betsy Cullen

1-, 2- and 3 day sessions, Half-Day session; selected dates March-Sept; corporate outings, individual lessons, Junior program (see page 173)

Rates $$

Instructors cover every aspect, introducing newcomers to golf and polishing the game for more advanced players. Program calls on state-of-the-art video with computer graphics to visualize students' swings. Take-home instructional tape with voice-over for continued learning. Provides one-on-one teaching within the group setting, class limited to 18, 6:1 student/teacher ratio. Includes accommodations in the lodge (nominal surcharge for cottages), all meals and golf fees, club fitting and discounted Tommy Armour equipment.

Three-day program (F-Sun, arrive Thu): 3 half-days instruction, total of 12 hours, 2 rounds of golf, 3 nights, 9 meals. Two-day program (Sat & Sun, arrive Fri): 2 days instruction, total of 12 hours, 1 round of golf, 2 nights, 6 meals. One-day (Sat): instruction plus 18 holes on-course training, 1 night (Fri or Sat), 2 meals. Half-Day program is a follow-up to measure progress.

Columbia Lakes Resort comprises 2,000 acres of magnificent trees, greens, fairways and clear lakes, constituting a year-round playground. Offers Gulf and lake sports (including fishing for trophy-sized bass in twin lakes covering over 300 acres), tennis academy, jogging, bocce courts, fitness center, pool, bike rental, assorted dining options. Horse-drawn carriage rides and tandem bikes permit guests to slow down and enjoy the countryside. Accommodations in colonial-style main club house or guest houses. Located one hour south of Houston's Hobby Airport.

■ Tom Fazio, 7,000-yard, 18-hole championship course, pronounced a true test of skill. Full practice facility.

UTAH

Exceller Programs Golf Schools

Radisson Park City
2121 Park Ave., P.O. Box 1778, Park City, UT 84060; 801 649-5000

Park Meadows Golf Course
2000 Meadows Dr., Park City, UT 84060

5-day, 4-day, 2 day; June-Aug; 5-day, summer

Rates: $$-$$$

Info: Exceller Programs Golf Schools, 800 424-7438. See page 4 for programs and methods.

Spacious rooms at the Radisson provide mountain views and all amenities. Offers indoor/outdoor pool, exercise facilities and hydrospa, indoor and outdoor tennis, handball, racquetball. Rich opportunities for hiking, fishing, hunting, and horse-back riding. Located 35 minutes from Salt Lake City International Airport.

■ Adjacent to the hotel, Park Meadows Golf Course was designed by Jack Nick-laus in the Scottish character, with arching bridges, scenic lakes and a traditional double putting green.

PARK CITY AREA

John Jacobs Practical Golf Schools

The Homestead
700 North Homestead Dr., Midway, UT 84049
800 327-7220   801 654-1102
4-day and weekends; May-Sept

Rates: $; commuter rate applies on weekends, inquire about lodging.

Info: John Jacobs Practical Golf Schools, 800 472-5007. See page 6 for programs and methods.

The AAA Four Diamond, Homestead is Utah's most complete resort. The Hitching Post Stables provides riding, hayrides and buggy rides, all within the resort's spa-cious mountain-side setting. Pools, tennis, all amenities. Offers spring-fed, natu-rally heated mineral baths. Acclaimed dining. Park City is the gateway to fishing, boating, sailing, tennis, mountain-biking, hot air ballooning, and hiking in the Wasatch and Unita Mountains. Cottages, suites or the hotel's own Bed & Break-fast.

■ The Homestead's course showcases spectacular mountain vistas as it mean-ders through Snake Creek Valley. Each hole offers five tee boxes, presenting never-ending challenges.

ST. GEORGE

Sun Desert Golf Academy

Dixie College
225 South 700 East, St. George, UT 84770; 800 545-GOLF

Pro: Mike Smith

4-day, (M-Thu), 6 day, (Sun-Sat), 6-day workshop; Nov-June; Junior program (see page 175)

Rates: $

Teaching pros, utilizing the latest techniques and high-tech video analysis, teach in first class facilities. Instruction focuses on fundamentals, management and con-fidence building. Located near glorious Zion and Bryce Canyon National Parks; 123 mi. from Las Vegas, NV. Regularly scheduled flights into St. George Airport.

Six-day program provides 20 hours instruction; 4 day program: 13 hours. Includes reserved tee times, golf fees, full use of practice facilities, video and computerized swing analysis, playing lesson, final tournament. Motel accommodations or more economical lodging in Dixie College dormitories; breakfast and dinner daily. Six-day workshop provides one-hour group instruction daily, reserved play on five courses, high tech video analysis, tournament and banquet, economical conference center lodging, breakfast and dinner daily.

■ Instruction at Indoor/Outdoor Golf Center with covered, air-cooled driving range and air-conditioned, indoor hitting cages and classroom. Tee times reserved on seven uncrowded courses shared by only 30,000 people amidst outstanding scenery; five 18-hole courses, two 9-holers; among them a new Ted Robinson design with three of its holes named among the finest he has ever designed.

> *Many golf schools offer specialized programs in the short game, course management and other areas. Check program listings.*
>
>

VERMONT

CHITTENDEN

Mountain Top Golf School

Mountain Top Inn and Resort
Mountain Top Rd., Chittenden, VT 05737; 800 445-2100
Director: Scott DeCandia
5-day; 3-day (Sun-W or F-M); 2-day weekend; May-Oct
Rates: $

Director Scott DeCandia, two-time National Long Drive Champion, is noted in the Guinness Book of World Records for his 350 yard drive – all carry. He offers a practical, results-oriented approach. Experienced instructors strive to discover each student's best means of gaining an understanding of the golf swing, of developing a longer drive, of putting, chipping and pitching with greater accuracy. Golfers are grouped according to skill, with novices taught the basics and advanced golfers experiencing a more aggressive curriculum. Students learn to analyze their own performance in order to institute corrections and improve every time out.

Six hours daily instruction, 4:1 student/teacher ratio, same instructor throughout to insure continuity. Employs video analysis and reviews; unlimited use of practice facility, personal instruction booklet, gift. Five-day program provides 30 hours instruction, scramble tournament, 5 nights. Three-day programs, mid-week or weekend, provide 20 hours instruction, 3 nights. Two-day weekend, Sat-Sun: 13 hours instruction, 2 nights. Lunch included; add $30 per day for breakfast and dinner.

Thirteen hundred acre resort nestled in the Green Mountains with water sports on its own 650-acre lake, swimming, sailing, fishing, canoeing, windsurfing; heated pool, horseback riding and instruction, tennis, trap shooting, mountain biking and hiking; sauna and whirlpool. Great stone fireplaces take the chill out of Vermont evenings. Refined dining by candlelight; 33 guest rooms plus 22 cottages and chalets with panoramic views. Located 10 miles northeast of Rutland.

■ A five-station, 25-acre learning center simulates actual playing conditions with a 5-hole, par 3 course, plus a classroom for video review and a 300 yard driving range with sheltered tee area. "Golf Around Plan" offers guests an opportunity to extend their stay and play any of the area's four 18-hole and three 9-hole courses at reduced rates.

STOWE

Roland Stafford Golf School

The Inn at the Mountain / Mt. Mansfield Resort
Mountain Rd., Stowe, VT 05672
800 253-4754   802-253-3000

Stowe Country Club, Mountain Rd., Stowe, VT 05672
802 253-4893

5-day, 2-day weekend, 3-day holiday weekends (Memorial, Labor Day and Columbus Day); May-Oct

Rates: $$

Info: Roland Stafford Golf School, 800 447-8894. See page 84 for programs and methods.

The AAA Four Diamond-rated Inn and condominiums rest against a backdrop of the Green Mountains in general and Mt. Mansfield, Vermont's highest peak, in particular. The resort offers rooms with steam bath and refrigerators, a Health and Fitness Center, tennis, varied dining and unlimited outdoor recreation, from mountain biking to scaling the cliffs at nearby Smuggler's Notch, to just plain sunning beneath Vermont's blue skies.

■ Three-and-a-half miles away, 18 challenging, hilly holes at Stowe Country Club, 6,213 yards, with breathtaking views.

STOWE

Natural Asset Golf Program

Stoweflake Inn and Resort
Box 369, Mountain Rd., Stowe, VT 05672
802 253-7355

Stowe Country Club, Mountain Rd., Stowe, VT 05672
802 253-4893

5-day Play with the Pro (M-F), 4-day Learn to Play (M-Thu), 3-day weekend (F-Sun), 2-day weekend; May-Sept

Director: Jim Beckett

Rates: $

Jim Beckett's revolutionary program centers on making golf instruction fun by using a student's own natural assets and routine body movements as the foundation for a consistent, repeatable swing. His instructors combine state-of-the-art video analysis, visual aids, the latest in teaching technology, drills, graphics and personal attention, while encouraging students to get in touch with their own individual rhythm, balance and tempo. Pros stress the psychological aspects of the game, dispelling anxiety and inducing confidence. All programs provide four hours instruction daily, 5:1 student/teacher ratio, maximum 15 students.

Five-day "Play with the Pro" includes three supervised rounds, 5 nights, breakfasts and dinners. Four-day "Learn to Play" provides on-course orientation, unlimited practice; surcharges for afternoon golf and Friday afternoon play with the pro; includes 4 nights, breakfasts and dinners. Three-day weekend: arrive before noon Friday and play with pro. Two- and-three-day weekend programs provide instruction and drills, 2 night, breakfasts.

AAA Four-Diamond inn in the heart of the Green Mountains, Stoweflake is located 30 minutes from Burlington International Airport, 10 miles from I-89. Accommodations range from deluxe resort units and suites to economical rooms in the country inn. Offers tennis, fishing, biking, hiking, windsurfing, indoor pool, health center, dining.

 A "healthy nine-iron away," 18 holes at Stowe Country Club, 6,163 yards, par 72, adjoining the Inn. Clubhouse, club rentals, locker facilities.

STRATTON

Stratton Golf School

Stratton Mountain Resort,
Stratton Mountain, VT 05155
800 843-6867   802 297-2200

Director: Keith Lyford

5-day, 2-day weekend, 2-day mid-week (begin M or W), May-Oct; 5-day on-course instructional plan, May & Sept

Rates: $$

Other locations: Scottsdale, AZ (Stratton Golf School is also know as Stratton/Scottsdale Golf School; programs vary slightly site-to-site)

Three-time collegiate All-American, former Tour player, and 1987 New England PGA champ, Director Keith Lyford subscribes to the theory: "You only remember 10% of the instruction you hear vs. better than 80% of what you see." Instructors combine extensive video teaching and stop action photography with close personal attention in small classes. They tailor a shot-by-shot improvement plan for golfers of all levels.

Six hours daily instruction, 5:1 student/teacher ratio, complimentary play after class, instruction booklet; use of Stratton Sports Center. Five-day program provides 4 days instruction, fifth day free play, graduation banquet. Five-day sessions in May and Sept offer more on-course instruction and tournament play. Two day programs provide 2 full days instruction, complimentary play on arrival day and after class. Lodging (5 or 2 nights) in 1- to 4-bedroom condominiums. Includes continental breakfast and lunch.

In the heart of the spectacular Green Mountains, the area offers some of Vermont's finest natural and man-made attractions. Stratton Mountain Resort complex offers health center, shops, restaurants, tennis (site hosts the Acura U.S. Women's Hardcourt Championships), mountain biking, summer theater and festivals. Accessible via airports at Albany, NY and Hartford, CT.

 Instruction centers on 22-acre Arnold Palmer-Geoffrey Cornish practice facility with classrooms, target greens, simulated conditions for all shots, covered practice shelter. Stratton's golf is comprised of Lake, Mountain and Forest courses, 27 holes designed by Geoffrey Cornish. The layout is rated one of the top resort courses in New England by GOLF Magazine and is the site of the McCall's LPGA Classic. Views are memorable.

WEST DOVER

The Golf School

Mount Snow Resort
Route 100, West Dover, VT 05356
800 451-4211   802 464-7788

Mt. Snow Country Club, Country Club Rd., West Dover, VT 05356
802 464-3333

5-day, 4-day and 3-day mid-week programs beginning Mon; 2-day weekend; May-Sept

Rates: $$

Info: The Golf School, 800 632-6262. See page 34 for programs and methods.

Enveloped by the Green Mountains of Vermont, the Mt. Snow area provides natural beauty and varied recreation from mountain biking to festivals, country fairs to summer theater. Accommodations in either Snow Lake Lodge or Resort Center Condominiums, both at the base of scenic Mt. Snow ski resort. Offers heated pools, lighted tennis courts; health club, paddle boats. Two and a half-hour drive from Albany and Boston; air service to Albany, NY or Hartford, CT.

▶ Nearby Mt. Snow Country Club is an 18-hole championship course, host to the New England PGA and New England Open. Its postcard-perfect fourth hole has been voted among the prettiest ten holes in the country. Site offers a large and complete practice facility.

VIRGINIA

HOT SPRINGS

Heritage Golf Schools

The Homestead
Hot Springs, VA 24445
800 336-5771   703 839-5500

3-day (F-Sun or M-W); June-July

Rates: $$$$

Info: Heritage Golf Schools, Winter Park, FL, 800 362-1469. See page 60 for programs and methods.

Built in 1832 and rebuilt in 1903, the Mobil Five Star, 600-room Homestead is an often-photographed, massive, colonnaded, Kentucky red brick edifice topped by a familiar clock tower. The ambiance is deep South and genteel. Activities abound: equestrian sports, indoor and outdoor pools, archery, bowling, carriage rides, nature walks, nightly movies and dancing, refined dining (coats and ties required). The service is that of a distinguished private club.

▶ Three courses: the Homestead and Upper and Lower Cascades. Homestead, a Donald Ross-design, dates from 1892; it was updated by Peter Lees and A.W. Tillinghast. Lower Cascades, opened in 1963, is a Robert Trent Jones design. The star of the threesome is the hilly, par 70, Upper Cascades, designed by William S. Flynn, and recognized as one of the world's finest courses.

The Kingsmill Golf School

Kingsmill Resort and Conference Center
1010 Kingsmill Rd., Williamsburg, VA 2318
800 832-5665   804 253-1703
Director: Tim Poland
3-day; spring-fall (no July classes); Juniors (see page 176)
Rates: $-$$, rates adjusted according to accommodations

How you look swinging the club is unimportant, according to pro, Tim Poland. What counts is how the swing feels and your ability to replicate successful hits every time. Tension, he tells his students, is the insurmountable barrier to swinging. The goal, therefore, is fluid motion. Beginning with short compact swings, students slowly extend the arc until they feel the action of the clubhead and understand how the motion results in a successful shot to target. Poland emphasizes tempo and rhythm and three fundamentals: grip, alignment and a comfortable, consistent set up.

Includes 2½ days instruction (15+ hours), 6:1 student/teacher ratio, limited to 6 students; up to 2 rounds of golf with shared cart. Provides 3 nights hotel or fairway villa accommodations.

Calling itself "the other Williamsburg," Kingsmill is a resort and residential community on 2,900 acres on the banks of the James River, three miles from Colonial Williamsburg. The resort provides four restaurants, 15 tennis courts, fishing, a complete fitness and sports club with an indoor lap pool, outdoor pool, game room, and a day camp for children ages 5-12 (May-Sept, M-Sat). Regularly scheduled flights into nearby Richmond, Norfolk and Newport News.

■ School's orientation and practice centers on the par 3, nine-hole Bray Links course. Resort offers an additional 36 holes comprised of Plantation Course and River course, a par 71, 6,800-yard, Pete Dye creation. Kingsmill is the home of the PGA Anheuser-Busch Classic. (A 28-minute, hole-by-hole, video playing-guide may be ordered by calling 800 345-9556.)

What to ask when you are choosing a Golf School

1. How many students can I expect in my learning group? How much time can I expect my pro to devote to me alone?

2. Will we be grouped according to skill to facilitate teaching?

3. Is there a curriculum and how will I be taught?

4. Are the instructors certified as teaching professionals? Are they schooled in this particular curriculum and method?

5. Are there hidden charges for golf fees, carts, videotapes, technical aids, take-home materials?

WINTERGREEN
Wintergreen Golf Academy

Wintergreen Resort, P.O. Box 706, Wintergreen, VA 22958
800 325-2200   804 325-2200
Director: Graeme Oliver
5-day (Sun-Th), 3-day (F-Sun); April-Oct
Rates: $$

A Scottish scholar of the game, golf director Graeme Oliver, creates an atmosphere in which learning, while intense, is memorable and enjoyable. The staff emphasizes fundamentals on which to build a sound game. Video analysis on the range and during on-course training is central to the program, to enable instructors to visualize mechanics and help students to see and, therefore, "feel" the correct swing.

Personalized classes 4+ hours daily, 4:1 student/teacher ratio, limited to 24; includes all golf fees for afternoon playing lessons and golf on afternoon of arrival; extensive videotaping and take-home instructional tape. Accommodations in studio to 4-bedroom condos and 2 to 6-bedroom homes. Five-day program provides 4 nights; 3-day program: 2 nights. Mid-week 3-day/4-night instructional packages available on request. Meals not included.

Set atop the Blue Ridge Mountains and encompassing the historic Rockfish Valley, the 11,000-acre Wintergreen is larger than some national parks. It provides five pools, a 25-court celebrated tennis facility, 25 miles of marked hiking trails, a 20-acre lake for fishing, swimming and boating. Resort boasts the Wintergarden Spa, plus an English-oriented equestrian center, guided mountain biking, a complete children's program for ages 2½-12, numerous restaurants. Accessible from airports at Richmond or Charlottesville or Greensboro, NC.

■ Golf Magazine has awarded Wintergreen a Silver Medal as one of the "Top 50 Golf Resorts in the U.S." Play two courses: the challenging, mountaintop, Ellis Maples-designed Devil's Knob and the engaging Stoney Creek in the valley, each with its own clubhouse. Stoney Creek, a Rees Jones-design, has been named by Golf Digest among America's Best Resort Courses.

WASHINGTON

PORT LUDLOW
Destination Golf Schools

Port Ludlow Golf & Meeting Retreat
9483 Oak Bay Rd., Port Ludlow, WA 98365
800 732-1239   206 437-0272
Director: Lyndon Blackwell
3-day; April-Sept
Rates: $, tuition only; lodging package ($) provides 3 nights.

Emphasis is placed on fundamentals for students of all ages and abilities. Ten hours of instruction is tailored to individual needs, touching on all aspects of the game. A maximum of 12 students are accommodated with two PGA instructors. On-course teaching bridges practice and solo play. Curriculum includes unlimited complimentary golf, a rules seminar and club fitting.

Located 1¹/₂ hours northwest of Seattle, Port Ludlow is on the Olympic Peninsula, placing it in the heart of salt and fresh water, mountains and forests. Accommodations three miles from the course provide spacious condominium lodging with up to four bedrooms, indoor and/or outdoor pool, tennis and a marina.

▪ 27 holes, three nines: Tide, Timber and Trail, designed by Robert Muir Graves and carved out of dense forest. Course sits high above Puget sound, affording spectacular views.

WISCONSIN

DELAVAN

Silver Sands Golf School of Wisconsin

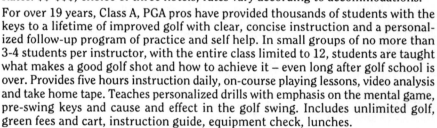

South Shore Dr., Dalavan, WI 53115
414 728-6120
Americana Resort Golf Club
Director: Wayne Rolfs
5-day, 3-day midweek, 3-day weekend; April-Aug
Rates: $$-$$$, choice of three hotels, rates vary according to accommodations.*

For over 19 years, Class A, PGA pros have provided thousands of students with the keys to a lifetime of improved golf with clear, concise instruction and a personalized follow-up program of practice and self help. In small groups of no more than 3-4 students per instructor, with the entire class limited to 12, students are taught what makes a good golf shot and how to achieve it – even long after golf school is over. Provides five hours instruction daily, on-course playing lessons, video analysis and take home tape. Teaches personalized drills with emphasis on the mental game, pre-swing keys and cause and effect in the golf swing. Includes unlimited golf, green fees and cart, instruction guide, equipment check, lunches.

*Choice of accommodations, 5, 4 or 2 nights, depending upon duration of program, at: Americana Lake Geneva Resort (Hwy 50 & U.S. 12, Lake Geneva, WI 53147; 800-558-3417), 350-room, 1,400-acre deluxe mega-resort with every possible diversion (details in the following entry); Hilton Inn on Lake Geneva (300 Wrigley Dr., Lake Geneva, WI 53147, 414 248-9181), 107-room hotel on the shores of Lake Geneva, with indoor pool, dining, walking distance to city center; Chateau Royal Inn (135 Main St., Lake Geneva, WI 53147, 414 248-9630), 44-room hotel overlooking wooded grounds and Hillmoor Golf Course, indoor pool.

▪ Learning center at Americana Resort, Lake Geneva. Two championship courses are ranked by Golf Digest among the top 100 courses in the country. The typically Scottish Briar Patch, the last course designed jointly by Pete Dye and Jack Nicklaus, is characterized by small greens and small rolling hills. The Robert Harris-designed Brute is longer, wetter and tougher.

LAKE GENEVA

Al Frazzini's Golf Course

Americana Lake Geneva Resort
Hwy 50 & U.S. 12, Lake Geneva, WI 53147; 800-558-3417
Director: Al Frazzini
5-day; May-Sept
Rates: $$-$$$
Info: Al Frazzini's Golf Course, 800 598-8127. See page **57** for programs and methods.

Thoroughly renewed and renovated, the former Playboy Hotel is now a family resort with nearly 350 rooms and an assortment of amenities, fitness pursuits and activities for the most discriminating guest. Spacious grounds with indoor and outdoor pools and tennis courts, stables, miniature golf, shooting, boating; several dining options and even an ice cream shop.

■ 36 holes. Refer to golf at the Americana resort in the previous entry.

LAKE GENEVA

John Jacobs Practical Golf Schools

Lake Lawn Lodge
Highway 50, Delavan, WI 53115; 800 338-5253   441 728-5511
4-day and weekends; May-Sept
Rates: $$
Info: John Jacobs Practical Golf Schools, 800 472-5007. See page **6** for programs and methods.

For over a century, Lake Lawn Lodge has attracted visitors for its rustic charm and heartland hospitality. Its location on the shores of Delavan Lake invites fishing, sailing and water skiing. The 275-acre site offers a 160 slip marina, an equestrian program, children's activities, a petting zoo, tennis, a baseball diamond, volleyball court, a health spa, dining in the finest American tradition, the list goes on and on. Charming Colonial rooms and suites in the main lodge, many with lofts, fireplaces and balconies. Located 45 miles southwest of Milwaukee, near Lake Geneva, one hour and thirty minutes from Chicago's O'Hare Airport.

■ The Dick Nugent course at Lake Lawn Lodge Golf Club is characterized by towering trees, strategically-placed bunkers which put shot-making skills to the test, and water – lots of water – with Lake Delavan coming into play. Stretches 6,418 yards, par 70.

LAKE GENEVA

John Jacobs Practical Golf Schools

Geneva National Golf Club
1221 Geneva National Ave, S. Lake Geneva, WI 53147; 414 245-7010
5-day and 2-day weekend VIP Schools with John Jacobs and Shelby Futch*
Rates: $$$, tuition only; accommodations on request
Info: John Jacobs Practical Golf Schools, 800 472-5700. See page **6** for programs and methods.

*Two masters, John Jacobs, "The Golf Doctor," and Shelby Futch, teaching editor of GOLF Magazine, conduct classes. Five-day program provides 5 hours instruction daily, 5 lunches, John Jacobs manual, video swing analysis, green fees and carts after class. Two-day program provides instruction Sat afternoon and Sun morning, a total of 8½ hours; includes John Jacobs manual of instruction and video swing analysis.

■ Geneva National's Arnold Palmer course, with five sets of tees and playing 7,193 from the championship level, is carved out of forested acres overlooking Lake Como – not Italy's but Wisconsin's. The Trevino course is said to be lighthearted and forgiving or a considerable challenge, depending upon the approach. A third course, this one by Gary Player, is planned for this serious complex. Located 45 minutes south of Milwaukee.

WISCONSIN DELLS

Galvano International Golf Academy

Scenic River Rd., P.O. Box 119, Wisconsin, Dells, WI 53965
800 234-6121   608 254-6361
Director: Phil Galvano, Jr.
3-day, Sun-W; April-Aug; Junior program (see page 177)
Rates: $-$$
Locations: three Wisconsin sites (see below); Ft. Meyers, FL

Established in 1941, Galvano International Golf Academy is the longest-running golf school in the nation. Bob Hope, Johnny Carson, Carol Burnett, Milton Berle and Dwight Eisenhower have all "galvanized" their game here. Instruction is targeted at combining a strong physical game with a powerful mental one. Instructors teach by concensus, combining the best techniques exhibited by golfing greats and adapting them to individual students. Students are oriented to a target line and helped to achieve square contact with the ball. Once they have mastered mechanics on the range, they take to the course to put their skills to practical use.

Three+ hours daily instruction, 3-4:1 student/teacher ratio; afternoon on-course play; includes golf fees, stop action videography and state of the art teaching aids. Details vary from resort to resort. All golf packages include three nights lodging at one of the following resorts:

Chula Vista Resort, Wisconsin Dells; 608 252-8366
Named 1991 Wisconsin Innkeepers Resort of the Year, Chula Vista is an affordable, family campus boasting 235 rooms and suites. Located on the cliffs of the Wisconsin River, the hotel offers indoor pool, varied dining, entertainment, spa, tennis, all the amenities, children's activities.

■ A 9-hole course with excellent practice opportunities. "All you need to improve your game."

Heidel House, Green Lake; 800 444-2812
Two-hundred room hotel situated directly on 7,325-acre Green Lake, Wisconsin's deepest, spring-fed, glacial lake. Spacious and lavish, it offers a wide assortment of activities, including live entertainment. Rated among the top resorts in Wisconsin.

■ 54 holes: three nationally recognized courses, named among the top 10 private courses in Wisconsin.

Cherry Hills Lodge and Golf Course, Sturgeon Bay; 800 545-2307

An elegant, 30-room gem with country club ambience, award-winning dining and an emphasis on golf and service, in a convenient and scenic horseshoe-shaped setting curving around the 18th hole.

■ 18-hole Cherry Hills Golf Course, lighted practice range and learning center, adjacent to the lodge.

Tell us how you fared at golf school. Complete the form at the back.

Tell us if "Golf Schools: The complete Guide" was helpful.

WYOMING

JACKSON HOLE

John Jacobs Practical Golf Schools

Wort Hotel
Corner of Glenwood and Broadway, Jackson, WY 83001
800 322-2727   307 733-2190

Jackson Hole Golf & Tennis Club, 5800 Spring Gulch Rd, Jackson, WY 83001
307 733-3111

4-days and weekend; Aug

Rates: $$$

Info: John Jacobs Practical Golf Schools, 800 472-5007. See page 6 for programs and methods.

Set against the majestic Grand Teton Mountains in an area rich in history, Western lore and natural beauty, Jackson Hole is the perfect spot for summer recreation. The 60-room, AAA Four-Diamond, Wort Hotel is a downtown historic landmark. Rebuilt in 1980 after a fire and completely redecorated in 1989, the Wort provides spacious rooms, concierge service, fitness center, skillful service, innovative dining, in the very center of lively, wild-Western, Jackson Hole. Direct daily air service from Denver and Salt Lake City.

■ Jackson Hole Golf Course, 10 miles north of town, has been rated among the top 25 public courses by Golf Digest magazine. Originally designed by Bob Baldock, the 7,168-yard, tree-lined course with spectacular views of the Grand Tetons was redesigned in 1967 by architect Robert Trent Jones, Jr. The Gros Ventre River creates water hazards on 12 holes; features elevated and contoured greens and 65 well-placed bunkers.

CANADA

See page 98 for programs and methods.

FAIRMONT HOT SPRINGS, BRITISH COLUMBIA

Swing's The Thing Golf Schools

Fairmont Hot Springs Resort
Hwy. #93/95, Fairmont Hot Springs, British Columbia, Canada V0B 1L0
800 663-4979 604 345-6311

3-day VIP session; June

Rates: $$-$$$, includes 3 nights, limited to 12 participants.

Info: Swing's The Thing Golf Schools, 800 221-6661. See page 98 for programs and methods.

Warmth comes naturally at this family-owned, rustic, 140-room lodge with Canada's largest, odorless, mineral hot pools (104-113°F) and a complete Spa program with Swedish massage, hydrotherapy, and private soaking pools. Nearly 1.4 million gallons of water flow through the gigantic pool complex which is drained nightly and re-filled by morning. Celebrated dining, nightly entertainment and a 265-site RV park a short walk from the pools. Located 1³/₄ hours southwest of Banff in the towering British Columbia Rockies at the headwaters of the mighty Colorado River.

▉ Two 18-hole courses: Mountainside and Riverside. Mountainside presents mountain and valley vistas as it winds through pine and spruce, culminating in crowned greens. Riverside incorporates the Columbia River among its water hazards. Each course prides itself on its separate club house facilities, pro shop and practice areas.

VILLE L'ESTÉREL, QUEBEC

Roland Stafford Golf School

Hotel l'Estérel, C.P. 38
Ville l'Estérel, QC, J0T 1E0
514 228-2571

5-day, 3-day weekend*; May-Oct

Rates: $$

Information: Roland Stafford Golf School, 800 447-8894. See page 84 for programs and methods.

*Arrive Thu; 6:1 student/teacher ratio

In the Laurentians, just one hour north of Montreal, the resort occupies 5,000 acres of lakes, forests and mountains. Features indoor pool, whirlpool, saunas, gym, volleyball, racquetball, seven tennis courts. At the marina: windsurfing, parasailing, water skiing and boating; 135 air conditioned rooms, a renown dining room. Includes breakfast and dinner daily.

▉ 18 hole mountain course designed by Canadian architect Jules Huot, a contemporary of Ben Hogan. First nine holes date back 25 years; second nine added in 1988. Plays 6,430 from men's tees, par 71. Host of the Canadian PGA, the l'Estérel Golf Club is the only course in Canada with a Ladies Pro-Am tournament.

JUNIOR SCHOOLS

ALASKA

ANCHORAGE

Elmendorf Junior Golf Clinic

Elmendorf Air Force Base - Eagle Glen Golf Course

Director: Ernie Hamby

One 8-week program (one day/week), June-Aug; $55, commuter only
Coed, ages 7-17, limited to 70

Info and registration: Eagle Glen Golf Course, Elmendorf AFB, AK 99506
907 552-3821

This complete instructional program, the only one in the entire state of Alaska, is open to military dependents and civilian youngsters. Three hours morning instruction over seven weeks, one day/week; on-course training after third session; closing tournament day. Fee includes all golf costs. According to the director, "Moose are charged double."

■ The 18-hole Eagle Glen Golf Course, considered one of the top courses in Alaska, was designed by Robert Trent Jones and opened in 1971. It is subject to aerial demonstrations by genuine eagles several times a week.

ALABAMA

AUBURN AND TUSCALOOSA

Tiger-Tide Golf Academy

University of Alabama and Auburn University

Directors: Dick Spybey and Mike Griffin

Three 4-day sessions (Regular and Elite), Sun-Thu, June, 22nd year
Coed, ages 10 through high school junior year
Regular Session; $495 (commuter $300), limited to 40
Elite Session, 0-10 handicap; $595 (commuter $400), limited to 20

University of Alabama at Tuscaloosa: two 4-day sessions (one Regular, one Elite)
Auburn University: one 4-day Regular session

Info and registration: P.O. Box 2564, Auburn, AL 36831
205 348-3692   205 752-0675

Dick Spybey, PGA, is director of Golf and Men's Golf Coach at University of Alabama; Mike Griffin is director of Golf and Men's Golf Coach at Auburn University. Instruction at all sessions is by PGA and LPGA pros, collegiate coaches and college golfers. Covers fundamentals, trouble shots, rules, etiquette and course strategy. Provides on-course playing lessons, video swing analysis and competitions.

Elite enrollment (0-10 handicap) for juniors interested in collegiate and/or pro golf. Both programs include 4 nights lodging in University dorms (2/room), all meals, round the clock supervision, evening recreation and camaraderie. Tuscaloosa is reached by commuter aircraft from Birmingham Airport. Auburn is a 35 minute drive from Columbus (GA) Airport; inquire about airport transfers.

■ At Tuscaloosa, students play the 18-hole Harry Pritchett Golf Course on campus, with a two-tiered driving range, short game practice facilities and clubhouse. At Auburn: the 54-hole Grand National Golf Course(s).

ARIZONA

SCOTTSDALE

Exceller Programs Golf Schools

7500 E. Butherus, Scottsdale, AZ 85260; 800 424-7438   602 998-1038
Director: Dave Bisbee

Junior clinic series (2+ hours instruction, 5-8 sessions) at Exceller Golf Learning Centers at Amherst, NH; Geenville, SC; San Francisco, CA; Scottsdale, AZ; $140, commuter only, summer

Learning Center Junior Memberships: weekly tournaments, interclub competitions; summer, $20

Coed, ages 4-18

Info: Exceller Programs Golf Schools; 800 424-7438. See page 4. Programs vary from site to site.

Scottsdale site: Crackerjax Golf Center

SCOTTSDALE

GOLFWEEK College Prep Academy

Marriott's Camelback Inn, 5-day session, Dec
Info: GOLFWEEK College Prep Academy, Winter Haven, FL
813 294-5511.
See page 137 for programs and methods.

SCOTTSDALE

John Jacobs Practical Golf Schools

Marriott's Camelback Golf Club
7847 North Mockingbird Ln, Scottsdale, AZ 85253; 800 24-CAMEL

2-day weekend, commuter only; $89, June & July
Coed, ages 13-16

Info and registration: John Jacobs Practical Golf Schools, 800 472-5007. See page 6 for programs and methods.

John Jacobs' proven method is taught by the school's own instructors; morning classes, 7 am-noon; includes green fees and carts after 1 pm.

■ At Camelback Golf Club, two championship USGA courses: the 18-hole, long, Jack Snyder-designed Indian Bend Course and the earlier, more compact, 18-hole, 6,559-yard Padre Course designed by Red Lawrence.

T E M P E

Arizona State University Golf Academy

Arizona State University, Tempe, AZ

Directors: Randy Lein and Linda Vollstedt

Three 4-day sessions, June; $595 (double session $1,190), 5th year
Coed, ages 10-17

Info and registration: Randy Lein and Linda Vollstedt, ASU, 306 ICA Building, Tempe, AZ 85287; 602 965-3262

ASU coaches, Randy Lein and Linda Vollstedt, made collegiate golf history when ASU's men's and women's teams won their respective NCAA championships – a never-before achieved feat. They join seasoned instructors and past and present collegiate greats in delivering daily instruction and directing intramural competitions. Evening speakers on history, rules, equipment and course management. Final tournament; families invited to closing awards reception.

Four nights lodging in University dorms; includes all meals; bus depot and airport transfers.

◼ Karsten Golf Course at ASU, with complete practice facilities.

> *NCAA regulations stipulate: "No student who is eligible for admission to a member NCAA institution or has started classes for his or her senior year in high school is allowed to participate in summer sports camps." For the most part, private camps and resorts do not follow this directive.*

C A L I F O R N I A

P A L O   A L T O

Stanford University Golf Camp

Stanford University, Palo Alto

Directors: Tim Baldwin and Wally Goodwin

Five 6-day sessions, June & July; $795; commuter $695, 5th year
Two coed sessions, three sessions for boys only; ages 9-17 (high school seniors and graduates exempted)

Info and registration: U.S. Sports Development, 919 Sir Francis Drake Blvd., Kentfield, CA 94904; 800 433-6060. See Stanford Golf School for Adults (see page 19).

Tim Baldwin and Wally Goodwin, directors of Stanford's women's and men's golf programs, respectively, field a team of personally selected instructors skilled in teaching youth at all levels. Over 35 hours instruction plus evening on-course training at this serious golf camp where campers receive not only grounding in the fundamentals but an appreciation for the game, its history, etiquette and what it can offer each golfer. Final day tournament, awards ceremony and barbecue. Component for tournament level golfers stresses practice routines, mental aspects and opportunities for collegiate competition; allows extra playing time. Five nights lodging in Stanford University dorms (2/room). Fully supervised program includes all meals and golf fees, evening recreation. Located 30 miles south of San Francisco.

▆ 18-hole Stanford University Golf Course with complete practice facility.

PEBBLE BEACH

FCA Junior Golf Camps (Fellowship of Christian Athletes)

Fort Ord Golf Course, 5-day program
Info: FCA, 904 273-9541. See page135 for programs and methods.

PEBBLE BEACH

The Ultimate Junior Golf Clinic

P.O. Box 1129, Pebble Beach, CA 93953
800 321-9401

Professionals: John Geertsen, Jr; Ben Alexander

Two 5-day sessions, June and Aug; $1,875, 4th year
Coed, ages 10-18, limited to 20

Info: The Golf Clinic, Pebble Beach, California, 800 321-9401. See page 20 for details.

Johnny Miller, Tony Lema and Mike Reid were junior participants here under the Geertsen teaching tradition. Instruction covers all aspects, plus course management and positive mental attitude; 5:1 student/teacher ratio; includes all golf fees, written materials, individual video swing analysis, take-home hour-long instructional tape, gifts, welcoming party, daily transportation.

Provides five nights lodging at the private Robert Louis Stevenson School in the heart of the Pebble Beach Forest, all meals and recreation, round the clock supervision, RT transfers to Monterey Municipal Airport.

▆ Students play the world famous Pebble Beach course; daily instruction at Poppy Hills.

SACRAMENTO

Northern California PGA (NCPGA) Junior Resident School

California State University of Sacramento
Director: Richard McShane

One 6-day session, June; $695, 13th year; coed, ages 12-17
Day clinics at Haggin Oaks Golf Course: "Wee Swingers, ages 5-8;
Beginner Camp, ages 8-17; Intermediate Day Camp, ages 12-17

Info and registration: Haggin Oaks Golf Shop, NCPGA, 3645 Fulton Ave., Sacramento, CA 95821; 916 481-4507

A number of PGA and LPGA Tour players hit their first golf balls at this camp. Golf Digest, the National Golf Foundation, Sacramento Boy Scouts of America, and the Association of the Retarded attest to its quality. All phases of golf are taught in personalized morning clinics with a 12:1 student/teacher ratio and an emphasis on maximizing each student's potential. Afternoons, students learn course management, playing with their instructors.

Resident tuition covers all meals, five nights accommodations in CSUS dorms, all golf fees and full supervision. Evening recreation on campus.

■ 36 holes at Haggin Oaks Golf Course, an Alister MacKenzie design, on the oak-studded site of the former J.B. Haggin Rancho Del Paso Mexican land grant. (MacKenzie is best known for carving out Cypress Point Golf Course at Pebble Beach.)

SAN FRANCISCO

Exceller Programs Golf Schools
Junior Clinic Series. See page126.

SANTA ROSA

Sports America Tours Junior Golf Clinic
1415 Fulton Rd., Ste. 211, Santa Rosa, CA 95403
800 876-8551   800 995-9333   619 452-0908
One 5-day, June; $595, 2nd year
Coed, ages 15-18, limited to 6-8

Variety is the key to this school which operates on the move. Four days instruction (1¹/₂ hours daily) at two sites, covering every aspect of the game. Students play four different courses. The diversity of instruction and play enables them to identify their own strengths and those of the courses and to compare their performance under various conditions.

Five nights accommodations at the centrally located, 138-room Days Inn of Santa Rosa (2/room) with restaurants and shops nearby; includes lunches, transportation to clinics and courses, one dinner celebration; does not include breakfasts or other dinners. Day-time supervision and 10 pm bed checks. Optional airport transfers.

■ Students play at Windsor Golf Club, par 72, home of the Nike Sonoma County Open; newly renovated Sonoma Golf Club, par 72, small greens and tight dog legs; Fountaingrove Resort and Country Club, par 72, Ted Robinson-design, a tight, hilly course; Bodega Harbor Golf Links, a Robert Trent Jones, Jr.-design, a scenic, oceanside, par 70.

Professionals disagree about whether left-handed juniors should be encouraged to shoot lefty. Some suggest that parents should not dissuade natural tendencies and should follow the youngster's left-handed patterns. Others suggest that juniors try out the golf swing lefty and righty and make a determination on which feels the most comfortable. Or let a professional golf teacher help decide.

COLORADO

ACADEMY

Falcon Youth Golf Camps

United States Air Force Academy

Professionals: Gene Miranda; assistant, Schott Davis

Camp #1, one 5-day session, boarding, all skill levels; $500
Camp #2, one 5-day session, boarding, for competition golfers; $550
Camp #3, one 5-day commuter session, all skill levels; $280

Coed, ages 11-17, June, 5-day, M-F, 14th year

Info and registration: Air Force Academy Athletic Association, USAF Academy, CO 80840; 800 666-8723   719 472-1895

A well known tradition, Falcon Golf Camp covers all fundamentals and strokes, course management and psychology. Instructors utilize video analysis to aid retention. Students are tested on skills, rules, and etiquette. Competition Camp (#2) is structured for juniors who break 100 and look forward to college competition; covers college choices and the application, practice routines and the mental approach to competitive golf.

Lodging (5 nights, Sun-Thurs) in cadet dormitories with supervision by cadet and officer counselors. Includes all meals, awards, photograph, evening recreation, all golf fees; transportation to and from Colorado Springs Airport.

▐ Eisenhower Golf Courses, 36 holes on campus, Blue and Silver courses. The Robert Trent Jones, Jr. Blue Course was recently rated third best in Colorado by Golf Digest.

GUNNISON

Rocky Mountain Family Golf School

Family and parent/child programs; juniors welcome accompanied by an adult.
Info: 303 932-2644   303 641-0451. See page 25 for details

VAIL

Colorado Section Junior Golf Academy

Roost Lodge, 1783 North Frontage Rd. W, Vail, CO 81657
303 476-5451

One 5-day, 4 night session; $475, 16th year
Coed, ages 13-18, limited to 48

Info and registration: Colorado Section PGA, 12323 E. Cornell Ave., Aurora, CO 80014; 303 745-3697

Designed for intermediate and advanced junior golfers, the school delivers intensive teaching by top notch pros from the Colorado Section of the PGA. Daily instruction emphasizes fundamentals plus on-course training. Golf Digest sports psychologist, Don Green, presents the mental aspects of golf. Leading Colorado section, PGA playing pros will be paired with students for play. As a finale, students are entered in the annual Tom Whitehead Junior Invitational Tournament.

Students are transported to Vail Monday morning from a central location in Denver and returned Friday. Accommodations at The Roost Lodge in Vail, 72 rooms, with pool, Jacuzzi, sauna, country inn atmosphere. Supervised program includes all meals, golf fees and tournament entry fee.

■ 18-hole courses and training facilities at Vail Golf Club and nearby Singletree Golf Club, Edwards, CO.

> *It is most likely that your child will be covered by the camp's blanket insurance policy. If this is not the case, you will be asked for a small additional fee or proof that you carry insurance.*
>
>

FLORIDA

AMELIA ISLAND

Ron Philo's Golf School

Amelia Island Plantation, P.O. Box 3000, Amelia Island, FL 32035
800 874-6878

Director: Ron Philo

Three 5-day sessions, Sun-F; June-Aug; $1,100, 1st year
Coed, ages 12-17, for juniors with some experience

Info: Ron Philo Golf School, page 31, for resort and golf information.

School selects for competent junior golfers with an interest in preparing for competition. The father and son team of Ron Philo Sr. and Jr. augment the school's PGA teaching staff with counselor-interns from professional golf management programs. Provides eight hours golf-related activities daily, including range instruction (8:1 student/teacher ratio), on-course training on Amelia Island's three courses, video analysis, competitive events. A sports psychologist will explore the mental aspects of competition and the importance of a winning frame of mind.

Includes full use of the facilities with supervision by the resort's recreational staff. Condo lodging (4/unit) with live-in counselor, round the clock supervision, three buffet meals daily.

BOCA RATON

Dave Pelz Short Game School

Boca Raton Resort & Club

Juniors, ages 13-17, accompanied by an adult

Info: 800 833-7370. See page 32 for description of programs and methods.

BOCA RATON

Welby Van Horn Tennis & Golf Camps

Boca Raton Resort & Club
501 E. Camino Real, Boca Raton, FL 33431
800 327-0101   407 395-3000

Eight 6-day sessions, June-Aug; $770/week; combination tennis/golf program $720/week (multi-week campers add $65 for each Sat night)
Coed, ages 8-18

Info and registration: Welby Van Horn Tennis & Golf Camps, P.O. Box 259 Gracie Station, New York, NY 10028; 800 424-4550   212 734-1037

Tennis great Welby Van Horn staffs his golf school with instructors skilled in teaching youth. Program provides 33 hours instruction, 4:1 student/teacher ratio, video analysis, written evaluations; optional strength training. Culminates with tournament and awards ceremony. Competition program for tournament caliber golfers emphasizes preparation for college varsity. Includes resort accommodations, all meals, 24-hour supervision.

Boca Raton Resort provides deluxe air conditioned rooms (6 nights, 2/room), private bath, TV and refrigerator; three pools, 34 tennis courts, wind surfing, jet skiing, sailing, volleyball, fitness center, junior activity room. Program features weekly trips, dances, movies, barbecues, game and show nights.

■ Two 18-hole championship courses: the beautifully manicured, tropical Resort Course on the grounds and, a few miles away, the more difficult Country Club Course.

GAINSVILLE

Gator Golf Camps

University of Florida at Gainsville

Director: Buddy Alexander

Two 4-day sessions, M-Th, June; $595, 5th year
Coed, ages 11-17, limited to 45

Info and registration: The Gator Golf Camp, P.O. Box 2313, Gainsville, FL 32602 904 375-4683, ext. 4720

Under coach Buddy Alexander, U of Florida has maintained a winning tradition. He brings together a staff of PGA pros and members of the University's golf team to coach juniors of all abilities. Provides 30+ hours instruction on all aspects; includes golf psychology, rules, etiquette, preparation for competition. Includes age-appropriate competitions, seminars. Player/Coaches Panel discusses collegiate golf.

Includes all meals, lodging in university dorms, round the clock supervision, swimming, movies, bowling; transfers to Gainsville Regional Airport.

■ University's 18-hole course and complete practice facilities.

HAINES CITY – ORLANDO AREA

GOLFWEEK College Prep Academy

Grenelefe Golf and Tennis Resort, two 5-day sessions, June and Dec
Info: GOLFWEEK College Prep Academy, 813 294-5511. See page 137 for programs and methods.

JACKSONVILLE

Osprey Golf Camp
University of North Florida, Jacksonville
Director: John Brooks
One 5-day, July; $375, 2nd year
Coed, ages 11-17
Info and registration: University of North Florida Athletics, 4567 St. Johns Bluff Rd. S., Jacksonville, FL 32224; 904-646-2535
1991 NAIA Golf Coach of the Year, John Brooks, heads the University of North Florida golf program. His camp is staffed with PGA pros and collegiate coaches, with members of the UNF golf team as counselors. Emphasis is on personalized instruction in classes with a 5:1 or better student/teacher. Campers experience daily instruction, videotaping of their swings to encourage correction, four competition rounds and exposure to rules and course management.

Students are lodged (4 nights, 2/room) in Osprey Hall on the UNF campus; includes three meals daily, beginning Sun and concluding with lunch on Thurs. Program is fully supervised. Includes airport transfers.

■ Students are transported by camp staff to and from Jacksonville Golf and Country Club, an 18-hole facility with practice areas.

MELBOURNE

United States Senior Golf Academy
Holiday Inn - Indian River Colony Club
5-day session; Juniors of all ages accepted with parent or guardian.
Info: United States Senior Golf Academy, 800 654-5752. See page 38, for programs and methods.

NAPLES

David Leadbetter Golf Academy Junior Golf School
Quail West Golf and Country Club
6303 Burnham Rd, Naples, FL 33999; 813 592-1444
Director: David Leadbetter
Two 7-day sessions, June; $1,350
Coed, 12-17, limited to 20
Info: See page 46 for further details.
Leadbetter's celebrated scientific approach is transmitted by a staff of trained and certified PGA teaching pros who develop a strong link between the physical and mental aspects of golf. In classes with a 5:1 student/teacher ratio, importance is placed on providing the necessary building blocks to establish strong character and encourage confidence and self esteem. Includes seven hours intensive teaching daily, videography, competitions, two rounds of golf at Quail West, supervised practice, lectures and films, awards banquet.

Offers varied recreation: swimming, tennis, racquetball, fitness training, an Everglades Wilderness Adventure and a cruise on the Gulf. Fully supervised program provides seven nights at the 69-room Comfort Inn (9800 Bonita Beach Rd., Bonita

Springs, FL 33923, 813 992-5001), all meals and airport transfers.

■ Classes are conducted at the new Quail West Golf and Country Club. Set on more then 200 acres of lakes and natural preserves, the 18-hole course was designed by Arthur Hills and Associates.

ORLANDO

Arnold Palmer Golf Academy

Arnold Palmer's Bay Hill Club
9000 Bay Hill Blvd., Orlando, FL 32819; 800 523-5999   407 876-2429
One 5-day Junior Advance session, commuter only, May; $500
Parent/Child sessions; June, July, Nov and Dec; $1,200/pair
Coed, ages 14-18
Info: See page 44 for further details.

For juniors with some proficiency; imparts 20 hours instruction, daily organized competition, unlimited golf and practice, video analysis, lunch, gifts and awards. Personalized and straightforward instruction by PGA pros trained in the Palmer method, with emphasis on fundamentals, good golf manners and a winning frame of mind.

Parent/Child, 2-day program includes 16 hours instruction, videotaping, instruction book and tape, daily playing lessons, gifts, awards. Includes 2 nights double occupancy at the Bay Hill Club.

■ The resort's 27 hole course is ranked among the world's leaders. Full practice facility.

Make the most of your child's first set of clubs. John Jacobs, the golf school giant (see page 6), is a source for equipment for young golfers, beginning as early as age eight or nine. The Junior Golf Club Program offers discounted junior clubs and discounted up-sizing (new grips and shafts, loft and lie alteration) every two years, as your child grows. Once juniors are 15 or 16, the Club accepts the set in trade on a new purchase. You might inquire whether a club fitter at your local pro shop or golf outlet offers a similar service.

PALM BEACH GARDENS

PGA National Junior Golf Academies

1000 Avenue of Champions, Palm Beach Gardens, FL 33418
800 832-6235   407 627-7593
Director: Mike Adams
Three individual Junior programs:
Junior Golf Academy: Two 4-day sessions, June and July (Tu-F); $750, coed, ages

7-18, 16th year

Situated at the home of the PGA, Junior Golf Academy provides a total of 24 hours instruction. Includes team competition, on-course play, final tournament and awards ceremony. Five nights lodging at PGA National Resort and Spa (2/room), all meals and golf fees, welcoming party, round the clock supervision, RT transfers to West Palm Beach Airport.

Young Lions Junior Development School: One 4-day session, commuter only, July, Tu-F; $750, coed, ages 16+, limited to 24 golfers with 0-9 handicaps

An intensive program for aspiring collegiate and pro golfers; accentuates competitive skills. Includes all related golf fees, green fees and carts; provides breakfasts and lunches; does not include lodging; contact school for information on accommodations.

Parent Child: 3-days, fall; $1,200/pair, coed, juniors ages 8-19

Provides quality time and quality instruction; includes recreational program; tuition only, inquire about accommodations at PGA National Hotel and Spa.

Info: See page 52 for further details.

PGA National Resort and Spa (400 Ave. of the Champions, Palm Beach Gardens, FL 33418; 800 633-9150 or 407 627-2000), a 335-room, 2,340-acre Mobil Four Star facility with an AAA Four Diamond rating. See page 52.

▪ Five championship 18-hole courses, 90 holes in total: Champion, Haig, Squire, General, and Estate. Plus state-of-the-art learning and practice facilities.

PONTE VEDRA BEACH

Fellowship of Christian Athletes

FCA Golf, Box 664, Ponte Vedra Beach, FL 32004; 904-273-9541

5-day sessions at 9 locations, see sites below; Sun-Thu, June-Aug; $200 to $460 (varies according to site), coed, ages 13-18, 16th year

Established in 1977, FCA's National Golf Ministry provides a vehicle for the enjoyment of golf and the pursuit of spiritual growth. Between 50 and 80 youngsters are grouped by skill and attend daily instruction and competitions. Features "huddles," motivational group discussions led by college or young adult golfers. Instruction is donated by PGA, LPGA, Nike Tour and club professionals. Includes all practice and green fees, on-site expenses, lodging, meals, FCA Bible, shirt, prizes, insurance, airport transfers. Scholarships available.

California: Pebble Beach

Fort Ord Golf Course, 5-day, Aug, 50 students; $360

Situated on the windswept, cypress-lined Monterey Peninsula. Campers housed off-site.

▪ Students play Fort Ord course; generous practice facilities.

Florida: Palm Beach Gardens

PGA National Golf Club - PGA National Resort, 5-day, June, 60 students; $400

A Four Star, Four Diamond, 335-room, luxury resort situated on the 2,340-acre PGA National community, offering deluxe accommodations and recreation.

🏴 Five championship courses. See previous listing.

Florida: Ponte Vedra Beach
TPC at Sawgrass - Marriott at Sawgrass, 5-day, July, 60 students; $415
A top resort and golfer's paradise, the 535-room Marriott offers deluxe and varied recreation and accommodations. Forty minutes from Jacksonville International Airport.
🏴 Home of the Players Championship and famed Sawgrass Golf Club, 99 holes.

Georgia: Pine Mountain
Callaway Gardens Golf Club and Resort, 5-day, July, 50 students; $400
An 800-room, Mobil Four Star resort on the famed, 12,000-acre Callaway Gardens, a horticultural paradise comprised of gorgeous gardens, woodlands, lakes and wildlife, with every possible recreational opportunity. Transfers to Columbus Airport.
🏴 Site of the annual PGA Buick Southern Open; 63 top-rated holes of golf.

Indiana: Indianapolis
Eagle Creek Golf Course - Best Western Waterfront Plaza, 5-day, July, 60 students; $250
Located 150 miles northeast of St. Louis in an area rich with man-made and natural attractions.
🏴 Site of past U.S. Publinx Championship; regarded as one of the finest public golf facilities in the country. Acclaimed Pete Dye-David Pfaff, 18-hole championship layout, playing 7,154 yards from the back tees. Instruction at elaborate, newly renovated family golf center.

Mississippi: Oxford
University of Mississippi - Ole Miss Golf Course, 5-day, Aug, 50 students; $200
Situated north of the historic town of Oxford. Lodging in University dorms.
🏴 One of the finest and most challenging courses in the state.

North Carolina: Southern Pines
Pine Needles Lodges and Country Club, 5-day, July, 80 students; $460
Family-owned Pine Needles offers rustic comfort amid natural beauty in the heart of golf country. Located 70 miles south of Raleigh.
🏴 Owned by leading LPGA figure, Peggy Kirk Bell. Offers complete practice facilities and championship golf. Pine Needles will host the 1996 U.S. Women's Open.

Texas: Woodlands
Woodlands Resort, 5-day, June, 50 students; $400
Deluxe, 268-room resort and conference center in the vicinity of Houston.
🏴 Two 18-hole championship courses. The Tournament Players Course, site of the annual Shell Houston Open, provides its practice area. Students play the North Course, one of the finest layouts in the state.

Wisconsin: Green Lake - Lawsonia Golf Course
Green Lake Conference Center/Lawsonia GC, 5-day, June, 50 students; $275
Located 40 miles from Fon Du Lac Airport (transfers provided). Lodging in Green Lake Conference Center, offering a range of recreational opportunities.

▶ The 36-hole Lawsonia Golf Course (Links and Woodland courses) ranks as one of the best golf facilities in the Midwest. Students practice on outstanding ranges and greens.

TARPON SPRINGS

Innisbrook Junior Golf Institute

Innisbrook Resort and Country Club
P.O. Drawer 1088, Tarpon Springs, FL 34688; 800 456-2000   813 942-2000
Director: Lew Smither, III
Three 5-day sessions, July; $900; $475 commuter, 11th year
Coed, ages 10-17, limited to 16
Info: See page 59 for further details.

School delivers a solid understanding of fundamentals, including rules and etiquette; 30 hours individualized instruction from top-flight, PGA pros at the school's dedicated practice facility; daily on-course training, videotaping with analysis for at-home continued learning.

Provides six nights lodging in 2-bedroom suites with a resident counselor assigned to each; all meals, all related golf fees. Supervised intramural sports. RT transportation from Tampa International Airport, gift pack, all related service charges. Round the clock supervision.

▶ Sixty-three holes of golf: Copperhead Course is rated Florida's #1 course by GolfWeek and one of "America's Greatest" by Golf Digest. Sandpiper, a shotmaker's course, has been recently reconfigured to 27 holes, the shortest of the three championship courses; the Island course, voted "Most Interesting" by a panel of writers and pros, is a hilly par 72, 7,000 yards from championship tees.

WINTER HAVEN

GOLFWEEK College Prep Academy and Championship

175 Fifth St., S.W., Winter Haven, FL 33880; 813 294-5511
Director: Buddy Alexander
Four 5-day sessions at 3 sites (see below); June, Aug and Dec; $1,495, 1st year
Coed, ages 13-17 (through junior year of high school), limit 100/session

Director Buddy Alexander's teams have won 35 titles and produced 25 All-Americans. His schools prepare serious junior golfers for competitive college golf. Instruction conducted by coaches of the winningest collegiate teams in the nation, plus touring pros, college advisors and golf industry experts. Four-part curriculum furnishes college preparation (recruitment, scholarships, careers, etc.), technical instruction (total game plus constructive practice routines), game enhancement (psychological readiness, club selection, fitness, pre-shot routines), and academic championship (3-day, college-style, 54-hole tournament against a strong field to gain exposure to top college coaches and industry professionals).

Includes four nights lodging (2/room), all meals, full supervision, airport transfers, all golf fees, equipment and apparel package. Parents are welcome to observe and/or vacation at discounted rates.

Haines City, Florida (Orlando area):
Grenelefe Golf and Tennis Resort, 3200 State Rd. 546
Two 5-day sessions; June & Dec
Secluded, 950-unit resort with all amenities, on 1,000 acres; 30 minutes from
Disney World, less than an hour from Orlando Airport.
▶ Three outstanding courses, including the Robert Trent Jones Grenelefe West,
ranked Florida's #1 course for six years and repeatedly named among the
nation's top 100. Complete practice facility.

Dallas, Texas:
Hyatt Regency DFW, International Pkwy - DFW Airport
Bear Creek Golf & Racquet Club
One 5-day session, Aug
A full-destination, 1,390-room modern hotel at DFW Airport with a dazzling
array of amenities.
▶ Two world-class,18-hole Ted Robinson courses at Bear Creek, rated among
the top 50 in the country by Golf Digest magazine. Complete practice facilities.

Scottsdale, Arizona:
Marriott's Camelback Inn and Golf Club, 5402 E. Lincoln Dr.
One 5-day session, Dec
Renown resort carries Mobil Five-Star and AAA 5-Diamond designations, year
after year. European Spa, and all comforts and services.
▶ 36-hole golf complex includes the Padre Course, a Red Lawrence design, a
tight shotmaker's layout, and Indian Bend, perfect for big hitters at 7,014 yards.

GEORGIA

ATHENS

Georgia Junior Golf Academies
University of Georgia, Athens

Junior Golf Academy: Three 4-day sessions, Sun-Thu, June-July; $495; boys, ages
10-17, 9th year, Director Maxie Boles

Junior Girls' Golf Academy: One 4-day session, Sun-Thu, June; $425; girls, ages
10-17, Director Beans Kelly

Advanced Junior Golf Academy: One 2-day session, Thu-Sat, June; $295; boys, ages
14-17, Director Joe Inman

Info and registration: Georgia Junior Golf Foundation, 121 Village Pkwy, Bldg 3,
Marietta, GA 30067; 800 949-4742   404 955-4272.

Qualified professionals deliver instruction on every aspect of the game, employing
the latest teaching aids, including swing trainer, caddy cam, graph check camera
and tempo master. Boys' and girls' 4-day programs include daily instruction, 4:1
student/teacher ratio, same instructor throughout, students grouped according to
skill, on-course instruction, competitions, early evening golf.

Four nights dorm lodging, all meals; supervision by collegiate golfer counselors.
Closing Awards luncheon open to families of students.

Advanced Junior Golf Academy accords intensive personalized training and play with leading coaches and PGA teaching pros, emphasizing correct practice routines to reach one's potential as a golfer. Two-nights lodging at the Athens Ramada Inn, all meals and supervision.

■ All students play the 18-hole U of Georgia Golf Course, with complete practice facilities; Advance Academy plays additional neighboring courses.

PINE MOUNTAIN

FCA Junior Golf Camps (Fellowship of Christian Athletes)

Callaway Gardens Resort, 5-day program
Info: FCA, 904 273-9541. See page 135 for details.

SEA ISLAND

Golf Digest Instruction Schools

The Cloister, 5-day Parent-Child session, July; $4,150/pair, coed, ages 12-18

Info: Golf Digest Instruction Schools, 800 243-6121. See page 30 for programs and methods; see page 61 for resort information and golf.

STATESBORO

Georgia Southern University Eagle Golf Camp

Georgia Southern University
Director: Doug Gordin
One 5-day session, July; $415, commuter $250, 8th year
Boys, ages 9-17 (high school seniors and graduates exempted), limited to 40
Info: Georgia Southern Golf Camp, Landrum Box 8082, Statesboro, GA 30460
912 681-9100

Doug Gordin, in his 11th year coaching the GSU golf team, has planned a program strong in the basics and implemented by a staff of respected professionals. Collegiate golfers serve as counselors and reduce the student/teacher ration to 4:1, providing personal attention. Grouped according to age and skill, students receive 5½ hours instruction daily. Camp culminates with an 18-hole tournament and an informal awards dinner.

Campers are based in air-conditioned dorm rooms (2/room, 4-nights) with live-in counselors and coaches; includes three all-you-can-eat meals daily. Airport and bus transfers provided.

■ Meadow Lake Golf Course, Statesboro's newest course, with two large putting greens and a huge practice tee.

In case of minor injury at a University-based sports camp, your child will likely first be seen by a trainer. Trainers are thoroughly versed in treating athletic-related strains, sprains, bruises and swellings.

ILLINOIS

GALENA

Eagle Ridge Golf Academy

Eagle Ridge Inn and Resort
U.S. Route 20, Box 777, Galena, IL 61036; 800 892-2269 815 777-2444
Director: Laura Schlaman

Six 2-day sessions, June-Aug; $300, commuter $240
Coed, ages 8-16, limited to 20
Info: See page 66 for further details.

Five hours instruction daily by PGA teaching pros, on fundamentals, rules, etiquette and finesse, in classes with a 4:1 student/teacher ratio. Features video analysis and on-course play with instructors.

Includes all golf fees, lodging, meals, full teen recreation program with round the clock supervision by experienced youth staff. Transfers to Dubuque. Commuter rate includes meals and recreation, no lodging.

Celebrated resort located on 6,800 rolling acres in the northwest corner of Illinois. Offers cycling, tennis, a complete fitness center, pool, sun deck, entertainment, even an ice cream parlor.

▌ 45 holes of golf. The North and South courses have been named among the top resort courses in the country. The 9-hole East Course is scenic and challenging.

NORMAL

Illinois State University Golf Camp

Illinois State University
Director: Harland Kilborn

One 5-day session, June; $295, commuter $195, 15th year
Coed, 10-17 (grades 7-11, graduating seniors ineligible), limited to 50
Info and registration: Illinois State University, 7130 Horton Field House, Normal, IL 61761; 309 438-3635

Harland Kilborn, Men's coach at ISU and Central Illinois Player of the Year in 1990, is supported by a team of teaching pros and clinicians. Each golfer receives individual instruction and participates in group clinics, on-course strategy sessions and tournament competition. Classes limited to 5:1 student/teacher ratio. The school makes extensive use of personal videotaping and viewing films from the USGA and National Golf Foundation.

Students housed in an air-conditioned ISU dorm (2/room, 4 nights). Camp staff supervises and lives in. Includes 11 meals (Mon breakfast-Thu lunch), all golf and recreation fees.

▌ 18-hole Illinois State University Golf Course, with large practice area; Royal Links par 3 course and driving range.

Band-aids, band-aids, band-aids. Bring a generous supply.

SAVOY

University of Illinois Summer Camp

University of Illinois

Directors: Paula Smith and Ed Beard

One 5-day session, July; $395, commuter $300, 15th year

Coed, ages 12-18 (high school seniors and graduates ineligible), limited to 50

Info and registration: 113 Assembly Hall, 1800 S. First St., Champaign, IL 61820; 217-244-7278.

Paula Smith and Ed Beard, Women's and Men's head coaches of the Fighting Illinois golf teams, have a string of championships and accomplishments to their names. They bring their expertise to the camp to enable youngsters to become more effective on the golf course. The curriculum integrates proper fundamentals with the correct attitude, good sportsmanship and concentration. Classes with 6:1 student/teacher ratio include videotaping for replay and analysis, sessions on rules and etiquette, on-course instruction and tournament-play by age and ability.

Includes round the clock supervision by coaches and summer housing staff, residence hall lodging (2/room, 5 nights), 15 meals, swimming and putt-putt. Located 2½ hours from Chicago, five minutes from Champagne.

■ Practice and play on University of Illinois golf facilities at Savoy and its 18-hole "Blue" course.

INDIANA

BLOOMINGTON

Sam Carmichael's Junior Golf School

Indiana University

Director: Sam Carmichael

Four 5-day sessions, June; $550, 5th year

Two sessions for boys, two sessions for girls; ages 10-17, limited to 50

Info and registration: Sam Carmichael's Junior Golf School, Indiana University, Assembly Hall, Bloomington, IA 47405; 812 855-7950

Indiana Women's Golf coach for nine years and Men's coach and Golf Director since 1989, Sam Carmichael knows his way around coaching young people and making certain that learning golf is fun. His staff is comprised of PGA and LPGA members, high school coaches, and members of the Indiana golf team who act as counselors and maintain round the clock supervision. Golfers are grouped according to age and playing ability. Instruction is concentrated on the fundamentals with on-course instruction stressing course management. Includes video analysis and monitoring.

Five nights accommodations in a nearby sorority house. Includes all meals and golf fees; recreational swimming at Indiana's Olympic size outdoor pool, evening lectures and weight training. Transfers to Bloomington Airport or bus depot with advance notice.

■ Championship IU Golf Course; full swing instruction at IU's 10-acre driving range; short game teaching on five practice areas and greens.

CULVER

Culver Summer Specialty Camps

Culver Military Academy

Director: Frederick D. Lane; Pro: Johnny Meyer

One 2-week session, August; $875, 20th year
Coed, ages 11-16, limited to 50

Info and registration: The Culver Educational Foundation, P.O. Box 138, Culver
IN 46511; 800 221-2020

Johnny Meyer, contributing editor of GOLF Magazine, brings his own extended
coaching staff from Monroe, Louisiana to the impressive colonial-style campus of
Culver Military Academy, for a concentrated, two-week, specialized golf program.
Golf is one of the school's ten educational/sports opportunities which range from
SCUBA diving to sailing to golf. Instruction is personalized, with a 5:1 student/
teacher ratio and a curriculum stressing fundamentals, attitude, sportsmanship,
etiquette, and course management. Five hours daily instruction utilizes videography
and still photography, drills, intramural competition and on-course training.

Students are housed in 60, A-frame, cedar cabins on Culver's campus and experience a virtual paradise of extracurricular recreation: movies, dances, crafts,
ice skating, socials, non-instructional athletics, bonfires, swimming and many
other pursuits. Mandatory non-denominational Sunday chapel (Friday Jewish
services/Sunday Catholic mass). Transfers to O'Hare Field, Chicago, and South
Bend Airport.

◾ 9-hole course with practice facility on campus. Advanced golfers travel to nearby
18-hole courses.

INDIANAPOLIS

FCA Junior Golf Camps (Fellowship of Christian Athletes)

Eagle Creek Golf Course, 5-day program
Info: FCA, 904 273-9541. See page 135 for programs and methods.

PLYMOUTH

United States Golf Academy

Swan Lake Golf Resort
Juniors under 16 accepted with a parent or guardian
Info: 800 582-7539 or 219 935-5680. See page 38 for programs and methods.

W·EST LAFAYETTE

Purdue Boys' Golf Camp - Purdue Girls' Golf Camp

Purdue University

Directors: Joe Campbell and Susan Stump

One 5-day session of each camp, Sun-Thu, June; $270, commuter $205, 17th year
Boys/girls, grades 5 through 12 (graduated high school seniors not eligible), limited to 50-80

Info and registration: Purdue University, 1586 Stewart Center, Room 110, West
Lafayette, IN 47907; 317 494-3216.

Purdue Boys' Golf Camp is led by Purdue's veteran head coach, Joe Campbell. The Girl's counterpart camp is headed by PGA, Class A member and Purdue golf coach, Susan Stump. They draw their staff from the university's athletic department, supported by high school coaches, top amateur athletes and qualified counselors. In classes limited to 8:1 student teacher ratio, juniors progress through five teaching stations focusing on all shots. Provides on-course training and competition. Parents and friends of campers are invited to attend closing awards ceremony.

Camps provide four nights lodging and all meals in Owen Hall, close to all Purdue's athletic facilities. Offers handball, squash, swimming, basketball, etc. Program is fully supervised.

■ Two 18-hole courses.

IOWA

Cyclone Country Golf Camp
Iowa State University
Director: Dale Anderson
Two 6-day sessions, June; $425, 24th year,
Coed, ages 11-to beginning high school seniors, limited to 80
Info and registration: P.O. Box 1995, Ames, IA 50010; 515 232-3999
Dale Anderson, dean of the Big Eight Golf Coaches, calls on some of Iowa's best known academic coaches to train junior golfers. Their goal is to teach fundamentals and techniques and to emphasize sportsmanship, a winning attitude and course management – all keys to golfing success. Daily instruction with 3-4:1 student/teacher ratio, stop action photos, on-course playing lessons and evening golf activities.

Five nights dorm accommodations, cafeteria-style food "and plenty of it."

■ Veenker Memorial Golf Course, rated fourth best course in Iowa, and the ISU range.

Cyclone Golf Academy
Iowa State University
Director: Julie Manning
One 5-day session, July; $299, 4th year
Coed, ages 10-beginning high school seniors
Info and registration: Cyclone Golf Academy, Strange Rd., Ames, IA 50011
515 294-6727
Under Julie Manning, head women's golf coach at ISU, head pro at Veenker Memorial Golf Course, and 1990-91 Big Eight Coach-of-the-Year, the school teaches individual techniques and fundamentals, as well as sportsmanship and the development of a winning attitude. A full schedule of instruction, play and activities is

planned daily. Coach Manning and the entire camp staff live in with campers in dorm lodging (4 nights), providing a secure environment. Three meals daily provided by ISU Food Service. Tuition includes all golf fees, evening snacks, swing analysis photos, and all recreation.

 Veenker Memorial Golf Course and the ISU range and practice center.

C E D A R   F A L L S

Iowa Section PGA Junior Golf Academy

University of Northern Iowa
Director: Kirk Stanzel
One 4-day session, June; $340, 13th year
Coed, ages 12-17 (high school graduates ineligible)
Info and registration: Golf Academy, PGA of America, Iowa Section, 1930 St. Andrews, N.E., Cedar Rapids, IA 52402; 319 378-9142

Iowa Section PGA professionals provide innovative teaching according to the newest research, in classes with a 4:1 student/teacher ratio. Includes video analysis, daily playing lessons and competitions supervised by PGA pros. Choice of evening recreation and educational programs. Fully supervised dorm lodging (4 nights), cafeteria meal program, PGA mementos and color group photo.

Pheasant Ridge Golf Course

I O W A   C I T Y

Iowa Summer Sports Camps

University of Iowa, Iowa City, IA
Directors: Diane Thomason and Lynn Blevins
One 5-day session, Sun-Thu, June; $220, commuter $170, 19th year
Coed, ages 10-18
Info and registration: University of Iowa Sports Camps, 216 Field House, Iowa City, Iowa 52242; 319 335-9714

Golf is one of dozens of sports camps offered by UI throughout the summer, with each one led by people tops in their field. The goal of the golf program is to expose young athletes to the fundamentals of the sound golf swing and to introduce them to the skills needed to be effective and successful. The camp is not only productive but enjoyable, with students divided into small groups for on-range and on-course instruction. Includes competitions, group meetings and discussion.

Facilities of the University are available, including the Field House Pool, and there is camaraderie among the many groups at the various sports camps on campus. Four nights lodging in supervised residence halls (2/room); cafeteria meals, evening movies and recreational sports. Students may choose sessions in other sports and attend several weeks in tandem. (Add $50 for three days and nights bridging the various programs). Includes transfers to Cedar Rapids Municipal Airport.

South Finkbine Golf Course, the Hawkeye's own 18-hole facility.

It is a big responsibility to oversee youngsters on a campus or in a resort. Junior golfers must abide by the rules and regulations laid down by staff and by the conventions of golf etiquette. It is likely that youngsters who repeatedly misbehave will be sent home at the discretion of the director.

KANSAS

LAWRENCE

Girls' Jayhawk Golf Camp
University of Kansas
Director: Jerry Waugh
One 5-day session, July; $425, commuter $375, 12th year
Girls, ages 7-18 (high school graduates ineligible), limited to 35-40
Info and registration: Girls Jayhawk Golf Camp, Inc., 3906 W. 10th Circle, Lawrence, KA 66049; 913 842-1907

University of Kansas Women's Golf Coach Jerry Waugh heads a PGA team skilled in coaching junior girls. The curriculum emphasizes fundamentals and shot making, with on-course training focused on good management, etiquette, specialty shots and rules. Youngsters are introduced to what it takes to play competitively. Classes limited to 5:1 student/teacher ratio with ample coaching for even beginner golfers. Video swing analysis and take-home tape.

Fully supervised program provides 5 nights room and board in Ellsworth Hall. Evening recreation and golf seminars. Located 35 miles west of Kansas City, 20 miles east of Topeka.

■ Alvamar Golf Course combines four championship, 9-hole courses: Jayhawk, Quail Creek, Hidden Valley and Sunflower, plus the Orchards, a 9-hole executive course. Alvamar, named best maintained course in the U.S., is host to the Kansas Open and others.

LAWRENCE

Jayhawk Golf Camp
University of Kansas, Lawrence
Director: Ross Randall
Three 5-day sessions, June; $430, commuter $360, 14th year
Boys, ages 10-18 (high school graduates ineligible)
Info and registration: Ross Randall Golf Camp, Inc., 2104 Inverness Dr., Lawrence KA, 66047; 913 842-1907 or 913 842-1714

Sectioned by ability, junior golfers receive full-time golf instruction from a team of qualified instructors led by Ross Randall, golf coach of the University of Kansas, named 1989 Big Eight Coach of the Year. Convinced that good early instruction stays with a golfer forever, Randall's program stresses proper fundamentals, shot-making, rules, etiquette and golf judgement. Includes video analysis and take-home tape, on-course training, evening sessions, end of week tournament and awards. Fully supervised program provides five nights dormitory lodging and meals. Located 35 miles west of Kansas City, 20 miles east of Topeka.

■ See Alvamar Golf Club in previous listing.

OVERLAND PARK
The Phil Ritson Golf School
Deer Creek Golf Club
Juniors admitted accompanied by an adult.
Info: 800 624-4653. See page 57 for programs and methods.

KENTUCKY

LOUISVILLE
Kentucky Section PGA Junior Golf Academy
University of Louisville and University of Kentucky at Lexington

Two 3-day sessions, two sites; $300
Coed, ages 11-18, limited to 40

Session #1: University of Louisville, Shelby Campus; Persimmon Ridge Golf Club, Louisville, June

Session #2: University of Kentucky; Man O' War Golf Learning Center, Lexington, July

Info and registration: Kentucky Section PGA Junior Golf Academy, P.O. Box 18396, Louisville, KY 40261; 502 499-7255

Separate staffs of PGA professionals instruct students on two University campuses. Curriculum is detailed and thorough, touching on every aspect of the game. Ample staff insures 3:1 student/teacher ratio; provides video analysis, on-course training, lectures on rules and etiquette, tournaments and awards. Area golf celebrities make guest appearances to discuss golf as a career.

Programs are fully supervised with one counselor for every 10 students. Three nights housing in university dorms, 2/room, with separate floors for boys and girls; cafeteria meals. Take-home gift, photo, workbook, personal videotape.

■ Both programs feature professional practice facilities and 18-hole courses.

MURRAY
Murray State University Golf School
Murray State University
Director: Buddy Hewitt
Two 5-day sessions; $325, commuter $225, 11th year

Coed, ages 10-17, limited to 40

Info and registration: Murray State University, Community Education Programs, 1 Murray St., Murray State University, Murray, KY 42071
502 762-4150, or 502 762-2187

Thirty-three years as Murray State's golf coach equips Buddy Hewitt to deliver quality golf education to juniors. Program covers all aspects and include six hours daily instruction, on-course playing lessons, video analysis and tournaments, in a relaxed setting. Early evening free play, golf movies and swimming. Five nights accommodations (2/room) in air-conditioned residence halls; cafeteria meals, full supervision.

■ 18-hole, 6,700-yard, championship Miller Memorial Golf Course provides two huge putting greens, a 300-yard, two-tier practice range and a 90-yard pitch shot area with green and sand trap.

LOUISIANNA

BATON ROUGE

Southern Junior Golf Academy

Louisiana State University, Baton Rouge

Director: Britt Harrison

One 6-day session, June; $450, commuter $350, 9th year
Coed, ages 11-17

Info and registration: Southern Junior Golf Academy, 4008 Irvine St., Baton Rouge, LA 70808; 504 383-8714

Britt Harrison, three-time All-American and LSU's Men's Golf Coach, heads a teaching team of PGA and LPGA professionals, augmented by LSU golfers as counselors. Students receive instruction in the fundamentals and engage in competition according to skill level. Instructors insure that golf learning is enjoyable with age and skill-appropriate competitions. Parents and friends invited to closing awards presentation.

Five nights lodging (2/room) in air-conditioned Broussard Hall, the university's athletic dorm. Cafeteria meals. Program is fully supervised. Includes off-course recreation: swimming, basketball and tennis. Transfers to and from Baton Rouge Municipal Airport.

■ LSU Golf Course with acclaimed practice complex.

> *Golf camps are exceedingly casual, but you may want to pack a tee shirt with a collar for tournament day. Include a swimsuit, pool towel, extra sneakers and a hat. Many schools present golfers with a tee shirt and cap or visor in a souvenir gift pack.*

MAINE

HARRISON

Camp Wigwam

Bear Pond Rd., Harrison, ME 04040; 207 583-2300
Director: Robert Strauss

7-week summer camp, June-August; $4,250, 83rd year
Boys, ages 7-17

Info and registration: (winter headquarters) 7111 Park Heights Ave., #812, Baltimore, MD 21215; 410-358-4466

Located on the shores of Bear Lake near the New Hampshire border, Wigwam is a traditional Maine boys camp where junior boys can concentrate on golf. The game is a mandatory activity for all campers, with two on-site collegiate golfers providing instruction. A professional instructor provides one day/week personalized teaching to motivated juniors. Practice is centered at a driving range on the camp grounds. Students may spend up to four afternoons of on-course play every week at two local courses, with Fridays reserved for intermural competition with other camps. Wigwam stresses participation and enjoyment of golf and extends a wide range of other instructional and recreational opportunities to campers.

KINGFIELD

Sugarloaf Junior Golf Camp

The Sugarloaf Inn
Mountainside Rd., Sugarloaf Mountain, Carrabassett Valley, ME 04947
800 THE-LOAF

Director: Scott Hoisington

Two 5-day sessions, June-July; $425
Coed, 7-18, limited to 20

Info: Sugarloaf Golf Club & School, Rte. 27, Box 5000, Kingfield, ME 04947; See page 70 for further details.

Five hours daily golf instruction by Sugar Loaf's accomplished golf staff, all with college degrees in education. Flexible programs provide video analysis, on-course playing lessons, unlimited use of practice facility, tournament with prizes.

Fully supervised program offers tennis, hiking, swimming, canoeing, mountain biking, health and fitness club – or all golf. Five nights lodging and meals in a dorm which houses the Inn's winter ski program. Located 3³/₄ hours drive from Montreal or Boston.

■ Designed by Robert Trent Jones, Jr., Sugarloaf Golf Course has been rated by Golf Digest as #1 course in Maine for four years in a row and one of the top 75 resort courses in the U.S.

NAPLES

Camp Skylemar

R.R. 1, Box 508, Naples, ME 04055; 207 693-6414
Directors: Herbert Blumenfeld and Lee Horowitz

7-week summer camp, $4,500; 4-week session $2,600; June-Aug, 45th year
Boys, ages 8-16, 140 campers

Info and registration: 7900 Stevenson Rd., Baltimore, MD 21208; 410 653-2480
(winter headquarters)

A traditional summer camp with a staff hand-picked for proficiency and as strong, mature
role models. Youngsters may major in golf, electing to spend instructional and recreational time on the camp's 6-hole course. More advanced golfers play at nearby Naples
Country Club. Campers, 14+, may elect to play daily.

> *Golf camps attract a wealth of talent – both campers and coaches.*
> *Young golfers who aspire to competitive collegiate golf often come to*
> *the attention of well-known coaches during summer golf programs.*

RAYMOND

Camp Nashoba North

198 Raymond Hill Rd., Raymond, ME 04071; 207 655-7170

Director: Sarah Seward Foley

8-week summer camp, $3,395; 6-week session $2,895; 4-week session $2,095
Coed, ages 10-15, 160 campers

Info: Nashoba Rd., Littleton, MA 01460; 800 448-0136 or 508 486-8236

Campers with basic golfing ability may elect golf as a major at this traditional summer
camp. Instruction, 3 days a week, at the camp's new two-hole practice course overlooking Crescent Lake. Fairways stretch 500 feet. Each hole has a 35-foot green,
with bunkers and practice areas. Proficient golfers play nearby nine holes at Bridgeton
Country Club, twice a week; includes all golf fees.

MARYLAND

COLLEGE PARK

Ronnie Scales Golf Camp

University of Maryland

Director: Ronnie Scales

One 5-day session; $260, commuter only, 21st year
Coed, ages 10-18, limited to 40

Info and registration: Ronnie Scales Golf Camp, University of Maryland Golf Course,
College Park, MD 20742; 301 403-4299

Personal daily instruction by University of Maryland PGA professionals under the
direction of UM's head pro, Ronnie Scales. Youngsters are encouraged to have a great
time while learning sound fundamentals. Provides 8:1 student/teacher ratio, individual videotaped instruction, on-course playing lessons and a full range of competitive activities: putting contests, sand contests, camp divisional championships.

■ 18 hole university course.

MASSACHUSETTS

BERNARDSTON

Crumpin-Fox Junior Camps

Crumpin-Fox Golf Club
Parmenter Rd., Bernardston, MA 01337; 413 648-9101
Director: Ron Beck

Two 3-day sessions, June; $160; members $135; commuter only
Ten-week program, Tues mornings, June-Aug; $75, commuter only; members $40
Coed, ages 8-15, limited to 24

Representing a sincere and serious commitment to young golfers, Crumpin-Fox has developed a program promoting maturity, good habits and sound values. Students are encouraged to derive satisfaction from improvement and to view golf learning as an educational and building process in their development. Concepts of fairness, perseverance, self control and healthy competition are taught, along with grip, stance and aim. Curriculum replicates Adult Golf Institute (see page 73).

■ Acclaimed Robert Trent Jones, Jr. course with complete learning facility simulating every golf problem and opportunity.

STOW

Stow Acres Introductory Junior Clinic

Stow Acres Country Club
58 Randall Rd., Stow, MA 01775; 508 568-9090.

3-evenings, Tu-Thu, 4-7 pm, selected dates, June-Aug; commuter only; $125
Coed, ages under 17

Info: See Stow Acres Country Club, page 77, for methods and details.

Nine hours instruction designed to get juniors started with the correct fundamentals to build a lifelong foundation. Includes introduction to all shots, club selection, rules and etiquette. Students are familiarized with warm up procedures, practice techniques and swing drills.

MICHIGAN

ANN ARBOR

University of Michigan Golf Camp of Champions

University of Michigan
Director: Jim Carras

Four 5-day sessions, June & July; $425; commuter $300, 14th year
Coed, ages 12-17, limited to 42

Info and registration: University of Michigan Golf Camp of Champions,
1000 S. State St., Ann Arbor, MI 48109; 313 998-7239

Jim Carras, Michigan's Men's Golf coach for ten years, leads a PGA coaching staff along with members of the University's golf teams in providing every participant with quality instruction, giving them the opportunity to develop skills and confidence. In classes with 5-7:1 student/teacher ratio, attention is paid to pre-shot routines and principles, laws of ball flight, grip and aim, shot-making and a full range of golf techniques. Includes daily on-course play and evening instruction.

Five nights lodging in West and South Quad residence halls; thoughtfully prepared cafeteria meals; lunches at the course. Program is fully supervised and includes nightly activities in residence halls.

■ The renown 18-hole, Alister MacKenzie University of Michigan Golf Course and practice facilities.

BIG RAPIDS

Ferris Golf Camp
Ferris State University
Director: Ron English

Two 5-day sessions, June & Aug; $410; commuter $310 (Premium for early payment)
Coed, ages 12-17, 20th year

Info and registration: Lifelong Learning, Alumni Bldg. 226, Ferris State University, 410 Oak St., Big Rapids, MI 49307; 616 592-3808

Named 1992 PGA Northern Chapter Teacher of the Year, Ron English has put together a teaching team of PGA pros and students from the university's golf management program. Classes are geared toward students of all levels, with a maximum 8:1 student/teacher ratio. Each player receives individual as well as group instruction, video analysis, on-course instruction.

Five nights accommodations in a modern residence hall; includes all meals, 24-hour supervision.

■ Katke Golf Course is home turf for FSU's Professional Golf Management program and for the golfing Bulldogs. A par 72, it occupies 145 acres and spans over 6,700 yards.

EAST LANSING

The Ken Horvath Golf Camp
Michigan State University
Director: Ken Horvath

Three 6-day sessions, Sun-F, July and Aug; $490 (add $75 for Saturday and Sunday to link two sessions); commuter $390, 23rd year
Coed, ages 13-17 (high school seniors and graduates ineligible)

Info and registration: Michigan State University, Sports Camps, 211 Jenison Field House, East Lansing, MI 48824; 517 355-5264

The MSU Spartans have returned to a position of power under Ken Horvath, now in his fourth year as head golf coach. He is in his 10th year heading MSU's junior golf camp, providing an atmosphere in which young golfers develop and refine their golfing skills and experience the correct attitudes needed to improve. Instruction by PGA pros and collegiate and high school coaches covers all points of the game and includes age- and skill-appropriate competition. Parents invited to view the concluding round of the camp's 36-hole tournament and awards ceremony.

Five nights lodging in Wonders Hall. According to campers: "Meals are excellent!"

The program is fully supervised.

◼ All instruction and play on MSU's 36-hole Forest Akers Golf Course, an acclaimed collegiate golf facility. Includes two driving ranges and ample short game practice areas.

MINNESOTA

BLOOMINGTON

Rob Hary, Jr. Golf School

Minnesota Valley Country Club
6300 Auto Club Rd., Bloomington, MN 55438
612 884-1744

Director: Rob Hary

Three 4-morning sessions, June & July; $90, commuter only, 15th year
Coed, ages 8-18

PGA golf pros and their assistants rotate students through assigned stations: driving, chipping, putting, pitching and bunker play, providing personalized teaching in a group setting. Instruction touches on rules, etiquette, strategy and equipment and emphasizes positive attitudes of honesty, fairness and good sportsmanship.

BREEZY POINT

Breezy Point Junior Golf Institute

Breezy Point Resort Golf Club, Breezy Point, MN 56472
800 328-2284   218 562-7811

Director: Jim McElhaney

Four 5-day sessions, June-July; $495
Coed, ages 8-18

Info: Breezy Point, 800 328-2284. See page 79 for methods and further details.

Instruction is directed at building a solid foundation for a lifetime of enjoyable golfing. Program provides 4½ hours range instruction daily followed by on-course training, with classes maintained at a strict 4:1 student/teacher ratio. A staff of five PGA pros oversees practice and emphasizes fundamentals. Provides full supervision, five nights resort lodging, all meals and varied recreation: movies, group tennis lessons, fishing, swimming, game room.

◼ Two 18-hole courses, Traditional and Championship, with learning facilities.

COON RAPIDS

Minnesota PGA Junior Golf Academy

Five golf clubs throughout Minnesota host programs. At:

Mankato Golf Club (south-central MN); Baker National Golf Club, Medina (Twin Cities metro area); Moorhead Country Club (northwest MN); Bemidji Town & Country Club (north central MN); Bunker Hills Country Club (Twin Cities metro area)

Directors: Bill Israelson and Peter Krause

Five 2-day commuter sessions*, June-July; $125, 16th year
Coed 13-18, for students with some experience, limited to 25 per session

Info and registration: Minnesota PGA Junior Golf Academy, Bunker Hills Golf Club, Hwy. 242 and Foley Blvd., Coon Rapids, MN 55448; 612 754-0820

Academy directors Bill Israelson and Peter Krause have had distinguished careers on the Tour and in teaching. They have a uniform teaching philosophy and a staff devoted to training youth. Students grouped according to skill, with a 6:1 student/teacher ratio for comprehensive instruction. Instructors utilize the latest teaching aids, including video analysis, to demonstrate principles of the swing and identify areas for improvement. Includes on-course instruction, putting tournament and competitive special events. Includes all golf fees and lunches.

*Primarily a commuter program, but the school will help out-of-towners find hosts.

■ Practice and play at five sponsoring courses.

MINNEAPOLIS

Minnesota Golf Instructional Camp

University of Minnesota at Minneapolis and St. Paul
Director: John Means

One 5-day session, June; $335; commuter $265, 12th year
Coed, ages 8-18 (high school graduates ineligible)

Info and registration: Golf Instructional Camp, U of Minnesota, 3812 Moccasin Ct., Burnsville, MN 55337; 612 625-5863.

Successful coach at the U.S. Military Academy at West Point for eleven years, John Means now turns his attention to Minnesota's "Gophers" and to the summer golf academy. Coach Means makes every day a new learning experience. Proficient instructors and members of the University's golf team train and supervise. Includes daily instruction, competition, practice and play; evening lectures on rules, etiquette and equipment.

The facilities of the Minneapolis campus are called into play to feed and house (5 nights, 2-3/room) participants. Nominal fee for air, rail or bus pick-up and drop-off.

■ 18-hole championship course at the Les Bolstad campus (St. Paul) of the University of Minnesota, with complete practice facility and par 3 training course.

If you have difficulty finding equipment for your left-handed junior golfer, have clubs fabricated by a club fitter. Often custom clubs are better and no more costly than those in sporting goods shops. And the club fitter may be able to extend the life of your youngster's set by lengthening the shafts and enlarging the grips as your golfer grows.

MISSOURI

OXFORD

FCA Junior Golf Camps (Fellowship of Christian Athletes)
University of Mississippi, 5-day program
Info: FCA, 904 273-9541. See page 135 for programs and methods.

MISSISSIPPI

UNIVERSITY

Ole Miss Golf Camp
University of Mississippi
Director: Larry Wagster

Two 5-day sessions, June; $370, commuter $320, 20th year
Coed, grade 10 to rising high school seniors, limited to 30

Info and registration: Ole Miss Golf Camp, U of Mississippi, Center for Public Service and Continuing Studies, P.O. Box 879, University, MS 38677; 601 232-7241

A former commissioned officer in the Marines and for 21 years a special agent of the FBI, Larry Wagster is an acclaimed golfer and head golf coach of Ole Miss. He applies his varied skills in a program which couples teaching sound golfing principles with toning and strengthening golf muscles. Organized according to proficiency, golfers receive group instruction on every aspect of the game.

Five nights housing in Ole Miss dorms, cafeteria meals, 24-hour supervision. Campers have access to the modern Ole Miss Student Union.

◼ Ole Miss Golf Club, a championship layout with large practice area and indoor teaching areas.

MONTANA

MISSOULA

Western Montana Junior Golf Academy
University of Montana
Director: Robert J. Veroulis

One 5-day session, June; $275, 7th year
Coed, ages 14-18, limited to 50

Info and registration: Western Montana Junior Golf Academy, P.O. Box 1183, Bigfork, MT 59911; 406 837-7302.

Directed by the head professional of Eagle Bend Golf Club in Bigfork, this camp is under the auspices of the Western Montana PGA Chapter. Leading area pros introduce new golfers to the game and sharpen the skills of those more experienced. Renown author and teacher, Carey Mumford, is guest instructor. The goal of the school is to establish a sound base on which to build a future of golfing pleasure. In skill groups, students receive comprehensive individual instruction on all aspects of the game, including elements of competitive golf. Instructors make use of videotaping and learning aids to teach the principles of the swing and pinpoint students' strengths and weaknesses.

Includes five-nights lodging in university residence halls, three meals daily, a kit of accessories and materials, extracurricular recreation and full supervision.

■ Missoula Country Club, Larchmont Golf Course and Highlands Golf Club lend their courses and learning facilities for practice and play.

NEBRASKA

LINCOLN

Nebraska Junior Golf Academy

North Forty Golf Course

One 3-day session, June; $285, commuter only, 1st year
Coed, ages 12-17, limited to 24

Info and registration: Nebraska Junior Golf Academy, Nebraska P.G.A., 9301 Firethorn Lane, Lincoln, NE 68520; 800 743-3383 or 489-7760

Golf is taken seriously in this commuter program, with heavy hitters doing the full-time teaching: Mike Cormell, 1991 Nebraska PGA Teacher of the Year; Rick Galliland, teaching pro for 18 years; Jerry Fisher, PGA pro and former Section champ, plus a dozen pros, part-time. Provides 17 hours instruction in classes limited to 4:1 student/teacher ratio and 36 holes of golf with the pros. Unlimited use of practice facility, lunch, gifts and tournament awards.

■ 9-hole, par 3, North Forty Golf Course with practice facilities.

NEW HAMPSHIRE

AMHERST

Exceller Programs Golf Schools,

Ponemah Green Golf Course
Junior Clinics and Learning Center Junior Membership program
See page 126 for details.

HUDSON

World Cup Golf School

World Cup Driving Range
9 River Rd., Hudson, NH 03051; 603 598-3838.

3-day junior camp (Tu-Th), total of 9 hours, summer; $30, commuter only,
Coed, ages 7-17

Info: See details of adult programs, page 82.

Most camps provide airport, bus depot, and rail station transfers at no cost or for a nominal fee. Notify the school well advance of arrival.

NEW MEXICO

ALBUQUERQUE

New Mexico Junior Golf School

University of New Mexico

Director: Henry Sandles

Two 4-day sessions for commuters, M-Thu, June; mornings for beginners, afternoons for beginner-intermediates; $45, 8th year

Coed, ages 7-17, 300 students

Info and registration: New Mexico Junior Golf School, University of New Mexico, Albuquerque, NM 87131; 505 277-4546

Sponsored in conjunction with Coca-Cola, the school brings together eight PGA, LPGA pros and coaches and a host of assistants and volunteers to teach youngsters the fundamentals of golf, rules, etiquette, care of the golf course and to start them on a lifetime of golf enjoyment and learning; 12:1 student/teacher ratio. Offers lunch, clubs, Coca-Cola tee shirts and lots of enthusiasm.

■ Complete UNM practice facility with three practice holes, two par 4s and a par 3.

SOCCORO

Sun Country Section PGA Junior Golf Academy

New Mexico Tech University

Director: Russ Moore

One 5-day session, June; $400, 13th year

Coed, ages 10-17, limited to 50

Info and registration: Sun Country PGA, Mountain Run Center, 5850 Eubank N.E., Suite B-72, Albuquerque, NM 87111; 505 271-1442

The goal of the academy is to assemble a topflight team of PGA instructors from the Sun Country Section of the PGA and to provide an atmosphere of discipline and intensity in which to teach the essentials of golf to young people. Instruction is geared toward beginning and intermediate golfers. Provides group clinics and exhibitions, videography with take-home tape and educational materials. Includes tournament activities, demonstrations and evening films and classes on course strategy, rules and etiquette. Morning classes followed by on-course training.

Five nights dormitory lodging and dining; full supervision and use of campus facilities: pool, tennis courts, weight room, Nautilus equipment, racquetball. Located 90 miles south of Albuquerque.

■ New Mexico Tech's 6,600-yard, 18-hole golf course, site of the New Mexico Open, Hilton Open and Sun Country Junior Championship. Practice facility.

Bring your tennis racquet and balls. There will be plenty of "down" time for recreation other than golf.

NEW YORK

KIAMESHA LAKE

The Concord Golf School

The Concord Resort Hotel
Accepts juniors ages 12+ in 4-day program with an adult. See page 85 for details.

MONTICELLO

Kutsher's Sports Academy

Monticello, NY 12701
800 724-0238   203 454-4991   914 794-5400
Director: Bob Trupin; Director of Golf: Joel Schwartz
8 week summer camp: June-Aug; $4295 (4 weeks, June-July, $2,445; 4 weeks, July-Aug, $2,195), 26th year
Coed, ages 7-17, total of 500 campers

Kutcher's is dedicated to the personal and athletic development of each and every camper. Juniors may elect to major in golf at this professional sports camp with acclaimed facilities and highly developed programs in dozens of sports. The powerful golf instructional team is headed by Joel Schwartz, now in his 17th season at Kutcher's. Staff act as strong role models, emphasizing good sportsmanship, fairness and a winning attitude. With guidance, campers select their own sports programs in 2-week increments, choosing from among the many offerings. Those majoring in golf receive two hours daily instruction plus on-course training, play, and tournament activities.

Campers bunk with contemporaries, grouped by age, gender and length of stay. Camp offers indoor and outdoor facilities for every team and individual sport, leisure areas, fitness center, lake and pool swimming, canteen, ice skating rink, a theater center, social program. Located in the Catskills, one hour from NYC.

■ Instruction centers on a 32-station range and the 7,157 Kutcher's Country Club Golf Course, with an instructor to each three students for on-course training (nominal additional charge for golf fees).

POUGHKEEPSIE

Falcon Youth Golf Camp

Dutchess Community College
Director: Richard L. Skimin

Two 10-day programs, June; $137, commuter only; coed; 8-10 am for ages 8-11, 10 am to noon for ages 12-18; 13th year

Players Golf Camp, 5-days, July, for juniors with two years Falcon experience; 8 am to 1 pm; $262, commuter only, limited to 16

Info and registration: Falcon Youth Golf Camp, 53 Rendell Rd., Poughkeepsie, NY 12601; 914 471-4500

To introduce young golfers to the game and instill fundamentals and good golfing habits. Ten-day program provides instruction on all aspects; employs videotaping and analysis, drills and teaching of effective practice routines.

Players Golf Camp, for golfers with some experience, provides instruction and on-course training with a 4:1 student/teacher ratio. Curriculum stresses course management, club selection and shotmaking.

■ Poughkeepsie Golf Range and various area courses.

SMITHTOWN

Mike Hebron's Boys and Girls Golf Camp

Smithtown Landing Golf Club
495 Landing, Ave., Smithtown, NY 11787
516 360-7618

One-day/week, total of 8 sessions, July-Aug; $195, commuter only, 15th year
Coed, ages 8-16, limited to 60

PGA Master Professional, Mike Hebron, accomplished golf teacher and author, is assisted by PGA pros experienced in teaching youngsters. Students are grouped according to skill (beginner, intermediate and advanced) and progress upward in specific categories (putting, chipping, pitching, fairway irons, sand shots, driving, etiquette, rules) in the course of the summer. Films and videotapes monitor each student. Group and personal recognition for achievement. Includes all instruction, green and practice fees.

NEW ROCHELLE

Pepsi Met PGA Jr. Golf School

Westchester Country Club - Marrott's Wind Watch Resort & Golf Club

One 3-day session at Westchester Country Club (North and Purchase Sts., Rye, NY 10580; 914 967-6000), 9 am-1 pm, limited to 60

One 2-day session at Marrott's Wind Watch Resort & Golf Club (1717 Vanderbilt Motor Pkwy, Hauppauge, NY 11788; 516 232-9800), 9 am-3 pm, limited to 50

Both sessions: coed, ages 9-17; July, commuter only; $175 each session ($150 for members of MET PGA Jr. Golf Assoc; both schools: $250), 19th year

Info and registration: Pepsi Met PGA Jr. Golf School, PO Box 268, Wykagyl Station, New Rochelle, NY 10804; 914 235-0312

Underwritten by Pepsi-Cola, the schools are staffed by instructors and apprentices from the PGA's New York Metropolitan section. For golfers of all abilities; 5-6:1 student/teacher ratio with three instructors at each of five different stations: chipping, half swing, full swing, pitching and putting. Intramurals keep the game fun, while drills, videography and supervised practice insure learning. Includes Pepsi and lunch, awards luncheon on final day.

Most University-based programs require campers to supply twin-bed sheets and a pillow case (pillow, too, in some instances), a blanket, towels and soap. Bring lots of tee shirts. Swapping is big.

NORTH CAROLINA

ARAPAHOE

Camp Sea Gull Golf Camp and Tennis Camp for Boys and Girls

Rt. 65, Box 1, Arapahoe, NC 28510; 919 249-1111

Director: Jim Hamilton

One 6-day session, Aug; $450, limited to 40

Coed, ages 9-16

YMCA-affiliated camp offers concentrated golf training by professional athletes and counselors with high professional standards and a special regard for teaching youth and promoting Christian values. Director Jim Hamilton, former co-captain of the University of Maryland team and now head pro at Oak Ridge Golf Center in Raleigh, NC, stresses character development and good sportsmanship. Both are emphasized in 6-8 hours daily individual and group instruction and participation. Schedule encompasses range and classroom sessions, free play, competition, rounds with professionals, seminars and multi-media presentations. Addresses all phases of golf.

Meals served family style in the camp's mess hall. Six-nights lodging in spacious cabins; two live-in counselors in each cabin group. Commercial bus and airport transfers from New Bern, NC; served by US Air and American Airlines.

■ Sea Gull's championship, 18-hole course with Bermuda grass greens and a nine hole, par 3 course at Camp Seafarer, nearby sister camp. Generous practice facility.

BUIES CREEK

Campbell University Golf School

Campbell University

Director John Crooks

One 5-day session; $450, 13th year

Coed, ages 10 through junior year in high school

Info and registration: Campbell University Golf School, Campbell University, P.O. Box 10, Buies Creek, NC 27506

919 893-4111, ext. 2458

A staff of college coaches, professionals and collegiate golf counselors instruct youngsters in all phases of golf in classes with a 4:1 student/teacher ratio. Teaching includes competitive drills, videotapes, films, lectures and tournaments. Daily on-course training and recreational golf.

Accommodations in air-conditioned residence halls, 24-hour supervision, dining hall meals, tennis and swimming. Raleigh-Durham Airport and bus depot transfers provided.

■ Keith Hills Country Club, Campbell's own 18-hole course, provides practice areas and play.

State your roommate preference early. With advance notice, it is likely that you and your buddy will be able to room together.

CHAPEL HILL

Coaches N.C. Golf School

University of North Carolina*

Director: Devon Brouse

Three 5-day sessions, June; $795, 17th year

Coed, ages 11-18, students may enroll for more than one session

*The school is a privately operated sports camp under the sole sponsorship of Devon Brouse Golf, Inc. and not by UNC.

Info and registration: P.O. Box 4402, Chapel Hill, NC 27515; 919 544-4655

North Carolina's Tar Heels have finished in the NCAA's Top 20 for twelve of the last fifteen years and have captured the Atlantic Coast Conference four times. Under Coach Devon Brouse, they placed second at the 1991 NCAA. His camp is imbued with his dedication to strong values and attitudes which are shared by a hand-picked staff of college coaches, PGA pros and UNC team members. The curriculum includes "academic enhancement:" a series of evening seminars on study skills, time and stress management and academic preparations for college golf. Emphasizes fitness, tournament preparation, course strategy, rules, equipment and psychology. Students take home a record of performance and a plan for future improvement.

Four nights lodging and cafeteria meals in air-conditioned Granville Towers. Nearby game room and pool. Includes Raleigh-Durham Airport transfers and discounted fare on U.S. Air and American Airlines.

■ Instruction and play at UNC's Finley Golf Course, host to numerous collegiate tournaments including the 1993 USGA Jr. Amateur Qualifier.

DURHAM

Duke University Golf School

Duke University

Director Rod Myers

Two 5-day sessions, Sat-Thurs, June; $750, 20th year

One session boys only; one coed session, ages 11-17

Info and registration: Duke University Golf School, Duke University, Durham, NC
Rt. 751 at Science Dr., Box 90551, Durham, NC 27708-0551
919 681-2494   919 493-1517

An outstanding staff is credited with Duke Golf School's success with golfers of all levels and abilities. Collegiate golfers serving as counselors reduce the student/teacher ratio to 4:1, resulting in small, homogeneous instructional groups. Full golf program includes daily instruction and play, early evening golf and lectures, strategy sessions, counselor exhibition round. Emphasizes mental aspects, rules and special situations. Students take home a complete instructional tape with their own swing analysis; 18-hole tournament with pizza and watermelon feast. Families welcome at Thursday's closing awards dinner (students may depart Fri am for convenience).

Six nights accommodations in air-conditioned dorms; includes all meals and supervision, swimming, movies.

■ Duke University's Robert Trent Jones-designed golf course and renovated practice range.

JACKSON SPRINGS · PINEHURST AREA

Bertholy-Method Golf Schools

Three-day program, coed, ages 14-20, year round, limited to 6; juniors must be accompanied by an adult; $600 tuition only (does not include Bertholy-Method Book II and swing pipe teaching tool)

Info: See Bertholy-Method Golf Schools, page 91.

PINEHURST

FCA Junior Golf Camps (Fellowship of Christian Athletes)

Pine Needles Lodges and Country Club, 5-day program
Info: FCA, 904 273-9541. See page 135 for programs and methods.

PINEHURST

Pinehurst Junior Golf Advantage Schools

Pinehurst Resort and Country Club
P.O. Box 4000, Pinehurst, NC 28374; 800 927-4653, ext. 8128
Director: Wayne Nooe

Six 5-day sessions, $820; one 5-day Advanced Junior Golf Advantage session (0-15 handicap), $875; June-July, 28th year
Coed, ages 11-17, limited to 48

Info: For further details, see Pinehurst Golf Advantage Schools, page 90 .

According to Wayne Nooe, golf education is not wasted on the young. In fact good early training pays off with a lifetime of enjoyment and appreciation for the game. Pinehurst presents a hands-on instruction program concentrating on fundamentals and proper golf etiquette. Includes instruction, drills, exercises, videotaped analysis, and playing lessons. Six 5-day programs are geared for beginners or as reinforcement for youngsters who already golf. Advanced Junior Golf Advantage School sharpens the skills of 0-15 handicappers and introduces them to the concepts of competitive play.

Five nights supervised accommodations in villas. Resort offers 28 tennis courts, five outdoor pools, three croquet courts, a 200 acre lake for sailing and boating, equestrian sports; gun club with skeet, trap and sporting clays; jogging trails, health club, refined dining.

▣ Seven famous championship courses.

PINEHURST

Pine Needles Youth Golfari™

Pine Needles Lodges and Country Club, Box 88, Pinehurst, NC 28374
919 692-7111
Director: Peggy Kirk Bell

9-day session, July; $1,140, 22 year
Coed, ages 10-18

Info: See page 92 for further details and adult programs.

Owner Peggy Kirk Bell, recognized as one of the five most influential women in golf, is a former LPGA Teacher of the Year and author of "Women's Way to Better

Golf." Her Golfari programs comprise a week of total immersion in golf. Provides nine days of concentrated teaching on all phases of golf, before and after video analysis and graph-check photographs, on-course instruction, friendly competitive events.

Eight nights accommodations (2/room) at the intimate, family-owned vacation spot, serving 140 guests. Includes round the clock supervision by PGA instructors and counselors, all meals, sauna, whirlpool, heated pool, tennis. Airport transfers.

■ A 6,603 yard, Par 71, Donald Ross-design, Pine Needles is the site of upcoming 1996, 51st U.S. Women's Open. Named one of the leading resort courses in the country by Golf Digest. Indoor driving/teaching facility.

RALEIGH

North Carolina State, Wolfpack Golf School

North Carolina State University

Director: Richard Sykes

Starter Day Camp, 5 morning sessions, June; $210, coed, ages 6-11

One 5-day session, June; $650, commuter $375, 5th year
Coed, ages 12-18, limited to 60

Info and registration: North Carolina State, Wolfpack Golf School, 3000 Ballybunion Way, Raleigh, NC 27613; 919 846-1536   919 515-3317

Richard Sykes, three-time Atlantic Coast Conference Coach of the Year, now in his 22nd year as N.C. State Golf Coach, is intent on promoting junior golf and helping to develop the talent of young golfers. His curriculum combines practice, play and fun. School provides individual and group instruction, videotaping, on-course training in strategy and management, rules, psychology, club fitting and tournament preparation.

Five nights lodging and dining in University Towers, an air-conditioned dorm on the N.C. State campus. Students have access to a game room, volleyball area and swimming pool. Coaching staff and counselors supervise round the clock. Round trip Raleigh-Durham Airport transfers for Sunday night arrival and Friday night departure.

■ 18-hole Wildwood Green Golf Club, with a double tee driving range, large short game practice areas, host to numerous tournaments including the U.S. Golf Tour Triangle Classic.

VASS - PINEHURST AREA

Woodlake Total Performance Junior Golf Schools

Woodlake Country Club
150 Woodlake Blvd., P.O. Box 648, Vass, NC 28934
800 334-1126   919 245-4031

Director: Tom Ream

Two 5-day sessions, July; $595; commuter $452, 2nd year
Coed, ages 9-18

Info: See Woodlake Total Performance Golf Schools, page 94.

The school replicates Woodlake's adult programs with the same PGA teaching pros and similar curriculum. Instruction focuses on fundamentals, etiquette and the rules of golf through instruction, drills and exercises. Afternoon playing lessons.

Five nights accommodations in 2-bedroom townhouses, two students/room with a counselor for every four campers; 24-hour supervision. Includes meals at Woodlake Country Club restaurant; swimming, boating, games and movies. Situated in the Sandhills of North Carolina, 20 minutes from Pinehurst and Southern Pines, RT airport transfers from Pinehurst Airport.

■ Instruction and play on Woodlake's 18-hole original Ellis and Dan Maples design. Two playing afternoons at the Southern Pines Country Club and Pinehurst #8 at Pinewild.

W I N S T O N - S A L E M

Jack Lewis Golf Camp*

Wake Forest University

Director: Jack Lewis

Four 2-week sessions, June-July; $1,950 (one week $975), 15th year

Coed, ages 9-18,

*Formerly Jesse Haddock Golf Camp; Coach Emeritus Haddock lectures.

Info and registration: Jack Lewis Golf Camp, Wake Forest University, P.O. Box 7567, Winston-Salem, NC 27109; 919 759-6000

This is a university and a camp where golf is taken seriously. An All-American three times while a student and now head coach at Wake Forest, Jack Lewis has led the "Deacs" to the NCAA twice – and he's still a rookie coach. He fields a winning team of professional instructors with outstanding playing ability and teaching skills. Members of the University team serve as counselors. Golfers are grouped according to age and ability. On and off-course instruction stresses sportsmanship and includes lectures, strategy sessions, videotaping, personal critiques, exhibitions, films and games. Personal, 1:1 attention and evaluation of each student's potential as a collegiate golfer. Guest appearances by golf greats. Final tournament.

Lodging (13 or 14 nights for 2-week session; 6 or 7 nights for 1-week session) in the new air-conditioned Arnold Palmer Dormitory (he's an alumnus), cafeteria meals. Access to tennis, basketball and playing fields.

■ Activities center at the new Haddock Center, one of the nation's premier teaching facilities. Play at 18-hole Tanglewood Golf Course, one of the University's three.

Make golf fun for kids. Play as a family and enroll youngsters in community or club clinics to introduce them to other young golfers. Don't get kids hung up on scoring before they have developed some skills. Keeping score can be discouraging at first.

OHIO

WOOSTER

Fighting Scot Golf Camp
College of Wooster
Director: Bob Nye

Two 5-day sessions, July; $495, 13th year
One session for boys only, one coed, ages 11-17

Info and registration: Fighting Scot Golf Camp, College of Wooster, Wooster, OH 44691; 216 263-2170

Entering his 29th year at the College of Wooster, Coach Bob Nye has molded the soccer and golf teams into perennial powers. His staff of high school and college coaches is augmented by collegiate golfers. Emphasis is placed on the highest principles of athletics and quality instruction. Classes are limited to 5:1 student/teacher ratio; includes video analysis and graph check photos. Closing 18-hole tournament, staff exhibition and contest night. Parents welcome at Friday evening's closing awards banquet.

The entire 320-acre campus is available to campers. Meals and recreation center around the Lowry Center student union and the Armington Physical Education Center, including its pool. Special programs bridge the two sessions for campers attending both.

■ Play and practice at the rolling and demanding L. C. Boles Memorial Golf Course and practice areas, the only course owned by a private college in Ohio.

OKLAHOMA

AFTON

Shangri-La Junior Golf Clinic
Shangri-La Resort
Rte. 3, Hwy 125 S, Monkey Island, Afton, OK 74331
800 331-4060   918 257-4204

Director: Marshall Smith; Head pro: Rick Reed

Two 3-day sessions, June, $650
Coed, ages 10-18, limited to 24

Info: See page 95 for methods and details of resort and golf.

Junior programs replicate Shangri-La's K.I.S.S. Golf Clinics for adults, sharing the same staff and methods. Provides 20 hours instruction, on-course training, tournaments and attentive supervision.

Shangri-La offers a wide range of extracurricular activities in its showcase Recreational Center, including bowling, Nintendo, indoor Olympic sized swimming pool, tennis courts, and much more. Plus outdoor attractions: swimming, fishing, biking and hiking. Fully supervised lodging in resort's Golden Oaks Lodge; hotel dining.

■ Two acclaimed courses with generous practice facilities.

EDMOND

South Central PGA Junior Golf Academy

Oklahoma Central State University

Director: Danny Hickman

One 4-day session, June; $385, 4th year
Coed, ages 11-17, limited to 50

Info and registration: South Central PGA Section, 2745 East Skelly No. 103, Tulsa, OK 74105; 918 742-5672.

Students develop their golf skills and character through the proven PGA training format and goal-setting principles promoted by the PGA staff assembled under the direction of Danny Hickman. Grouped by proficiency, eight students to an instructor, golfers receive comprehensive instruction on every facet of the game, including on-course training. Provides demonstrations, cameo celebrity appearances, group clinics, lectures on course strategy, history, rules, and etiquette. Utilizes video technology and feedback to teach swing principles and to pinpoint students' strengths and weaknesses.

Fully supervised dormitory lodging and meals at Central State University; transportation provided to course. Evening recreation.

■ Kicking Bird Golf Course, the home of past Oklahoma Opens and NCAA championships.

STILLWATER

Mike Holder's Oklahoma State Cowboy Golf Camp

Oklahoma State University

Director: Mike Holder

Two 6-day sessions, June (one week boys, one week coed); $750; two-week session $1,600, 16th year
Ages: 11-17 (high school graduates ineligible)

Info and registration: Mike Holder's Oklahoma State Cowboy Golf Camp, Oklahoma State University, Gallagher-IBA Arena, Stillwater, OK 74078; 405 744-7259

Director Mike Holder has been golf coach at OSU for 19 years, heading the winningest teams in college golf. His camp exposes young golfers to basic and advanced techniques of competitive golf as taught on collegiate and professional levels – and provides a good time doing it. Families are invited to view the camp's final tournament. Five-nights accommodations in air-conditioned, high-rise dorm accommodations, 2/room; "all you can eat" in college dining hall. Airport transfers included between Oklahoma City Airport.

■ 18-hole Lakeside Municipal Golf Course.

> *As a rule, students must bring their own clubs and golf shoes to Golf Camp. Inquire whether the school has rental clubs or can direct you to a source. Don't forget a golf glove.*

PENNSYLVANNIA

CHAMPION

Tri-State Section PGA of America Junior Golf Academy

Seven Springs Mountain Resort, Champion, PA

Director: Dennis J. Darak

One 3-day session, Wed-F, July; $300, 12th year
Coed, ages 12-17, limited to 60

Info and registration: Tri-State Section PGA Junior Golf Academy, 221 Sherwood Dr., Monaca, PA 15061; 412 774-2224; (Tri-Sate encompasses Western Pennsylvania, West Virginia and Maryland.)

Sixty fortunate golfers travel one hour east of Pittsburgh to the Seven Springs Mountain Resort for three days of golf learning with a host of PGA professionals from the greater Pittsburgh area. On a rotating basis, 20 pros committed to teaching junior golfers arrive daily to join a three-person permanent staff in delivering individualized, instruction. Juniors are grouped by age and ability in classes limited to 3:1 student/teacher ratio. Includes instruction at stations devoted to every aspect of the game, on-course training, two-day scramble tournament with prizes.

Lodging in an all-season ski lodge, 2/room; includes all meals and supervision, one free alpine slide ride, indoor pool and recreation in the lodge's gargantuan game room.

▉ Students are bused to Seven Springs Golf Course, 18-hole mountain layout with learning stations and ample practice facilities.

HAVERFORD

JKST Golf School

Haverford College

Director: Mike Hagan

Eleven 1-week sessions, Sun-Sat, June-Aug, minimum registration 2 weeks; $695/wk, commuter $360, 6th year

Coed, 10-18, limited to 25-30 students

Info and registration: JKST, Inc., 696 Raven Rd., Wayne, PA 19087; 215 293-0678

PGA golf directors, assisted by graduates of the Golf Management Programs of New Mexico, Mississippi and Ferris State universities, coach at this academy run by tennis great, Julian Krinsky. Enthusiasm and dedication for the game is communicated in up to six hours daily personalized teaching, 4:1 student/teacher ratio, employing videography and instructional golf films. On-course instruction 4 days/wk. Each student is evaluated as he or she progress through the curriculum which touches on every aspect of golf. Daily coaching staff meetings insure consistency and attention to detail. Includes preparation for competition; intramural and inter-camp tournaments.

Students have access to all the athletic facilities of the college, including pool, 45 outdoor and 28 indoor courts; game nights, dances, cook-outs, outings. All aspects of camp are fully supervised; campers are housed in modern residence halls, 1/room; buffet meals in the dining center; on-site nurses and trainer.

■ Six practice facilities. Campers practice, play and compete on seven area courses plus others for tournaments.

PHILADELPHIA

PGM Golf Clinics
Freeway Golf Course, Sicklerville, NJ
Director: Phyllis Meekins
Four 5-day sessions, July; $100, commuter only, 14th year
Coed, ages 7-17
Info and registration: P.O. Box 27531, Philadelphia, PA 19118; 215 247-3821

According to Golf Digest, LPGA professional Phyllis Meekins has "single-handedly redirected the lives of hundreds of underprivileged boys and girls." Her program of year-round clinics and four weeks of concentrated summer golf education has been replicated in Baltimore, Nashville and Memphis. The 68 year-old pro, who first picked up a club at 25 and earned LPGA credentials at 55, teaches solid basic fundamentals to build on and produce a "whole golfer." In five hours of instruction and play daily, with a 10:1 student/teacher ratio, pros teach from the green back to the tee on the premise that the short game accounts for a disproportionate number of strokes per hole.

Students are transported from the city to the course; includes playing privileges, snacks.

■ Minutes from Philadelphia, Freeway Golf Course offers 50 driving stations and ample short game practice areas.

SALTSBURG

Kiski Golf School
Kiski School, 1888 Brett Lane, Saltsburg, PA 15681
412 639-3586
Director: Dan Brooks
One 5-day session, July; $485, 10th year
Boys only, ages 10-18
Info and registration: Dan Brooks, Kiski Director, 3516 Sayward Dr., Durham, NC 27707; 919 681-2628 or 412 639-3586.

Coach Brooks's Duke University Women's Golf Team ranks second in the nation in Division I NCAA competition. He brings his expertise to coaching youth as assistant director of Duke's Junior Golf School and for the fourth year as director of Kiski Golf Camp. His team of winning coaches and Class A teaching pros provides technical training, both mental and physical, to all levels of young golfers in a 4 (or better):1 student/teacher ratio. The staff is comprised of an equal number of coaches and counselors and utilizes extensive personalized video instruction. Each student returns home with his own teaching tape for continued learning.

Fully supervised dorm accommodations just 100 yards from the first tee on the 300-acre Kiski School campus, 35 miles east of Pittsburgh; new dining hall, numerous athletic fields, swimming, evening videos.

■ Kiski School's own nine-hole course and practice area is dedicated to the school for the session.

SHIPPENSBURG

SU Golf Camp

Shippensburg University, Shippensburg, PA

Director: Charles Fields

5-day session, Sun-Thu, June; $260, commuter $185; plus $20 green fees
Coed, grades 7-12, mid to higher handicaps, limited to 24

Info and registration: SU Golf Camp, Office of Conferences, Cumberland Union Bldg., Shippensburg University, Shippensburg, PA 17257; 717 532-1256

Coaches and golf professionals teach skills and an appreciation of the game, covering all facets of golf and providing individual attention to each camper. The goal is to make each junior a more complete and confident golfer. Includes on-course training and PGA speakers.

Four nights accommodations (Sun-W) in college residence hall (2/room). Includes all meals, two parties, movie, surprise gift, use of university athletic facilities: tennis courts, indoor/outdoor basketball courts, handball courts, pool, weight training room and game room (additional fee). Commuter students may purchase meals for nominal charge.

▣ Practice facilities at Mayapple Golf Links in Carlisle, PA; campers will play a local course during the week.

> *Campers must provide a medical statement attesting to the state of their health along with a release for treatment. Notify the camp if you have allergies or an unusual condition.*

TYLER HILL

Tyler Hill Camp

Rte. 371, Tyler Hill, PA 18469; 717 224-4131

Director: Al Liebowitz; Operator: J. S. Jacobs

One 8-week summer camp session; $4,650, 38th year
Coed, ages 7-16, limited to 180 boys and 180 girls

Info and registration: Tyler Hill Camp, 144 Woodbury Rd., Woodbury, NY 11797; 516 367-6700

A traditional, sleep-away summer camp located on a 200-acre campus in Wayne County, less than 2½ hours from New York City. All campers receive 2-3 hours golf instruction per week; those "majoring" in golf receive up to two hours instruction daily, 4-5 days a week; 3:1 student/teacher ratio.

Tyler Hill offers virtually unlimited recreational opportunities, water sports on two lakes and outstanding athletic facilities, including 12 tennis courts. Programs stress friendship, sportsmanship, generosity, care and concern.

▣ Practice is centered on a top-class driving range; students play the camp's own professional nine-hole course, site of the former Wayne County Country Club.

STATE COLLEGE

Penn State Golf Camp

Penn State's University Park Campus

Director: Denise St. Pierre

Three 5-day sessions, Sun-Fri, June; $495, 15th year
Coed, grades 7-entering 12 (high school graduates ineligible)

Info: Penn State Golf Camp, Penn State University, 405 Keller Conference Center, University Park, PA 16802; 814 865-0561

Penn State's head Women's Golf coach, Denise St. Pierre, maintains her team among the top 50 in the country. The goal of her program is to improve students' swings through personally tailored, integrated teaching in classes limited to 10:1 student/teacher ratio and to transfer that learning to the course. Emphasis is placed on the swing-building process, proper practice habits and course management. Includes lectures, demonstrations, audio-visual teaching aids, drills and course manual. Parents invited to the camp's closing awards picnic.

The camp is conducted on Penn State's University Park Campus in State College, PA. Students are housed in residence halls (5 nights, Sun-Thu, 2/room). Program is fully supervised with counselors drawn from Penn State's varsity teams. Recreation includes swimming, racquetball and tennis.

▐ Two 18-hole courses, indoor practice area for inclement weather

STATE COLLEGE

Philadelphia PGA Junior Golf Academy

Penn State's University Park Campus

Director: Jeffrey T. Mowrer

Two-5-day sessions, Sun-F; July; $575, 7th year
Coed, ages 11-17

Info: Jeff Mowrer, 814 863-0254; Registration: Eric Loop, Penn State University, 410 Keller Conference Center, University Park, PA 16802; 814 863-1738

Expert instruction and fun characterize the Philadelphia PGA Golf Academy located in the scenic mountains of central Pennsylvania. Jeff Mower, M. Ed., golf professional at Penn State and a Class A member of the PGA, contributes his expertise in sports psychology, biomechanics and exercise science to the PGA's solid program of golf teaching. A staff of Philadelphia-area golf pros implements the program which places equal emphasis on skills development, playing performance, and acquired knowledge of the game. Provides computerized swing analysis, an evening academic series featuring speakers from the University faculty, and competitive intramural events.

Students are supervised by counselors drawn from Penn State's varsity golf teams and apprentice professionals from the Philadelphia PGA. Dorm lodging (5 nights, Sun-Thu, 2/room), all meals and recreational activities, including a hayride and bonfire.

▐ Spacious practice range and two golf courses.

> *Bring along a small amount of spending money for snacks and soft drinks. Almost everything else will be covered.*

SOUTH CAROLINA

GREENVILLE

Exceller Programs Golf Schools
Junior Clinic Series. See page 126.

GREENVILLE

Junior Golf Academy at Furman University
Furman University
Directors: Willie Miller, Michael Potter
Two 6-day sessions, Sat-Thu, June; $695, commuter $595, 11th year
Coed, ages 9-18 (excluding high school graduates), limited to 48
Info and registration: Junior Golf Academy, Furman University, Greenville, SC,
3300 Poinsett Hwy., Greenville, SC 29613; 803-294-9091

Furman is the alma mater of Brad Faxon, Beth Daniel, Betsy King and Dottie Pepper-Mochrie. The academy staff numbers coaching luminaries from Purdue, UNC and Clemson. Emphasizing golf fundamentals, classes are comprised of a maximum 12:1 student/teacher ratio, ample personal attention; includes audio-visual teaching aids, classroom seminars, on-course play, friendly mini-tournaments, equipment demonstrations, and celebrity guest appearances. All golf fees included. Beginner golfers are especially encouraged to apply.

Five nights accommodations (Sat-Wed) in ultra-modern, air-conditioned women's dorm; campus dining; includes all meals, all-you-can-eat salad and ice cream bar (commuter rate includes all but breakfasts and lodging); pizza party, Greenville Braves baseball outing, other diversions.

▣ Furman University Golf Course, totally dedicated to the school, provides practice and play. Host to numerous tournaments, including the annual Furman Pro-Am with returning celebrity alumni.

PAWLEYS ISLAND - MYRTLE BEACH AREA

The Phil Ritson Golf School
Juniors accepted with an adult. See page 51 for details.

TENNESSEE

FRANKLIN

Tennessee PGA Junior Golf Academy
Tennessee PGA Girls Golf Academy
Fall Creek Falls Resort Park - Legends Club of Tennessee/Belmont University
Directors: Joe Taggert, boys; Nancy Quarcelino, girls
6-day, 5-night sessions, Sun-F; $455, ages 11-17, 21st year, limited to 36
Boys, 4 sessions, June & July; Girls: 1 session (concurrent with boy's session), July
Fall Creek Falls Resort Park hosts four boys' sessions and one girls'; Legends Club of Tennessee, near Nashville, hosts one boys' session.

Info and registration: Tennessee PGA Junior Golf Academy, Tennessee PGA Girls Golf Academy, 1500 Legends Club Lane, Franklin, TN 37064; 615 790-7600

Over 4,000 junior golfers from 30 states have attended the academy since 1973. Experienced golf educators stress fundamentals, using stop-action video and eight-sequence cameras to film students' swings for analysis and correction. A computer measures clubhead speed and driving distance. Classes are grouped according to ability and limited to five students per teacher, with permanent PGA staff and visiting pros instructing. Tennessee's PGA celebrities make guest appearances and conduct clinics.

Boys' and girls' programs are independent, with the exception of meals and evening programs during the one coed week. Girls concentrate on skills at their own levels, with less emphasis on course play; tournament with awards. Boys play nine holes in the early morning followed by instruction, free time and an optional early evening nine-hole round and engage in an Academy Championship, competing at their own levels.

Fall Creek Falls sessions: meals, lodging (Sun-Thu) and evening programs in the Academy's group lodge. Legends session: fully supervised dorm lodging (Sun-Thu), 2/room) at Belmont University, cafeteria and golf course meals, transportation to the course and nearby recreation center. All programs include daily recreation, swimming and evening golf films.

■ Fall Creek Falls State Park: a Joe Lee-design, nearly 7,000 yards of bluegrass fairways and greens, selected by Golf Digest among the top 75 public courses in 1990. North and South courses (36 holes) at Legends Club of Tennessee, a Tom Kite-Bob Cupp design, with superb practice facilities.

TEXAS

AUSTIN

Academy of Golf Dynamics

The Hills of Lakeway, 45 Club Estates Pkwy., Austin, TX 78738
800 879-2008   512 261-8168

Three 3-day Parent/Youth programs, July & Aug; $1,200 each pair; $400 each additional child*
Coed, ages 9-18
Info: See page 108 for programs and methods.

Quality time for parent and child, learning the game or improving together. Concentrated instruction by PGA pros for golfers of all abilities, 3:1 teaching ratio; high speed video swing analysis, specialized swing enhancement devices, drills and training aids. Includes opening breakfast and graduation lunch. Located 30 minutes from Austin.

*Does not include lodging; inquire about condo and resort accommodations nearby.

■ Play centers on a Jack Nicklaus-designed, 500-yard driving range; a 7,500 square foot putting green and three complete holes: pars 3, 4, and 5, laid out to provide a wide range of challenges. Afternoon play at two courses in the Lakeway area. Graduates have privileges for one year at the Jack Nicklaus practice course.

COLLEGE STATION

Texas A&M John Jacobs Junior Golf Schools

Texas A&M University

Director: Bob Ellis

Four 5-day sessions, June and July; $500

Boys only, ages 13-17 (through junior year in high school), limited to 35

Info: John Jacobs Practical Golf Schools, 800 472-500. See page 6 for programs and methods.

John Jacobs method is taught by Texas A&M golf staff under the supervision of Bob Ellis, 1955 Ryder Cup winner, golf coach at Texas A&M, and veteran of 19 years conducting golf schools. Curriculum covers setup, grip, all shots, club construction, club fitting, etiquette and rules. Includes graph check photos and analysis, on-course training, 18-hole tournament and awards.

Five nights (Sun-Thu) dormitory lodging, all meals, 24-hour supervision, evening recreation program, swimming, movies, transfers to College Station Airport.

■ The University's 18-hole course.

DALLAS

GOLFWEEK College Prep Academy

Hyatt Regency DFW and Bear Creek Golf Club, 5-day program, Aug.

Info: See page 137 for details.

DALLAS

Scotty's Golf Park Junior Camp

8787 Park Lane, Dallas, TX 75231; 214 342-0373

Co-director: Sandra Haynie and Scott Ezell

Five 4-day sessions, mornings, coed, ages 6-10; $125, commuter only, June & July

Five 5-day sessions, afternoons, coed, ages 11-18; $125, commuter only, June & July

Comprehensive daily instruction by qualified PGA instructors; 5:1 student/teacher ratio, classes limited to 10. Utilizes videotaping and personal attention. Juniors progress through phases ranging from fundamentals and the full swing through problem shots and ultimately to playing lessons. Boys and girls, ages 6-10, receive 14 hours instruction over four days, 8:30 am - noon. Boys and girls, ages 11-18, receive 12 hours instruction, 1-3:30 pm.

■ 30-acre golf theme park with full range facilities, three practice greens; a four-hole, par 3 course.

Select clubs that are appropriate size. Second-hand shops and sporting goods stores carry inexpensive sets for growing youngsters. A beginner probably needs only 5, 7 and 9 irons, a putter and a 3 or 5 wood.

DENTON

Doug Egly/David Foster Boys and Girls Golf Camp

University of North Texas

Directors: Doug Egly and David Foster

One 4-day session, July; $395; commuter $260, 5th year

Coed, ages 9-17 (high school seniors ineligible)

Info and registration: Golf Camp, P.O. Box 13917, Denton, TX 76203; 817 565-3674 or 817 565-4404

Dave Foster, head coach of UNT's men's team, pairs with Doug Egly, head coach for UNT's women's golf team. The university's golf programs have produced four NCAA championship teams and a number of All-Americans, including PGA Tour players Don January, Rives McBee and Joel Edwards. The faculty is comprised of PGA pros and members of the university's golf team. Camp provides three days concentrated instruction on all aspects of the game, in classes with a 10:1 student/teacher ratio, followed by a final-day 18-hole tournament and awards presentation. Includes take-home videotape and all fees.

Fully supervised program furnishes four nights lodging (Sun-Wed) in air-conditioned dorms and all meals.

◪ Campus, 18-hole, newly renovated course with learning situations.

LUBBOCK

Texas Tech Junior Golf Academy

Texas Tech University

Director: Dr. Danny Mason

One 5-day session, Sun-Fri, July; $249, commuter $129, 11th year

Coed, ages 12-17 (junior high and high school students), limited to 40

Info and registration: Texas Tech Junior Golf Academy, Texas Tech University, Box 42191, Lubbock, TX 79409; 806 742-2352 ext. 247

Dr. Danny Mason, professor of health and physical education, has designed a program to teach the basics of the full swing: grip, posture, body movement, head position, and arc of the swing. Curriculum utilizes videotaped swing analysis and provides personalized teaching. Students work on the short game with one-on-one instruction based on progression. National Golf Federation films, videos and slides. Students are tested on rules. Closing tournament.

Fully supervised program includes five nights lodging (Sun-Thu) in open-air cabins on the campus, all meals and golf fees.

◪ Instruction and play at the nearby 9-hole Junction Country Club.

WEST COLUMBIA

Columbia Lakes Junior School

Columbia Lakes Resort and Conference Center

188 Freeman Blvd., West Columbia, TX 77486; 409 345-5151, ext. 532

Directors: Mark Steinbauer and Betsy Cullen

4-day program, July; $695, limited to 36

Coed, ages 12-18

Instructors at Columbia Lake's adult golf schools provide 24 hours of intensive instruction to young people, in a well-rounded, four-day program covering every aspect of the game. Includes three rounds of golf, competitions, team scrambles, rules quizzes, evening golf.

Golf is coupled with a full recreational program of social activities, movies, parties, and ongoing intramural competitions in swimming, ping pong, sand volleyball, goofy games and others. Four nights accommodations in the lodge at Columbia Lakes Resort and Conference Center, one hour south of Houston. Full supervision by collegiate counselors, includes 12 meals, green fees and awards.

■ Columbia Lakes 18-hole course, with full practice facility and learning center; 20 square foot tent shelter.

W O O D L A N D S

FCA Junior Golf Camps (Fellowship of Christian Athletes)
Woodland's Resort, 5-day program
Info: FCA, 904 273-9541. See page 135 for programs and methods.

U T A H

P R O V O

Brigham Young University Summer Camps
Brigham Young University

Director Bruce Brockbank

5-day Elite program, 0-12 handicap, July, limited to 30; $445, commuter $350; coed, ages 12-17

5-day Golf Intermediate, 13-20 handicap, June; limited to 30; $395, commuter $285; coed, ages 12-17

5-day Cubs Golf Day Camp, commuter program for beginners, July, limited to 40; $135; coed, ages 8-14

Info and registration: BYU Conferences and Workshops, 147 Harman Bldg, Provo, UT 84602; 801 378-4851 or 801 378-7685.

Young people from everywhere enroll in BYU's diverse sports programs to train with nationally known head coaches and to practice at some of the nation's finest facilities. Students receive comprehensive personal instruction from BYU's head golf coach Bruce Brockbank and newly retired, 31-year veteran coach, Karl Tucker, and a first rate teaching team. Program emphasizes correct application of sound golf mechanics and golf theory. Includes first and last day videotaping with coach commentaries, drills, supervised practice, personal training guidelines.

Elite program features 36 holes of championship golf, highly competitive closing tournament and awards banquet; Intermediate session furnishes 18 holes of competitive golf. Programs are fully supervised and include recreation with students in dozens of concurrent BYU sports camps. Residency in campus dorms (2/room), all meals (commuter includes lunch and dinner). All programs adhere to a strictly enforced behavioral and dress code.

Commuter Cubs program (M-F, 10 am-2 pm, campus practice range) is supervised by BYU's coaching team including Director Bruce Brockbank. Individual and small group instruction in the basics; includes swing analysis, attitude training, drills, demonstrations and fun competitions. Provides cafeteria lunches; school has limited supply of clubs.

■ Practice range on campus; Elite and Intermediate campers play area courses.

ST. GEORGE

Sun Desert Junior Golf Academy

Dixie College
225 S. 700 E., St. George, UT 84770
800 545-GOLF
Pro: Mike Smith

Three 5-day instructional programs, M-F (students may stay Sun-Sat), June; $299, commuter $249, 5th year
Coed, ages 10-17, limited to 20-25; for individuals and teams
Info: See Sun Desert Golf Academy, page 113, for further details.

Teaching pros, utilizing the latest techniques and high tech video and computerized swing analysis, provide 20 hours of comprehensive instruction and personal attention. Learning directed at golfers of all levels and high school teams. Growing program includes daily on-course training with an opportunity to play three uncrowded courses with supervision. Tournament and awards banquet. Evening review and activities.

Five or six nights lodging in Dixie College dorms with cafeteria meals; 24-hour supervision. Fly into Las Vegas for a Sky West Delta connection or bus transportation to St. George; includes transfers to and from St. George Airport and bus depot.

■ First class learning facility at Southgate Golf Club: covered, air-cooled driving range, teaching stations for putting, chipping, trouble shots, and special lies; air-conditioned, indoor hitting cages and classroom. Play Southgate (18 holes, par 70), Dixie Red Hills (9 holes, par 34) and St. George Golf Course (18-holes, par 73).

VIRGINIA

SOUTH BOSTON

Green's Folly Golf Camp

Green's Folly Golf Course, Rt. 1, Box 600, South Boston, VA 24592
804 572-4998
Directors: Bill Morningstar and Chris Dockrill.

Two 5-day sessions (one for individuals, one team session), July; $395, commuter $285, 8th year
Coed, ages 8-18

Bill Morningstar, golf coach of the Fightin' Christians of Elon College, has earned a nationwide winning reputation. Chris Dockrill, a former All-American player at Elon and golf director at Green's Folly, co-directs the camp. "Individual" camp directs customized instruction to each camper, with students grouped according to age and skill. "Team" camp provides an opportunity for high school teams and their coaches to live and practice together; individual and team instruction stresses competitive skills, cohesiveness and a collective winning attitude.

Supervised accommodations at nearby Day's Inn Motel (804 572-4941); meals at local restaurants and at the course; swimming, cable TV.

■ Daily play at Green's Folly Golf Course, the Gene L. Hamm-designed, 140 acre, 18-hole course built on the site of an historical, colonial era tobacco plantation, one of the best designed and most challenging courses in the area.

WILLIAMSBURG

The Kingsmill Golf School

Kingsmill Resort and Conference Center
1010 Kingsmill Rd., Williamsburg, VA 23185; 800 832-5665   804 253-1703

Director: Al Burns; Touring Pro: Curtis Strange

One 5-day session, June; $50, commuter only
Coed, ages 7-17, limited to 30-40

Info: Kingsmill Golf School, see page 118 for golf and resort information.

Program replicates Kingsmill's adult school, with the resort's regular PGA staff delivering instruction to juniors. Provides three hours instruction daily, ranging from the full swing through the short game and includes rules, etiquette and course management. Age-appropriate closing tournament and follow-up activities for campers throughout the golfing season. Program attracts area youth and vacationing juniors.

> *If your child seems like a "natural" golfer, invest in professional coaching or a good golf camp before he or she has a chance to develop bad habits. Contact the Junior Golf Association in your area for community programs.*

WISCONSIN

DELAVAN

Silver Sands Golf School

Three sites: Lake Geneva - Williams Bay - Wisconsin Dells

Director: Wayne Rolfs

Seven 6-day sessions, Sun-F, June-Aug

Five coed sessions, two for boys only; ages 10-17, limited to 25, 20th year; commuters 40% discount (rates below)

Hillmoor Golf Club - Chateau Royal Inn, Lake Geneva; $635; for experienced, older golfers

Christmas Mountain Village, Wisconsin Dells, $635; for experienced, older golfers

George Williams College, Lake Geneva Campus, $499; for all golfers

Info and registration: Silver Sands Golf School, South Shore Dr., Dalavan, WI 53115; 414 728-6120

In classes with a 5:1 student/teacher ratio, students are grouped according to skill. Instruction covers all facets of golf, with videotaping and instant swing analysis, drills and training. Provides on-course playing lessons, golf clinics and intramural tournaments, golf movies, lesson notebook, take-home swing analysis tape and practice summary.

Five nights: Chateau Royal Inn and Christmas Mountain Village, 2-3 students/room; George Williams College, dorm accommodations with bunk beds, 4/room. All meals at all sites, round-the-clock supervision; swimming, tennis, basketball, fishing, miniature golf, softball. Limousine transfers to and from Chicago's O'Hare Field.

◪ 18-hole courses at each site; learning-center ranges.

GREEN LAKE

FCA Junior Golf Camps (Fellowship of Christian Athletes)

Green Lake Conference Center-Lawsonia Golf Course, 5-day program

Info: FCA, 904 273-9541. See page 135 for programs and methods.

WISCONSIN DELLS

Galvano International Golf Academy

Chula Vista Resort, North River Rd., Wisconsin Dells, WI 53965

Director: Phil Galvano, Jr.

Seven 5-day sessions, Sun-Thu, June-Aug (inquire about extended stays); $439, 4th year

Coed, ages 10-17, limited to 30-32

Info and registration: Galvano International Golf Academy, Scenic River Rd., P.O. Box 119, Wisconsin, Dells, WI 53965; 800 234-6121. See page 122 for programs and methods.

The goal of instruction is to build a personalized swing and reach maximum power. Students are grouped according to age and skill. Covers all shots and focuses on increasing concentration and developing course strategy. Provides videography, class tournament and equipment analysis.

Numerous recreational opportunities at this family resort, including indoor pool, hiking, trips, movies, evening activities. Resort lodging and buffet meals in the dining room, 24-hour supervision.

◪ Coldwater Canyon Golf Course, 9-hole course adjacent to the resort. Comprehensive golf learning center.

> *Junior golf programs are "all you can eat" affairs. Good nutrition is a high priority at golf camp. And food is thoughtfully prepared to appeal to young appetites.*

CANADA

MANITOU

Manitou-wabing Summer Camp
McKellar, Ontario POG 1C0;   705 389-2410-1
Director: Ben Wise; Director of Golf: Howard Corley
Summer Camp: 7, 4, or 3 week sessions, June-Aug; major or minor in golf; full season $3,895, plus golf fees
One 1-week Intensive Golf Camp, Aug; $450, 1st year
Coed, ages 8-17
Info and registration: Manitou-wabing Sports and Arts Centre, 251 Davenport Rd., Toronto, Ontario M5R 1J9, Canada; 416 922-2447

Youngsters from all over the world are encouraged to reach their potential in sports, the arts and as individuals at this camp which stresses productivity and creativity. Located on the shores of Lake Manitou-wabing, 160 miles north of Toronto. Regular summer campers minoring in golf receive 1½ hours instruction three times a week plus frequent playing periods. Those who choose golf as their major receive 3-4 hours instruction and play every day. Campers participate in the other instructional and recreational programs of the camp.

One-Week Intensive Golf Camp provides a full week devoted to golf and nothing but golf, in a crash training program designed to produce the maximum results in the shortest time. Six to seven hours instruction daily at a neighboring course and on the camp's driving range. All programs include video analysis, lectures and golf films. Waterfront and recreational activities during free time.

Charter buses provide transportation from Toronto International Airport. Lodging in rustic, cedar cabins; dining hall meals, full supervision; wide variety of enriching, fun activities.

■ The camp boasts a newly installed driving range. Play and practice at the 18-hole, manicured Parry Sound Golf Course, 20 minutes away.

Golf camp is a formative experience in a lifetime of good sportsmanship and playing the game. Choose carefully, inquiring about the qualifications of instructors and their approach to teaching. Ask if you can observe the camp in action.

Professional Golf Management Programs (PGM)

Following is a selection of certification and degree-granting programs for men and women seeking careers in golf teaching, course and club management, golf-related business, public relations and merchandising. A number of programs offer financial aid and career placement. Professional Golf Management programs endorsed by the PGA of America are starred (*) below.

College of the Desert

43-500 Monterey Ave., Palm Desert, CA 92260; 619 341-2491   619 773-2577
Two-year program granting an Associate of Arts Degree in Golf Management. Courses offered in all aspects of country club management, including marketing, merchandising, landscape planning, turfgrass management and teaching golf. School's location in the golf course capital of the nation enhances job placement opportunities.

Ferris State University*

901 S. State St., Big Rapids, MI 49307-2295; 616 592-2380
Established in 1975 as the first program of its kind in conjunction with the PGA. Four and one-half year, work-study, degree-granting program for high school graduates with handicap of 8 or better; leads to a BS in business with a major in marketing. Students develop their golfing ability while learning operations, teaching, club and course organization. They fulfill post graduate requirements in anticipation of becoming Class A members of the PGA. Six-hundred acre campus located in west-central Michigan.

Golf Academy of San Diego

Whispering Palms Country Club, P.O. Box 3050, Rancho Santa Fe, CA 92067;
800 342-7342   619 756-2486

Golf Academy of the South

P.O. Box 3609, Winter Springs, FL 32708 (Orlando area);
800 786-0108   407 699-1990

Related two-year, four-semester, accredited programs combining golf and business management; graduates awarded four credits toward PGA membership. Limited to 40/semester, tuition $3,250/semester, enter Jan, May or Sept.

Mississippi State University*

P.O. Box NN, Mississippi State, MS 39762; 601 325-3161
Four and one-half year, degree-granting program in the College of Business and Industry leads to a bachelor's degree in business administration with a marketing major and includes 20 months on-the-job-training (co-op work) with Class A, PGA professionals at a golf facility, plus four, 16-hour PGA workshops. PGM graduates receive 24 credits toward the 36 required for Class A, PGA status. Open to high school graduates with a handicap of 8 or lower.

Mundus Institute - School of Golf Course Management

4745 N. 7th St., Phoenix, AZ 85014; 800 835-3727   602 248-8548
Full-time, 40-week program combining comprehensive training in golf and the business aspects of management of golf facilities at resorts, private and public courses and hotels. Includes golf history, golf shop operations, club repair, rules, tourna-

ment organization, first aid, merchandising, communications, business management, food and beverage management, turf and course culture, operations and
equipment. Tuition: $8,950, financial aid available.

New Mexico State University*

Box 30001, Dept. 5280, NMSU, Las Cruces, NM 88003-0001; 505 646-2814
Four and one-half year program in the College of Business Administration and
Economics leads to a bachelor's degree in business administration with a marketing major and includes 16 months on-the-job-training (co-op work) with Class A,
PGA professionals at a golf facility, plus four, 16-hour PGA workshops. PGM graduates
receive 24 credits toward the 36 required for Class A, PGA status. Open to high
school graduates with a handicap of 8 or lower. Combines solid academic credentials with work experience and PGA training.

Oglebay Institute

Wheeling, WV 26003; 800 624-6988, ext. 278
Two week-long programs, two consecutive years, totaling 22 hours of classroom
instruction/year. Business training and course management given in cooperation
with the National Golf Foundation, exclusively for municipal or daily-fee golf courses.
The only one of its kind in the U.S., the school is located on a 1,500-acre resort
and municipal park with 54 holes of golf, driving range and indoor teaching facility which provides a ready-made golf laboratory for would-be managers. Limited
to 100/class, $325/year.

Penn State/University Park Campus*

Golf Management Option, Penn State University, 203 Henderson Building South,
University Park, PA 16802-6505; 814 865-1851
The School of Hotel, Restaurant and Recreation Management of Penn State, the
largest university in Pennsylvania, offers a PGM program combining general aca-
demic requirements, leisure studies, extensive co-op experiences and yearly PGA
technical workshops. Open to high school graduate with a handicap of 8 or below.
Completion of the PGM program provides 24 of the required 36 credits for Class
A, PGA membership.

Professional Golfers Career College

P.O. Box 682, Murrieta, CA 92564; 800 877-4380 or 909 698-4380
Sixteen-month, four-semester, certificate-granting, vocational program in professional
course management. Located at Murrieta Hot Springs Resort, 45 miles north of
San Diego. Offers all facets of management training with full-time PGA golf instruction. Full-time placement office, limited to 30/class, $3,200/semester.

Golf Associations and Organizations

American Society of Golf Course Architects
221 N. LaSalle St., Chicago, IL 60601; 312 372-7090
With the goal of advancing the profession, the 47 year-old organization promotes
communication among professionals and the public about golf course design and
its practitioners.

Club Managers Association of America
1733 King St, Alexandria, VA 22313; 703 739-9500
CMA's 5,000 members manage 2,900 city, athletic, faculty, military, yacht, corporate and country clubs. Its foundation supports the advancement of club management and sponsors research, education and scholarships to students interested in the profession. Conducts professional development programs, career assistance; offers an in-house library and monthly magazine.

Golf Course Superintendents Association of America
1421 Research Park Dr., Lawrence, KS 66049; 913 841-2240
Originally the National Association of Groundskeepers of America, the nearly 70 year-old GCSAA advances golf course management and the dissemination of practical information. Provides certification, educational materials, continuing education and regional conferences on the concerns of its members. Publishes relevant literature, sponsors awards and contests. Open to course managers, employees and those in related businesses.

Golf Writers Association of America
c/o Jack Berry, P.O. Box 32054, Farmington Hills, MI 48332; 313 442-1481
Operating since 1946, 650-member group of newspaper, book and magazine writers from U.S., Great Britain, Europe and Australia sponsors awards for golfers and writers and promotes camaraderie among golf writers.

LPGA (Ladies Professional Golf Association)
2570 Volusia Ave., Suite B, Daytona Beach, FL 32114; 904 254-8800
Forty-three year old organization of Tour and professional women golfers promotes women's golf. Its growing Junior Girls Golf Club program interests and develops young golfers. Candidates for memberships must meet a number of qualifications including a playing ability test. New LPGA Foundation allows for donations to further the golf industry and the charitable aims of the organization (promotion of junior programs for girls and minorities, Catastrophic Illness Fund for members and the forthcoming LPGA Hall of Fame to be constructed in 1995 in St. Augustine, FL, in conjunction with the PGA).

National Association of Left-Handed Golfers
c/o Ken Ahrens, P.O. Box 801223, Houston, TX 77280-1223; 713 464 8683
Encourages the tendencies of left-handed golfers to swing lefty. Promotes left-handed golfers in a positive manner and advocates for availability and improvement of equipment for lefties. Now in its 58th year, group fosters camaraderie and acquaintanceship among left-handed golfers.

National Golf Foundation
1150 South U.S. Hwy. 1, Jupiter, FL 33477; 407 744-6006
The 58 year-old, 6,000-member research and consultative arm of the golf industry tracks golfer statistics, identifying trends and opportunities. It audits golf courses, monitors golf course construction, advances professionalism and encourages the growth of the industry; publishes newsletters, market reports and references, sponsors conferences. Membership open to businesses, educators, professionals, suppliers and associations involved in golf.

PGA of America (Professional Golf Association)

100 Avenue of the Champions, P.O. Box 109601, Palm Beach Gardens, FL 33401; 407 624-8400

Organization of 13,225 members and 9,256 apprentices (as of October, 1992), divided into 51 regional groups representing the nation's club professionals. Attaining PGA membership is a long process requiring study, apprenticeship, playing ability testing (PAT), an interview and work. PGA runs regional and national tournaments, educates teaching pros, regulates pro shops and equipment repair. Develops junior golfers, including minorities, through golf teaching, sponsorship of regional camps and through its "Junior Golf Journal."

PGA Tour

112 TPC Blvd, Sawgrass, Ponte Vedra Beach, FL 32082; 904 285-3700

Membership organization of golfers who earn their livings playing tournaments and through PGA Tour Partners whose membership benefits Tour charities; sponsors the professional Tour, Senior PGA Tour and Nike Tour.

Royal and Ancient Golf Club of St. Andrews

St. Andrews, Fife K Y16 9JD, Scotland

Dating from 1754, the ruling body of world amateur golf outside the U.S. and Canada. Conducts British Open, issues the Rules of Golf jointly with the USGA.

USGA (United States Golf Association)

Golf House, Box 708, Far Hills, NJ 07931; 908 234-2300

The venerable, hundred-year-old USGA is the volunteer organization formulating the 34 Rules of Golf in conjunction with the "R&A" (see above). Sponsors Rules workshops, publishes Golf Journal. USGA computes handicaps and course ratings, determines the conformity of golf equipment and conducts 13 national championship events (U.S. Open, U.S. Amateur, etc.), ten exclusively for amateurs. Encourages golf for young people and publishes annual Directory of Junior Golf Programs, listing 2,500 opportunities for youth. USGA catalogue sells apparel, memorabilia and books. Operates Golf House museum and library. Composed of 380,000 individual members and 7,700 club-members, as of mid-1993.

United States Golf Teachers Association

P.O. Box 3325, Ft. Pierce, FL 34948; 407 464-3272

Second largest organization of teaching professionals, with members from every state and 16 foreign countries. Runs seven-day teaching certification clinics in the U.S. and abroad. Promotes golf teaching profession and communicates with members through "American Golf Pro" newsletter.

World Amateur Golf Council

Box 708, Far Hills, NJ 07931; 908 234-2300

Sponsors biennial amateur men's and women's team Championships to foster friendship and sportsmanship among peoples of the world.

Junior Organizations and Associations

American Junior Golf Association

2415 Steeplechase Lane, Roswell, GA 30076; 404 998-4653
Seventeen-year-old, 3,000-member organization encouraging development and participation of young golfers through competition in the AJGA Tour. Displays skills of young golfers (ages 13 through high school) in regional tournaments; publishes monthly newsletter and Rules book.

LPGA Junior Girls Golf Club

2570 Volusia Ave., Suite B, Daytona Beach, FL 32114; 904 254-8800
New developmental golf program for girls ages 6-18, to create a network for girls to learn golf. Enrollment at five skill levels with appropriate theme- and age-related tournaments.

The Junior Tour

6905 Telegraph Rd., Suite 114, Bloomfield Hills, MI 48301; 313 642-6120
Eight-year-old organization to further competitive events and showcase young golf talent, endorsed by the U.S. High School Golf Coaches Association (c/o Jim Haimes, 800 925-1685) and ESPN, cable TV sports network. Runs seven national weekend tournaments from Nov through Feb, with a fixed 180 player field chosen during summer qualifiers.

Organizations for Physically Challenged Golfers

Association of Disabled American Golfers

c/o Greg Jones, 7700 E. Arapahoe Rd, Suite 350, Englewood, CO 80112;
303 220-0921
New group acts as a clearing house for information, conducts annual national tournament and represents the mutual interests of all disabled golfers and the golf industry.

Golf for Fun

c/o Director Bob Nelson, 3290 S. Reed Ct., Lakewood, CO 80227; 303 985-5851
Colorado volunteer organization with a volunteer board of directors to teach golf to people of all ages and all levels of disability, ranging from amputees to brain injured individuals. Hourly lessons with close personal attention, classes limited to 10; financial aid available. Annual fund-raising golf tournament for disabled and non-disabled; annual participant tournament.

Golf School for the Blind

c/o Joe Spoonster, 673 Ardleigh Dr., Akron, Ohio 44303; 216 864-5967
Ten year-old resource for instructors and programs in the U.S., providing information on teaching methods and learning devices. Programs located in Akron, Ohio; matches golf instruction programs with instructors and facilities in locales around the country.

National Amputee Golf Association

c/o Bob Wilson, Box 1228, Amherst, NH 03031; 800 633-6242

4,100-member organization teaches PGA pros and physical therapists to teach physically challenged golfers; conducts 24 regional tournaments; produces "The Amputee Golfer" magazine.

National Handicapped Sports

451 Hungerford Dr., Suite 100, Rockville, MD 20850; 301 217-0960
84-chapter advocacy organization promoting participation on behalf of handicapped athletes. Services 60,000 handicapped persons, families and friends, providing programs and information. Runs fitness instructor certification workshops, programs for parents of disabled children. While the group does not run golf programs, it is a resource for information and trains physically challenged athletes in other sports.

United States Blind Golfers' Association

c/o Bob Andrews, 3094 Shamrock St. N, Tallahassee, FL 32308; 904 893-4511
Promotes participation and education for sight-impeded golfers, sponsors tournaments, publishes "The Midnight Golfer" newsletter.

Commemorative Golf Sites

Golf House

Golf House, Box 708, Far Hills, NJ 07931; 908 234-2300
Museum and library protects the history and tradition of golf. Contains Bobby Jones room, artifacts, art, memorabilia, and literature celebrating the past to the present. Research library, rotating exhibits, gift shop. Free and open to the public daily.

PGA World Hall of Fame

PGA Blvd., Pinehurst, NC 28374; 800 334-0178   919 295-6651
Operated by the PGA of America; features exhibits on the Ryder Cup, history of Golf, golf-related art, memorabilia, gift shop; $3/person, open daily.

Rules of Golf

United State Golf Association, in conjunction with Royal and Ancient Golf Club of St. Andrews, has compiled 34 far-reaching rules covering all aspects of play. Rules workshops for professionals and amateurs running tournaments and interested golfers are offered at:

Mundus Institute Rules of Golf Workshop

4745 N. 7th St., Phoenix, AZ 85014; 800 835-3727   602 248-8548
Annual one-day session sponsored by the School of Golf Course Management. Provides certificate of completion and official rules book.

PGA-USGA Rules of Golf Seminars

Four-day seminars for those who officiate at tournaments; for amateurs and as a refresher for pros. Sept-March at various locations throughout the U.S., including Florida and California. Each of the 34 rules is explored in depth as well as the countless situations which arise in play. $175, tuition only. Accommodations will be suggested by course organizers. Inquire: PGA of America (Professional Golf Association), 407 624-8400 or USGA (United States Golf Association), 908 234-2300.

Index

The Index lists States, Schools, Resorts and Organizations.
- The page number for each school's Headquarters is indicated in bold type. There you will find methods, teaching techniques and programs.
- (J): Junior programs are printed in italics and noted with "(J)"
- (A&J): Sites at which schools are operated for Adults and Juniors

Tell us about your Golf School experience:

School _____

Site _____

_____

Remarks _____

_____

_____

_____

_____

Your Name/Address/Telephone (optional): _____

_____

_____

☐ Yes, "Golf Schools, The Complete Guide" was helpful

Suggestions for the next edition _____

_____

_____

Mail to: First Person Press, 25 Allen Road, Swampscott, MA 01907

- -

Include the following schools in the next edition of "Golf Schools, The Complete Guide"

School _____

Address _____

_____ Telephone: _____

Contact person _____

Remarks _____

Mail to: First Person Press, 25 Allen Road, Swampscott, MA 01907